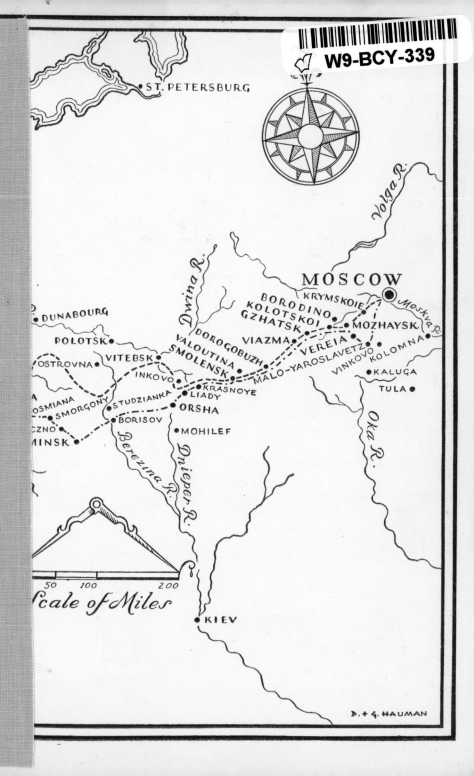

ST. PETERSBURG

MOSCOW

Volga R.

KRYMSKOIE
BORODINO
KOLOTSKOI
GZHATSK
VIAZMA
MOZHAYSK
Moskva R.
DOROGOBUZH
VALOUTINA
VEREIA
DUNABOURG
SMOLENSK
MALO-YAROSLAVETZ
VINKOVO
KOLOMNA
POLOTSK
INKOVO
KALUGA
OSTROVNA
VITEBSK
KRASNOYE
TULA
Dwina R.
OSMIANA
SMORGONY
STUDZIANKA
LIADY
ORSHA
CZNO
BORISOV
MINSK
MOHILEF
Oka R.
Berezina R.
Dnieper R.

50    100    200

Scale of Miles

KIEV

D. + G. HAUMAN

# NAPOLEON'S
# RUSSIAN CAMPAIGN

# NAPOLEON'S
## *Russian Campaign*

BY COUNT PHILIPPE–PAUL DE SÉGUR

*TRANSLATED FROM THE FRENCH*
*BY J. DAVID TOWNSEND*

*WITH AN INTRODUCTION BY*
*WILLIAM L. LANGER*
*COOLIDGE PROFESSOR OF HISTORY*
*HARVARD UNIVERSITY*

******** ********

HOUGHTON MIFFLIN COMPANY BOSTON

The Riverside Press Cambridge

# INTRODUCTION

**\*\*\*\*\*\*\*\***

## by *William L. Langer*

ÉGUR'S vivid and stirring account of Napoleon's invasion
of Russia, of the French occupation of Moscow and
of the Grand Army's disastrous retreat in the late autumn
of 1812 easily ranks with the classics of military narrative.
It first appeared in 1824 under the title *Histoire de
Napoléon et de la Grande Armée pendant l'année 1812*,
and within three years ran through ten editions. At the same
time it was translated into almost all European languages,
versions in English appearing in both London and Phila-
delphia in 1825. Many generals and soldiers who had participated in this famous campaign paid tribute to its accuracy
and objectivity. To this day it remains not only one of the
most readable but one of the most reliable narratives of
Napoleon's ill-starred adventure.

The author, Count de Ségur, was a member of a distinguished French family which, like many others, was
all but ruined by the French Revolution. Count Philippe-
Paul aspired to a literary career, but at the age of nineteen
enlisted in the army and thereafter participated in most of
the campaigns of the Napoleonic period. Though an ad-
mirer of the Emperor, he was by no means uncritical of him
and his despotic regime. During the Russian campaign

v

Ségur served as Quartermaster-General and therefore had unusual opportunities to see and hear what went on at imperial headquarters. The picture he gives of Napoleon, driven on by fate, at times irresolute and at critical moments weighed down by sickness, is an extremely human one, which eminent historians have found psychologically convincing.

Count de Ségur meant his book to rate not only as history, but as literature. His narrative — vivid, dramatic and always moving — evokes brilliantly the character of the period and the epic suffering of the great expedition. This is a book, then, that well deserves re-publication. It is here presented in a new and more modern English translation and somewhat shortened by the omission of technical military detail much of which would be meaningless to the present-day reader. Since interest in Napoleon and particularly in his Russian campaign has never flagged, it is hoped that in this new English version this fine piece of military literature will take yet another lease on life.

# TRANSLATOR'S INTRODUCTION

********

THIS BOOK has had a curious history. After a popular reception on its first publication, it was out of print and well on the way to being forgotten when General de Ségur died at the advanced age of ninety-three. During the last years of his life, however, the aged historian had been engaged in compiling his *Mémoires,* which were not published until after his death in 1873. Two of the seven volumes of this work, the fourth and fifth, were a reprint, with a few minor changes, of the original *History.*

In 1894 a considerably abridged version of this part of the *Mémoires,* prepared by a grandson of the author, was brought out by Firmin-Didot of Paris under the title *Campagne de Russie, Mémoires d'un Aide de Camp de Napoléon.* It is this version which we have translated, though we have worked directly from the 1910 Nelson edition. We have taken the liberty of further abridging it, leaving untranslated material dealing with military maneuvers which we feel would only serve to slow up the narrative and confuse the twentieth century reader. The earlier English translations of the book have long been out of print in America.

No one was better qualified than General de Ségur to write an account of the disastrous campaign of 1812. For fifteen years, as Napoleon's aide-de-camp, he was able to observe the great man at close range — intelligent witness of both his triumph and defeat. In his own words, "I was less an actor than a witness (in this campaign), never leaving the Emperor's side for more than a few feet, and then only to deliver several of his orders and see that they were carried out." The portrait painted against the background of these experiences was so little complimentary that many staunch Bonapartists took offense at it. One of them, General Gaspard Gourgaud, considered Ségur's implications insulting to the Emperor's memory, and challenged him to a duel in which Ségur was wounded. It is true that the Napoleon who emerges from the pages of this history is far more vulnerable, far less heroic, than the figure generally encountered in biography and legend. Here the Emperor is represented in a state of moral and physical collapse — so reduced that at times the reader will find himself almost pitying the giant.

Count de Ségur was no *parvenu*, ennobled by a grateful sovereign, as were most of Napoleon's marshals, but the scion of one of the most illustrious families of France. His grandfather, Marquis Philippe-Henri de Ségur, was a marshal of France and minister of war under Louis XVI. His father, Count Louis-Philippe, had accompanied Rochambeau to America, and later was the popular ambassador to the court of Catherine the Great. Philippe-Paul adopted a military career, and by the time he was thirty had won the rank of general and been made one of Napoleon's aides-de-camp.

Several generations of Ségurs earned a living by their pens. Both Philippe-Paul and his father were elected to the French Academy. A nephew of our author married the daughter of Rostopchin, reputed to be the incendiary of Moscow, who, signing herself *Comtesse de Ségur, née Rostopchine,* became famous as a writer of children's books, several of which are still popular in France.

It seems most likely that Tolstoy had a copy of the *History of Napoleon and the Grand Army* by him when he was writing *War and Peace.* The similarity between the two works is too great to be accidental; and it cannot be argued that both Tolstoy and Ségur were drawing upon some common source: this *is* the source. It was to Ségur that later historians turned for those details of behavior and conversation which only an eyewitness could provide.

Chapters 29 and 34 of Part X of *War and Peace,* in which Napoleon is shown in his tent before the battle of Borodino, are built up out of scraps of information given in Chapter III of the present work. There we find the incident of the reception of the portrait of the King of Rome, and that of the distribution of special rations to the Old Guard, the conversation between Rapp and the Emperor with this definition of war: "The art of being stronger than the enemy at a given moment," the statement, "I don't yet see my chessboard clearly," and the intimate description of Napoleon's illness. Tolstoy puts into the Emperor's mouth, as he stands proudly on Poklonny Hill, the very words Ségur gives us: "La voilà donc enfin cette fameuse ville! Il était temps!"

In another place this similarity is even more striking. Napoleon has ordered a squadron of Poles to ford the Viliya River. Ségur writes: "At first they advanced in order, and when they were beyond their depth they still forged manfully ahead. They swam together to the middle of the stream, but there the swift current swept them apart. Then their horses took fright. Helplessly adrift, they were carried along by the violence of the current. They no longer tried to swim, and lost headway completely. Their riders splashed and floundered in vain. Their strength failed finally, and they gave up the struggle . . . But it was for their country and her liberator that they were sacrificing themselves. As they were about to go down, they turned toward Napoleon and shouted *Vive l'Empereur!*"

Tolstoy puts it thus: "Hundreds of Uhlans galloped in after him. It was cold and uncanny in the rapid current in the middle of the stream, and the Uhlans caught hold of one another as they fell off their horses. Some of the horses drowned, and some of the men; the others tried to swim on, some in the saddle and some clinging to the horses' manes. They tried to make their way forward to the opposite bank. . . . and were proud that they were swimming and drowning in this river under the eyes of (the Emperor). . . . As soon as they had got out in their soaked and streaming clothes they shouted *Vivat* and looked ecstatically at the spot where Napoleon had been."

I wish to record my gratitude for assistance rendered in the course of this arduous task by: my French-born wife who was a constant help in the unraveling of the good general's knotty sentences; my daughter Mary who typed and revised much of the final draft of the manuscript; my friend Vladimir Monosson who read parts of the manuscript for spelling of the Russian proper names; and my daughters Paulette, Jeanne, and Catherine, who from beginning to end have been patient listeners and advisers.

J. DAVID TOWNSEND

# CONTENTS

\*\*\*\*\*\*\*\*

# NAPOLEON'S
# RUSSIAN CAMPAIGN

# MARSHALS OF FRANCE

\*\*\*\*\*\*\*\*

## *With titles conferred by Napoleon*

BERTHIER, LOUIS ALEXANDRE —
                    Prince of Wagram and Neuchâtel
BESSIÈRES, JEAN-BAPTISTE — Duke of Istria

DAVOUT, LOUIS-NICOLAS —
                    Duke of Auerstaedt, Prince of Eckmuehl
LEFEBVRE, FRANÇOIS-JOSEPH — Duke of Danzig

MACDONALD, ALEXANDRE — Duke of Taranto

MORTIER, ADOLPHE — Duke of Treviso

MURAT, JOACHIM — King of Naples

NEY, MICHEL — Duke of Elchingen, Prince of the Moskva

OUDINOT, NICOLAS-CHARLES — Duke of Reggio

VICTOR, CLAUDE (PERRIN) — Duke of Belluno

BEAUHARNAIS, EUGÈNE DE — Viceroy of Italy (not a marshal)

# CHAPTER I

********

## Crossing the Niemen

NAPOLEON had moved his troops in Poland and East Prussia from Koenigsberg to Gumbinnem. At the close of the spring of 1812 he reviewed several of his armies. He spoke to the soldiers in a jovial, bluff, often brusque manner, fully aware that by these simple, war-hardened men bluntness was looked upon as sincerity; rudeness as strength; haughtiness as true nobility; while the refinement and elegance that certain of the officers brought with them from the Paris salons were considered signs of weakness and faint-heartedness. Gentle speech was like a foreign language which they did not understand, and whose tones struck them as ridiculous.

According to his custom, Napoleon walked along in front of the ranks. He knew what wars each regiment had fought with him. He halted before the oldest soldiers, mentioning to one the battle of the Pyramids; to another, Marengo; to another, Austerlitz, Iena, or Friedland, accompanying his words with a familiar tap on the shoulder; and the veteran who believed he had been recognized by his Emperor felt himself grow in stature and glory before his envious, less experienced companions.

As Napoleon went down the line he did not overlook the younger soldiers. It seemed that everything about them

interested him, and that their slightest wants were known
to him. He questioned them: did their captains take proper
care of them? Were they getting their pay? Did they need
any equipment? He even asked to see their knapsacks.

He halted at the center of the regiment. There he inquired what officers' billets were vacant, and in a voice
which could be clearly heard asked who most deserved promotion. He called those whose names were mentioned and
questioned them: how many years of service? What campaigns? Any wounds? Any meritorious actions? Then he
appointed them officers and had them installed immediately,
all of which delighted the soldiers. They told themselves
that this great emperor who judged the nations in the mass
still troubled himself about their well-being — down to the
meanest detail. They felt that they were his eldest, his true
family. In this manner Napoleon instilled in them the love
of war, of glory, and of himself.

Meanwhile the army was advancing from the Vistula to
the Niemen, and was now not far from the Russian frontier.
From right, to left, or from south to north, the army was
drawn up along the Niemen. At the extreme right, coming
from Galicia, Prince Schwartzenberg with thirty-four
thousand Austrians; on their left, coming from Warsaw and
moving toward Bialystock and Grodno, the King of West-
phalia at the head of seventy-nine thousand two hundred
Westphalians, Saxons, and Poles; farther to the left, the
Viceroy * of Italy who had effected the junction of his
seventy-nine thousand five hundred Bavarians, Italians, and
French near Marienpol; next, the Emperor with two hundred
thousand men commanded by Murat, the Prince of Eckmuehl, and the Dukes of Danzig, Istria, Reggio, and Elchingen. These troops had marched from Thorn, Marienwerder,

* Eugène de Beauharnais, Napoleon's stepson. — J.D.T.

and Elbing; and on June 23 were gathered in one compact body near Nogarisky, about a league above Kovno.

Everything was ready. From the Guadalquivir and the shores of Calabria to the banks of the Vistula, six hundred and seventeen thousand men (of whom four hundred and eighty thousand were already present), six companies of engineers, one siege train, several thousand wagons of provisions, innumerable droves of cattle, one thousand three hundred and seventy-two pieces of cannon, and thousands of artillery and hospital wagons had been mustered and were now stationed a short distance from the Russian river.

Napoleon, who until now had traveled in a small carriage, mounted his horse at two o'clock in the morning. Under cover of the darkness he reconnoitered this frontier, which he would have to cross again in darkness five months later. As he reached the riverbank his horse suddenly fell, throwing him to the sand. A voice exclaimed, "This is an ill omen! A Roman would turn back!" It is not known whether it was Napoleon himself or one of his retinue who uttered these words.

His reconnaissance completed, he gave the order that the following nightfall three bridges should be thrown over the river near the village of Poniemen. Then he withdrew to his quarters. He spent part of the day in his tent and part in a nearby Polish mansion, lying without energy in the breathless, muggy heat, trying in vain to get a little sleep.

When night had fallen he approached the river. A small boatload of sappers were the first to be sent across. To their great surprise they were able to set foot on Russian soil without meeting with any resistance. They found peace there: they had left war on their side. All was calm on this foreign soil which had been painted to them in such threatening colors. However, a single Cossack officer commanding a night patrol soon appeared. He was alone, and seemed to think he was in the midst of peace, wholly unaware that all Europe in arms was at hand. He asked the intruders who they were. "Frenchmen," they told him. "What do you want?" he questioned further. "And why have you come to Russia?" One of the sappers answered bluntly, "To make war on you! To take Vilna and set Poland free!"

The Cossack withdrew into the woods, whereupon three of our soldiers, carried away by enthusiasm or to see how matters stood in the forest, fired their muskets. Thus the insignificant noise of three shots — to which no one replied — advised us that a new campaign was opening, that a great invasion had begun. This first signal of war made the Emperor violently angry, either from prudence or presentiment.

Three hundred light infantrymen were quickly dispatched across the river to cover the erection of the bridges. Then out of the valleys and woods streamed the French columns. They advanced in absolute silence to the riverbank, invisible in the thick darkness. You had to touch them to know they were there. All fire, down to the faintest spark, had been forbidden. The men slept with their weapons in their hands, as if in the presence of the enemy. The standing rye, wet with heavy dew, provided beds for the men and food for the horses.

The chill of night which made it hard to sleep, the darkness that lengthened the hours and exaggerated our needs, the dangers of the morrow — all contributed to the solemnity of the situation. But the expectation of a day of glory sustained us. Napoleon's proclamation had just been read. The men repeated in whispers the most memorable passages in it, and the spirit of conquest fired our imagination.

The Russian frontier stretched before us. Through the

gloom our eager eyes strained to see into this glorious promised land. We imagined we heard the joyful shouts of the Lithuanians at the approach of their deliverers. In our mind's eye we saw the river lined with their imploring hands. Here we had nothing; there, everything would be lavished on us. The people would flock to supply all our needs: we should be surrounded by love and gratitude. What mattered one bad night? Day would shortly appear, bringing its warmth and illusions . . . Day did appear! And it revealed to us only barren stretches of sand and dismal black woods. Then our disappointed eyes turned back upon ourselves, and we felt pride and hope swell again in us at the impressive sight of our assembled army.

Perched on the highest hill, about three hundred feet from the river, we saw the Emperor's tent. Around it, every hill, slope and valley was covered with men and horses. When the sun had risen on this swarming soldiery and their glistening arms, the signal was given, and in three columns the multitude began to move forward toward the bridges. They could be seen winding down the short uncovered slope which separated them from the Niemen, stretching out and narrowing down in order to cross the bridges, and finally setting foot on that foreign soil which they were soon to devastate and litter with their vast wreckage.

Enthusiasm ran so high that two divisions of the vanguard, contending for the honor of crossing first, almost came to blows, and were restrained with difficulty. Napoleon was impatient to set foot on Russian territory. Without faltering he took that first step toward his ruin. He stood for a time at the head of the bridge, encouraging the soldiers with his look. All saluted him with their usual *Vive l'Empereur!* They seemed more excited than he; perhaps his heart was heavy with the responsibility of so great an aggression, or his weakened body could not bear such excessive heat, or perhaps he was simply disconcerted at finding nothing to conquer.

At length, overcome by impatience, he suddenly galloped off across country and plunged into the forest which skirted the river. He urged his horse on at top speed. In his eagerness it seemed as though he wanted to overtake the enemy all by himself. He rode on in that direction for more than a league without encountering a living soul. Finally he had to turn back to the bridges whence, accompanied by his guard, he descended the river toward Kovno.

We thought we heard the rumble of cannon, and listened as we rode along to determine where the battle had broken out; but with the exception of several bands of Cossacks, the only enemy we encountered that day or on the following days was the heavens. Indeed, the Emperor had hardly crossed the river when the air was shaken by a faint rumble. In a short time the sky had grown black, the wind had risen, bringing to our ears the sinister crash of thunder. The threatening sky, this land without visible shelter, threw a gloom over our spirits. Several of our men, recently so enthusiastic, were terrified as though this were an ill omen. They fancied that the fiery clouds had piled up over our heads and were bursting on this country to prevent our entering it.

This thunderstorm was as grandiose as our undertaking. For several hours the clouds grew thicker and blacker over the entire army. From one end to the other, for fifty leagues around, the troops were everywhere endangered by the lightning and overwhelmed by the downpour. Roads and fields were flooded. The unbearable heat changed suddenly to a disagreeable cold. Ten thousand horses perished along the way or later in the forced bivouacs. Great quantities of provisions were abandoned on the sand, and many men died from exposure to the elements.

A convent sheltered the Emperor from the first fury of the storm. Before it was over, however, he set out for Kovno where everything was in complete disorder. The thunder faded away in faint rumbles, the rain ceased, the wind died down, and the horror disappeared as quickly as it had risen. The majority of the army thought of this catastrophe only as an ill-timed natural accident rather than as a condemnation of the colossal aggression — for which, of course, they were not responsible; they found in it only an excuse for raging against fate and heaven that, by chance or intentionally, had given them such a terrible warning.

That same day a more personal misfortune was added to these general trials. Above Kovno, Napoleon was annoyed to find that the bridge over the Viliya had been destroyed by the Cossacks, preventing Oudinot from crossing. He shrugged this off scornfully, as he did everything that thwarted him, and ordered a squadron of Poles to ford the river. These picked troops obeyed without a moment's hesitation.

At first they advanced in order, and when they were beyond their depth they still forged manfully ahead. They swam together to the middle of the stream, but there the swift current swept them apart. Then their horses took fright. Helplessly adrift, they were carried along by the violence of the current. They no longer tried to swim and lost headway completely. Their riders splashed and floundered in vain. Their strength failed, and finally they gave up the struggle. Their doom was certain; but it was for their country and her liberator that they were sacrificing themselves. As they were about to go down, they turned toward Napoleon and shouted, "Vive l'Empereur!" We

noticed three in particular who, their mouths still above
water, repeated the cheer and immediately sank. The army
was gripped with horror and admiration.

Meanwhile Napoleon had given prompt and explicit
orders to do all that could be done to save the greater part
of the men, though without betraying the slightest emotion,
either because he had learned to master himself, or because
in wartime he considered the gentler emotions a sign of
weakness and a bad example for the army, or, finally, because he foresaw greater disasters compared to which this
was as nothing.

Napoleon was two days marching from Kovno to the
narrow passes which defended the plains around Vilna. He
did not show himself until he had news from the outposts.
He expected that Alexander would oppose his entering this
capital city * and he was encouraged in this hope by the
sound of scattered shots. When word was brought to him
that the town was not to be defended, he advanced in a
worried, dissatisfied mood. He accused the generals of the
advance guard of having allowed the Russian army to
escape. It was Montbrun — the most active of all — whom
he reproached most bitterly, losing his temper to the point
of threatening him. Words without effect, violence without
consequence, less to be condemned in a man of action than
simply noted as a proof of the great importance he attached
to a prompt victory.

Though still in a rage, he exercised his customary shrewd-
ness in his preparations for entering Vilna, ordering that he
should be preceded and followed by Polish troops. But,
more interested in the retreat of the Russians than in the

* Vilna was the capital of Lithuania which country, after being absorbed
in Poland for four hundred years, had fallen to Russia in the Third Partition
of Poland in 1795. — J.D.T.

expressions of admiration and gratitude of the Lithuanians, he crossed the city at top speed and hastened to the outposts.

The Russian army had disappeared. We had to press on in pursuit.

# CHAPTER II

********

## From Ostrovna to Viazma

FOR A WHOLE MONTH, since the crossing of the Niemen,
our army had kept hot on the trail of the Russians.
On the twenty-fifth of July Murat was approaching Ostrovna
at the head of his cavalry. Domon, Du Coëtlosquet, and
Carigan, with the 8th Hussars, were marching in an unbroken column along a broad road lined on each side with
splendid birches. About five miles from the town the hussars
reached the foot of a hill, at the top of which they spied a
feeble enemy detachment composed of three regiments of
cavalry and six cannon. The position was not defended by a
single sharpshooter.

The officers of the 8th thought that they had been preceded by two regiments of their own division who were
marching through the fields at the right and left of the road,
but hidden by the thick trees. The fact was that these
regiments had halted. The 8th, already well in advance of
them, kept on up the hill, believing that the troops they
saw in a little wood about a hundred and fifty feet ahead
were those two regiments that must have gone by them without their noticing it.

The immobility of the Russians completed this illusion,
so that when the generals were ordered to charge, they

thought a mistake had been made. They sent an officer ahead to reconnoiter, and marched on without suspicion. Suddenly they saw the officer struck down and run through as the enemy opened fire on their ranks. Without pausing to spread out their forces, they plunged into the wood and charged the cannon. With their first impetuous rush they captured the weapons, and they had little difficulty in overcoming the regiment forming the center of the line. Then they fell upon the regiment on their right, which was standing as though stupefied with amazement, and attacking it from the rear, they promptly dispersed it. In the flush of this second success they noticed the third regiment on the left retreating in great disorder. Mustering all their forces, they turned quickly about and charged this third adversary in full flight, and completely routed it. Emboldened by this success, Murat drove the remainder of the Russian forces into the Ostrovna wood, where he would have followed them had he not been checked by violent resistance.

Our position at Ostrovna was well chosen as it commanded a broad view and we could see everything from it, without being seen. It intersected an important highway, the Duna River lay on its right, a ravine in front and thick woods at the left. Moreover, it was within a short distance of our stores and commanded the roads to Vitebsk, the capital of that province. Count Osterman rushed up to defend it. Murat, as careless with his life even now when he was a victorious monarch as he had been when an unknown soldier, persisted in his attack on the wood, despite the bullets which came pouring out of it. He soon realized, however, that a surprise attack would be out of the question here. The position won for him by the 8th Hussars was being vigorously contested, and his advanced column, composed of the divisions of St. Germain and Bruyères, of the

8th Infantry, was going to have to hold out against an entire army.

The French forces defended themselves as victors always do, by attacking. Each Russian corps that came up to assail our flank was in turn attacked. The cavalry was pushed back into the wood, and the infantry was routed at saber point. We were growing weary of winning when Delzons' division appeared on the scene. The King * promptly ordered him to the right to follow the retreat of the enemy who were disorganized and were no longer contesting the victory.

The ravines there were several miles long. That evening the Viceroy rejoined Murat, and the next morning they saw that the Russians had taken a new position. After checking the advance of the enemy's left flank, the two princes were designating the positions that were to serve as points of defense or departure for the troops when a sudden clamor rose on their left. Twice the cavalry and infantry on that side had charged the enemy, twice they had been beaten back; and now the emboldened Russians were streaming out of the woods, shrieking wildly as they came. The daring and fire of attack had now shifted to them, the uncertainty and astonishment of defense had fallen to the French.

A battalion of Croats and the 8th Regiment put up a vain resistance. Their line was rapidly diminishing: in front the ground was littered with their dead, in the rear the plains were covered with the wounded and men withdrawing from combat. It was the beginning of a defeat. But General D'Anthouard rushed up with his artillery, General Girardin hurled the 106th against the enemy's right, General Piré fell upon their left, and together they turned the tide of battle, and the Russians retreated into their forests.

* Murat, the King of Naples, Napoleon's brother-in-law. — J.D.T.

The enemy, however, was still obstinately defending a thick wood whose advanced position broke the continuity of our line. The 92nd Regiment, astonished at the heavy fire issuing from the wood, dazed by the rain of bullets, stood still, not daring either to advance or to fall back, restrained by two conflicting emotions, shame and fear, yet doing nothing to rid themselves of either. General Belliard, closely followed by Roussel, galloped up to revive their spirits by his words and example, and the wood was taken. But this region was furrowed with ravines which protected the Russian retreat, and the whole army finally disappeared into a forest some five miles deep, the last screen hiding Vitebsk from our view.

After such a violent fight, the King of Naples and the Viceroy were undecided as to whether their troops should venture into so thickly wooded an area. When Napoleon approached, they galloped up to him, showing him what had been done and what still remained to be done. Napoleon went to the top of the high hill nearest the enemy's position, from which point his genius, dismissing all obstacles, immediately fathomed the mystery of the wood and the extent of the mountains. Without hesitation, he issued orders, and the forest which had checked the bold assault of the two princes was crisscrossed from one end to the other. That night Vitebsk, looking down from its double hill, could have seen our light troops emerging on the surrounding plains.

At that point everything seemed to conspire to delay the Emperor — the night: the multitude of enemy fires covering the plain, an unfamiliar terrain which had to be reconnoitered before his divisions could be sent forward and, above all, the time required for a vast number of soldiers to issue from the long, narrow passes through which they were marching. A general halt was ordered to give time to take a breather, reconnoiter, rally forces, eat and prepare arms for the following day. Napoleon slept in his tent on a rise to the left of the highroad, behind the village of Kukowiaczi.

On the twenty-seventh the Emperor was at the advanced posts before dawn. The first rays of the rising sun showed him, at last, the Russian army camped on a plateau which commanded all the approaches to Vitebsk. The Luczissa River flowed at the bottom of a deep bed encircling the base of this position. Before it, a body of cavalry ten thousand strong and some companies of infantry were drawn up in a line of defense. The infantry was in the center on the main road, its left flank extending to a grove of tall trees. The cavalry was all on the right, in a double line, backed up by the Duna.

In the course of the morning there were several bloody encounters. Murat again covered himself with glory in a sharp but brief skirmish with the Russian vanguard, forcing both cavalry and infantry back across the ravine of the Luczissa. Thus the enemy army of eight thousand men was assembled in one mass on the opposite bank. At eleven o'clock Napoleon ordered the fighting to cease, so that he might survey the entire front line in peace, and plan a decisive battle for the next day. He proceeded to station himself on a knoll among the light troops, with whom he ate his lunch. While he was engaged in observing the Russians, one of their bullets wounded an officer who was dangerously close to him. The remaining hours of the day were spent in studying the terrain and waiting for the other regiments to come up.

Napoleon announced a battle for the following day. His parting words to Murat were, "Tomorrow at five o'clock, the sun of Austerlitz!" These words partly explain his suspension of hostilities in the heat of success. The soldiers, in high spirits, were surprised at this inaction, coming at the moment when they had overtaken the army whose incessant flight was wearing them out. Murat, whose hopes of battle had been disappointed day after day, pointed out to the Emperor that Barclay * would not have put on so bold a front except to allow him to withdraw all the more quickly in the night. Unable to convince his sovereign, Murat went and rashly set up his tent on the bank of the Luczissa, almost in the enemy's camp. This position would allow him to overhear their faintest preparations for retreat, perhaps to prevent it, and it appealed to his venturesome nature.

Murat was mistaken, yet he appears to have seen the more clearly. Napoleon was right, yet events decided against him. Such are the tricks of fortune! The French Emperor had rightly judged the intentions of Barclay, who had decided to wage the battle in order to give Bagration, whom he believed to be in the neighborhood of Orsha, time to join him. The news of Bagration's withdrawal toward Smolensk brought to him in the evening, caused him to change his plans suddenly.

At dawn on the twenty-eighth of August Murat sent word to the Emperor that he was going to pursue the Russians, who were no longer anywhere to be seen. Napoleon stubbornly clung to his opinion, and persisted in assuming that the entire Russian army was close at hand, and it was necessary to advance cautiously. Thus a great deal of time was lost. At length Napoleon got on his horse; he realized he was wrong as he rode ahead and found himself shortly in the center of the camp that Barclay had just abandoned.

* Michel Barclay de Tolly (1761?–1818), Russian field marshal of Scottish origin. Born in Livonia. Tolstoy calls him a German, perhaps because at one time Riga, his birthplace, belonged to the Hanseatic League of N. German cities. — J.D.T.

Everything he saw there spoke of a mastery of the science of war: the favorable situation of the camp, the symmetrical layout of its parts, the exact and exclusive observance of the use for which each had been designed, and the resultant order and cleanliness. Moreover, nothing had been left behind, not a weapon or personal possession, no tracks — nothing to indicate the route the Russians had taken in their sudden nocturnal flight. There was more order in their retreat than in our victory! Defeated, they left us as they fled the sort of lessons by which the victorious never profit, either because success thinks it has nothing to learn, or because we put off improving ourselves till misfortune has struck.

A Russian soldier found asleep behind a bush was the only fruit of a day which was to have been decisive. We then entered Vitebsk, which we found as completely deserted as the Russian camp. All the roads were reconnoitered in vain. Had the Russians marched toward Smolensk, or had they gone back up the Duna? At length an independent band of Cossacks enticed us in the latter direction, while Ney took the former. We covered about fifteen miles through thick dust, in suffocating heat, halting at nightfall near Agaponovtchina.

*

## Vitebsk

While the men, completely exhausted and half starved, were quenching their thirst with muddy water, Napoleon, the King of Naples, the Viceroy, and the Prince of Neuchâtel *

---

* Prince de Neuchâtel: Louis-Alexandre Berthier, one of Napoleon's marshals. — J.D.T.

held a council of war in one of the imperial tents pitched in
the courtyard of a country seat on a hill at the left of the
main road.

Napoleon said, "So the victory we have all so keenly desired and so long looked forward to, which each passing day
has made more necessary, has slipped through our fingers
again, as it did at Vilna! It is true that we caught up with
the Russian rear guard. But did it belong to their army?
Isn't it likely that Barclay has stolen off in the direction of
Smolensk? How far must we pursue these Russians before
they decide to give battle? The necessity of organizing
liberated Lithuania, of setting up hospitals and supply
depots, of establishing a central point for recuperation, defense, and subsequent departure on a line of operation
which is growing longer and longer every day — shouldn't
all this make us decide to stop here on the border of old
Russia?" . . .

Having made this decision, Napoleon disposed the various
corps of his army on a line extending from the Duna to the
Dnieper, then he returned to Vitebsk with his guard. There
on the twenty-eighth of July, in the imperial quarters, he
took off his sword and threw it down on the maps covering
the table, exclaiming, "Here I stop! I want to collect myself, rally my forces, rest my army, and organize Poland. The
campaign of 1812 is finished. The campaign of 1813 will
do the rest."

With the liberation of Lithuania the objective of the
conflict had been attained, yet it seemed that the war had
hardly begun. Places alone had been overcome, and not
men. The Russian army was still intact, and its two flanks,
separated by the ardor of an initial attack, had just been
reunited. We were in the finest season of the year. Such was
the situation when Napoleon decided to halt on the banks

of the Dnieper and the Duna — a decision which he thought
irrevocable. He was better able to deceive others concerning
his intentions since he was deceiving himself.

The Emperor could now be seen wandering about the city
and its outskirts as if studying the center he was going to
occupy for a protracted period. All sorts of establishments
were planned. Thirty-six ovens with a daily capacity of
twenty-nine thousand pounds of bread were set up. And he
did not stop at the purely utilitarian but thought also of
adornment. For instance, he ordered his guard to tear down
some stone houses which spoiled the appearance of the palace
square, and to clear away the rubbish. He gave thought to
winter pleasures. Actors would be brought from Paris to
Vitebsk, and since this city was empty of civilians, feminine
spectators might be drawn to it from Warsaw and Vilna.
His lucky star was his guide in those days. If only he had
never mistaken the promptings of his impatience for the
inspiration of genius!

That very same day he challenged an administrator with
these remarkable words: "As for you, sir, your business is to
provide for our needs here." Then, in a voice that could be
heard by his officers, "For we shall not repeat the folly of
Charles XII." * But very soon, indeed, his actions contradicted his words, and everybody began to wonder at his
carelessness in issuing orders for such a large establishment.

Besides, the moderation of Napoleon's first speech had
not deceived the members of his household. They recalled
how, at the first sight of the empty Russian camp and the
deserted city, hearing them rejoice over this conquest, he
had turned sharply on them and cried, "Do you think I have

---

* Charles XII, King of Sweden, known as "The Madman of the North,"
after a number of successes in Europe was crushed by the Russian army
(July 8, 1709). — J.D.T.

come all this way just to conquer these huts?" They also knew that he never made more than the most sketchy plans even for his great projects, but generally acted on the spur of the moment, which was in keeping with his impulsive nature.

Napoleon was confident that he would receive fresh proposals of peace from Alexander, and he was kept busy for a while by the weakened condition of the army. The interminable lines of sick and stragglers must be given time to rejoin their regiments or get into hospitals. These hospitals had to be set up, supplies had to be collected, horses rested or replaced. Furthermore, we had to wait for the ambulances, the artillery, and the pontoons which were still dragging after us across the Lithuanian sands. The Emperor's correspondence with Europe demanded his attention, but most serious of all, a burning implacable sky halted everything. For such is the Russian climate: the weather is always extreme, intemperate. It either parches or floods, burns or freezes the earth and its inhabitants — a treacherous climate, whose heat weakened our bodies as if to soften them for the cold which was soon to attack them.

The Emperor was not the least of the sufferers from the heat, but when he had been refreshed by rest and still did not see any deputation arrive from Alexander, and when all his first orders had been carried out, he became impatient. We noticed that he was restless; either because as with all men of his nature, inaction lay heavy upon him and he preferred danger to the boredom of waiting; or because he was excited by the hope of gain which, in most men, is stronger than the pleasure of keeping or the fear of losing.

It was then that the image of a defeated, subjugated Moscow began to obsess him. There lay the end of his fears, the fulfillment of all his hopes. Possessing it, he would have everything. From that moment, it could be predicted that this fiery, restless genius, accustomed to short cuts, would not wait eight months when the final destination was in his grasp, so close that it could be reached in only twenty days.

We must not, however, be too quick to condemn this extraordinary man for weaknesses common to all men. He will speak for himself, and we shall see to what extent his political position complicated his military position. Later on, we shall be still less inclined to blame the resolution he took, when we see how the fate of Russia hung on just one more day of health, which failed Napoleon on the field of Borodino.

At the outset he did not dare acknowledge even to himself such a bold project, but little by little he got the courage to look at it squarely. Then he began to deliberate, and the great irresolution which had been tormenting his mind took hold of his body as well. He could be seen wandering about his apartments as if haunted by this dangerous temptation. He was unable to keep in one place; every few minutes he picked up, laid down, and picked up again some piece of work. He walked aimlessly up and down, asked what time it was, remarked about the weather, then stopped, humming a snatch of song, then resumed his walking.

In this state of perplexity he spoke a few disconnected words to whomever he chanced to meet. "Well, what are we going to do? . . . Shall we stay here? Shall we advance? . . . How can we stop now on the road to glory?" Without waiting for an answer, he moved on, seeming to be looking for someone or something that could help him make up his mind.

At length, overtaxed by the burden of so momentous an idea, and overcome by the terrible uncertainty, he threw himself down on one of the cots he had had brought into his chambers. Because of the stifling heat he was wearing only light undergarments. In this manner he spent a great part of his days at Vitebsk. When his body was at rest his mind was all the more active. "How many reasons have I for going to Moscow at once!" he would say. "How can I bear the boredom of seven months of winter in this place? . . . Am I to be reduced to defending myself — I who have always attacked? Such a role is unworthy of me . . . I am not used to playing it . . . It is not in keeping with my genius."

Then, his mind made up, he suddenly sprang to his feet, as if he did not want to give his reflections the time to plunge him back into a state of painful uncertainty. Filled with plans for the successful termination of his conquest, he rushed to the maps which showed him Smolensk, and Moscow, great Moscow, the holy city. He repeated over and over these names which filled him with pleasure and kindled his desire. Fired with this formidable conception as he was, he seemed to possess at that moment the very genius of war. His voice hardened, his eyes glittered, his expression became fierce. We drew back from him in mingled fear and respect. But in a short time, once his plans were laid and his order of march traced out, the storm within him subsided; and freed from the burden of this awesome conception, his features resumed an expression of serene, gentle good humor.

It was very important to him that his decision should not displease his staff. But every one of the men opposed him in some way, each according to his character; Berthier, with a long face, lamentations, even tears; Lobau and Caulaincourt with frank disapproval, displayed in the former by a chilly rudeness, understandable in so intrepid a soldier, and in the latter by resistance to the point of almost violent obstinacy. The Emperor spurned their observations with a show of

temper, and addressing himself to his aide-de-camp* particularly, as well as to Berthier, he exclaimed, "I've made my
generals too rich. All they dream of now is following the
hunt and flaunting their elegant carriages in Paris. I sup-
pose they have lost their taste for war!" Since no rejoinder
was possible to such an attack on their honor, they hung their
heads and submitted. In a fit of temper, Napoleon had once
said to a general of his Guard: "You were born in a bivouac,
and in a bivouac you will die!"

Marshal Duroc also expressed his disapproval, at first by
a cold silence, later by brief answers, insistence upon the dry
facts, and curt remarks. The Emperor told him, "Of course
I see clearly that the Russians only want to lure me on.
Nevertheless, I must extend my line as far as Smolensk,
where I shall establish headquarters. If by the spring of 1813
Russia hasn't made peace, she is ruined. Smolensk is the
key to two main roads — one to St. Petersburg, the other to
Moscow. We must take possession of it so that we may
march on the two capitals simultaneously. In Moscow, we'll
destroy everything; in St. Petersburg we'll keep everything.
Then I'll turn my arms against Prussia and make her pay the
cost of the war."

Then came Daru,† a man rigidly upright and inflexibly
firm. The question of the march on Moscow was taken up
with him, in the presence of Berthier only, and was debated
for eight consecutive hours. When Napoleon asked his
minister for his opinion of this war, the latter replied, "It is
certainly not a national matter. The importation of some
English goods into Russia,‡ even the creation of the king-
dom of Poland are not sufficient reasons for waging war with

---

* To General de Ségur, probably. Ségur wrote in his *Mémoires:* "Several
times I referred to myself without, however, mentioning my name." — J.D.T.
† Pierre-Antoine Daru, Minister of War under Napoleon.
‡ In violation of France's Continental Blockade.

such a remote country. Neither your troops nor ourselves see the object or the necessity for such a conflict. Everything warns us to stop where we are."

The Emperor protested, "There's been no blood shed as yet! and Russia is too great to surrender without a fight. Alexander cannot negotiate until there has been a decisive battle. If necessary, I'll seek that battle in their holy city itself, and I'll win it! Peace awaits me at the gates of Moscow. If Alexander's honor is preserved and he still holds out, I'll negotiate with the Boyars,* or even with the large and enlightened population of this capital. They will understand what is in their best interest, and know the meaning of liberty." After a moment he added, "Besides, Moscow hates St. Petersburg. I will benefit from this rivalry. Why, the results of such jealousy are incalculable."

Thus in the heat of discussion Napoleon revealed his hopes. Daru answered simply, "Your army has already diminished by one third, either through desertion, famine, or disease. If supplies are scarce in Vitebsk, what will it be like farther on?"

To this Berthier added, "If we extend our line any farther, the Russians will have in their favor our long drawn-out flanks, lack of food, and especially their terrible winter; while if we stop here you will have winter on your side, and will become the master of this war by keeping it within your reach, instead of following its deceitful, wandering, undecided flight."

The Emperor listened quietly to the arguments from the two men, interrupting them from time to time with some penetrating remark, asking questions that suited his purpose, or changing the subject when he was cornered. But in the

* Napoleon did not seem to know that this class of Russian aristocrats had been abolished by Peter the Great. — J.D.T.

end, no matter how disagreeable the facts were that he had to hear, he listened patiently and answered in the same fashion. Throughout all these discussions his words, manners, and gestures were remarkable for the same ease, simplicity, and good nature that he nearly always preserved in private life. This explains why, despite so many misfortunes, he is still loved by all those who were close to him.

Still not entirely satisfied, the Emperor summoned successively several other generals of his army. The questions he asked indicated what answers he expected, and some of these officers, born soldiers and accustomed to explicit obedience, were as submissive in these interviews as on the field of battle.

We felt that we had gone too far to draw back now; that a victory was necessary to extricate us quickly, and that Napoleon alone could give it to us. Moreover, continued hardship had purged our ranks. Those who remained were unquestionably the pick of the army, in mind as well as in body. What trials had they not had to withstand, to have come so far! The boredom of inaction and the discomforts of their wretched camps were real torture for such men. To remain where they were seemed unbearable; to retreat, impossible; there was no choice for them but to advance.

At that time their ambition was still boundless, and everything aroused their passion for glory. They had been swept into a limitless undertaking. How can we calculate the influence that so powerful an emperor had over them, or the spur he had given them — he who had been capable of saying to his soldiers after the battle of Austerlitz, "Give my name to your children: I permit it. And if one worthy of us should be found among them, I will leave him all that I possess, and make him my successor!"

Meanwhile, the junction of the two wings of the Russian army in the vicinity of Smolensk had forced Napoleon to draw the corps of his own army closer together. No signal for attack had been given, but war was all around him and seemed to be tempting his genius by its gains and stimulating it by its reverses. It was about this time that we learned at Vitebsk that the advance guard of the Viceroy had been successful in a skirmish at Suraij, but that in the center near the Dnieper, at Inkovo, Sebastiani had been overcome by superior numbers.

Thereupon, Napoleon wrote to the Duke of Bassano,* charging him to issue daily bulletins to the Turks informing them of fresh victories. It did not matter whether these communications were true or false, as long as they delayed their treaty with the Russians. Even while he was so engaged a deputation from Red Russia arrived in Vitebsk and informed Duroc that they had heard the report of Russian cannon proclaiming the Treaty of Bucharest.† Duroc conveyed this news to Napoleon who was horrified to hear it. He no longer had to wonder at Alexander's silence.

This event made an immediate victory all the more necessary; any remaining hopes of peace were destroyed. The Emperor had just read Alexander's proclamation. Intended for crude people this document was in crude language, as the following passages from it will prove: "The enemy, with unequaled perfidy, threatens the destruction of our country. Our brave soldiers want to throw themselves on his battalions and destroy them; but we will not sacrifice them on the altar of this Moloch. There must be a general uprising against this universal tyrant . . . He has come with treachery in his heart and loyalty on his lips to enslave us with the help of his legions of slaves. Let us drive this plague of locusts out! Let us carry the Cross in our hearts, and steel in our hands!

* Hugues-Bernard Maret, Minister of Foreign Affairs. — J.D.T.
† The Turks had been at war with Russia since 1806. By the Treaty of Bucharest, May 28, 1812, they made peace and surrendered Bessarabia to the Russians. — J.D.T.

Let us pluck the fangs out of this lion's mouth, and over-throw the tyrant who would overthrow the earth!"

Napoleon was furious. The abusive language, the suc-cesses, the reverses, all combined to spur him. The advance of Barclay's troops in three columns toward Rudnia which had been revealed to him by the defeat at Inkovo, and Wittgenstein's vigorous defensive, heralded a battle. Now the choice would have to be made between an immediate conflict and a long, painful, bloody, unaccustomed defensive, difficult to maintain at this distance from our reinforcements and encouraging for our enemies.

Napoleon made the choice and his decision, without being rash, was as grand and bold as the undertaking. His ma-neuver was so well planned, his lieutenants were trained to such a degree of punctuality, precision, and secrecy that within four days, while the Russians, taken by surprise, looked in vain for a single French soldier in front of them, Napoleon had succeeded in moving a mass of one hundred and eighty-five thousand men around the left flank and to the rear of an enemy that for a moment had been bold enough to believe they could surprise him.

On the tenth of August the Emperor gave the order to advance. In four more days all his army would have to be assembled on the left bank of the Dnieper, near Liady. On the thirteenth he left Vitebsk where he had remained just fifteen days.

*

## Smolensk

At three o'clock on the fifteenth we came in sight of Krasnoye, a town built entirely of wood, which a Russian regiment tried to defend. They halted Ney's advance only as long as it took him to fall upon them and scatter them. When we were in possession of this city we saw beyond it a body of Russian infantry, six thousand strong, in a two-column formation, several squadrons of which were covering the retreat. This was Neverovski's corps, and they retreated like lions leaving on the battlefield twelve hundred dead, a thousand prisoners, and eight pieces of artillery. To our cavalry belonged the honors of the day. The attack was as fierce as the defense was stubborn, and our men were all the more to be praised as they had used only the sword against both sword and fire. Neverovski, almost annihilated, retreated within the walls of Smolensk, leaving a band of Cossacks to burn the forage, but sparing the farmhouses.

After a first unsuccessful attack on Smolensk — an attack which cost him two thirds of his soldiers — Ney withdrew to a wooded, sandy knoll overlooking the Dnieper. He was studying the city and the surrounding country when in the distance, on the other side of the river, he saw what he took to be a great mass of marching troops. He lost no time in informing the Emperor and led him to the top of the hill through the underbrush and along ravines to protect him from the Russian fire. From his high post Napoleon saw long black columns marching in a cloud of dust, shot through with the glitter of an enormous number of weapons, advancing so rapidly they seemed to be running. It was the joint forces of Barclay and Bagration, nearly a hundred and twenty thousand men — the entire Russian army!

At the sight Napoleon, beside himself with joy, clapped his hands, exclaiming, "At last! I have them!" There was no doubt about it, the great army was hurrying to enter Smolensk with the intention of crossing it and deploying beneath its walls, there to wage the battle we had so ardently desired.

The moment which was to decide the fate of Russia had come at last!

The Emperor hurried along the lines and assigned to everyone the position he was to occupy. Davout with Count Lobau would spread out on Ney's right; the Guard would be in reserve in the center, and farther along, the army of Italy. The position of Junot and his Westphalians was pointed out, but they had taken the wrong direction and got lost. Murat and Poniatowski were to hold the right. These two generals were already threatening the city, but Napoleon ordered them back to the edge of a thicket, leaving unoccupied in front of them a wide plain extending from the thicket to the Dnieper. This was the battlefield we were offering the enemy. The French army thus posted had no cover to the rear; we were backed by narrow ravines and precipices; but retreat was of little importance to Napoleon who thought only of victory.

Meanwhile Barclay and Bagration were marching rapidly back to Smolensk, the one hoping to save the city by battle, the other to direct the flight of the inhabitants and the evacuation of the stores. They had determined to leave us nothing but ashes. The two generals with their troops arrived out of breath on the steep right bank of the river, and they did not breathe again till they found themselves once more masters of the bridge connecting the two cities.

Then Napoleon harassed the enemy with a swarm of sharpshooters, hoping to draw them to the left bank so that he could wage battle the next morning. It is said that Bagration would have let himself be drawn on, but Barclay would not expose him to this temptation and dispatched him toward Elnia, while he himself took charge of the defense of the city.

In the evening of the sixteenth Bagration began his withdrawal toward Elnia. Napoleon had had his tent set up in the center of the front line, almost within cannon range of

Smolensk, on the edge of the ravine encircling the town. He summoned Murat and Davout. Murat declared that he had noticed movements in the Russian ranks that looked very much like retreat; since crossing the Niemen he had grown accustomed to seeing them escape, and could not believe there would be a battle the next day. Davout was of a contrary opinion. The Emperor of course believed what he most desired.

On the seventeenth Napoleon was awakened at the crack of dawn by the expectation of seeing the Russian army drawn up in front of him; but the battlefield he had prepared for them was still deserted. Nevertheless he clung to his opinion, which was shared by Marshal Davout. Dalton, one of this marshal's generals, had seen Russian battalions come out of the city and take battle position. The Emperor let himself be beguiled by this hope, which Ney and Murat tried in vain to shatter. While they were hoping and waiting, Belliard, having grown weary of the uncertainty, called a small body of cavalrymen to follow him, and drove a band of Cossacks into the Dnieper at a spot above the city. From there he saw that the road to Moscow on the other side of the river was black with artillery and marching troops. There was no longer room for any doubt; the Russians were in full retreat. The Emperor was informed that he would have to give up hope of battle, though the distance from our side of the river was not too great for our cannon still to do considerable damage to the fleeing enemy.

Belliard even proposed that a part of the army should cross the river and cut off the retreat of the Russian rear guard, entrusted with the defense of Smolensk; but the horsemen sent out to look for a ford rode five miles without finding one, merely drowning several horses. There was, however, a wide and safe crossing a couple of miles above the city. Napoleon in his restlessness rode a short distance in that direction, but got tired and came back.

From then on Napoleon appeared to look on Smolensk as nothing more than a halting place, to be captured by storm, and at once. But Murat, prudent when he was not excited by the presence of the enemy, opposed this decision. It was true that he and his cavalry would not be involved in this operation, yet so violent an effort seemed useless to him, since the Russians were withdrawing on their own initiative. When it was proposed that we should pursue them he was heard to exclaim, "Since they don't want a battle, we've chased them far enough. It's high time we stopped!"

The Emperor retorted, but no further record of this conversation has been preserved. However, some words the King let fall at a later date give an idea of the subject of their disagreement. "I threw myself on my knees before my brother-in-law and implored him to stop. But he couldn't see anything but Moscow. Honor, glory, rest — everything was there for him. This Moscow was going to be our ruin!" One thing is certain: when Murat parted from Napoleon his features were marked by real suffering, his movements were jerky as if he were shaken by deep, repressed emotion, and the word "Moscow" fell from his lips several times.

Not far from there, on the left bank of the Dnieper, we had set up a powerful battery on the spot from which Belliard had first noticed the enemy's retreat. But the Russians opposed us with two even more formidable batteries, and our cannon and ammunition wagons were being blown up one after another. The King drove his horse straight into this inferno, dismounted, and stood motionless. Belliard warned him that he was going to get himself killed to no purpose and without glory, but Murat's only reply was to walk closer to the danger. Those around him could no longer doubt that he had lost hope in the outcome of the war, that he foresaw a disastrous future for himself, and was deliberately courting death as the only means of escape. Nevertheless Belliard persisted, pointing out that his rashness would only result in the loss of all their lives. "Then go away, all of you!" cried Murat, "and leave me alone here!" But they refused to leave him. Then the King, swinging around in anger, tore himself away from the place of slaughter, like a man saved against his will.

A general attack had been ordered. Ney was to storm the fortress, Davout and Lobau the sections of the city lying outside the walls, Poniatowski, already on the banks of the Dnieper with sixty pieces of cannon, was to go back down the river as far as the suburbs, and cut off the garrison's way of retreat by blowing up the enemy's bridges. Napoleon wanted the artillery of the guard to batter down the outer wall with their five-inch guns; but the artillerymen, knowing these guns to be powerless against such a mass of masonry, disobeyed and opened fire on the covered way, which they swept clean.

In the course of the action one of our battalions that had presented its flank to the Russian fire had one whole row mowed down by a single ball — twenty-two men felled by one shot!

All the efforts were successful, except Ney's attack which should have been decisive, but was negligently executed. The Russians were quickly driven back within the city walls. All who had not the time to crowd in were killed, but our own attacking columns left a long, broad trail of blood and wounded and dead behind them.

When we reached the city walls we took shelter from the enemy's fire in the outworks we had seized. The firing continued, the crackling of the muskets, doubled in volume by

the echo from the walls, growing louder and louder. The
Emperor, unable to endure it any longer, wanted to withdraw his troops. Thus the mistake Ney had made the day
before with one battalion would have been repeated by an
entire army. The first cost three or four hundred men; the
second had already cost five or six thousand. Davout, however, persuaded the Emperor to persevere in his attack.

At nightfall Napoleon withdrew into his tent which was
placed on a safer spot than the night before. Count Lobau,
who had occupied the moat, which he finally found untena-
ble, had a number of shells dropped on the city to drive out
the enemy's troops. Almost immediately, from several
different points, thick columns of smoke began to rise, soon
to be lit up with the ruddy reflection of flames, and shot
through with sparks. Then long bursts of fire sprang up
everywhere. At first they looked like a great number of
isolated conflagrations, but before long they had melted
together and formed one vast flame, swirling and twisting
into the sky, covering the city and consuming it with a sinister roar.

Count Lobau was appalled by this great disaster, which
he believed to be his work. The Emperor, seated in front of
his tent, contemplated the dreadful spectacle in silence.
Neither the cause nor the result could be determined yet,
and the troops spent the night under arms.

About three o'clock in the morning one of Davout's noncommissioned officers ventured to the foot of the city wall,
and scaled it silently. Emboldened by the complete stillness
around him, he made his way into the town. Suddenly he
heard men speaking in a Slavonic tongue. Taken by surprise
and trapped, the Frenchman was debating whether to take
his own life or surrender when the first rays of the morning
sun showed him that those whom he had taken for enemies

were Poles belonging to Poniatowski's army. They had been the first to enter the city after Barclay's departure.

As soon as Smolensk had been reconnoitered and the gateways cleared of debris, our army marched in. We passed through the smoking ruins in military formation, with our martial music and customary pomp, triumphant over this desolation, but with no other witness to our glory than ourselves. Spectacle without spectators, victory almost without fruits, bloody triumph, of which the smoke that hung heavy around us was a symbol only too clear!

When day came and various reports had sufficiently enlightened the Emperor, he realized that here, as at the Niemen, at Vilna, at Vitebsk, the mirage of victory which lured him on, which he seemed so often on the point of grasping, had once more eluded him. He determined, however to continue pursuing it.

*

## Valoutina

A short distance from Smolensk the highroad to St. Petersburg turned abruptly from the river. Two marshy tracks branched off from it on the right, the first five miles from Smolensk, the second five miles farther on. They wound through a wooded region and rejoined the Moscow road after a long circuit. The fleeing Barclay did not hesitate to risk his forces, with so many wagons and horses, on those narrow, tortuous roads. His long heavy column was forced to toil along the two arcs of a circle of which the road from Smolensk was the span. As usually happens under such circumstances, the forward march was constantly halted by overturned wagons, broken trees, and wheels or horses stuck in the mud.

And all the time the noise of French firing was drawing nearer and nearer, until it seemed to come from ahead of the Russian column, closing off the outlets to safety which they were striving so hard to reach.

At length after a trying march the head of the convoy came in sight of the highroad. To reach the same point the French still had to force the heights of Valoutina and cross the Kolowdnia.

At Valoutina there was a bloody encounter between the main body of the Russian army and the forces of Ney, Junot, and Gudin, in which the last-named general had both his legs shattered by a shell. Removed to Smolensk, he died within a few hours.

During this action the whole army wondered why the Emperor, while forcing three generals to compete for the same objective independently of each other, had not been on hand to give that sort of cohesion to the effort which was impossible without him. But he had returned to Smolensk, either because he was tired, or had not anticipated so important a battle, or simply because, being obliged to look after everything at the same time, he could not give himself fully to any one thing. Also, matters relating to the government of his empire and Europe, held up by the previous days' activities, had been accumulating; and he had to run through his correspondence and dispose of the civil and political affairs that were beginning to be embarrassing. Besides, it was urgent and a matter of pride to him that his communications should be dated from Smolensk!

When Borelli, an officer of Murat's staff, came to bring Napoleon the news of the serious clash at Valoutina, the Emperor at first refused to see him. He was so preoccupied that a minister had to insist before he would admit the

officer. He was visibly affected by Borelli's report, and asked,
"What do you say? Aren't there enough of you? The enemy
has sixty thousand men? Then this is a battle!" And he
inveighed against Junot's disobedience and inaction. When
Borelli informed him of the death of Gudin, the Emperor's
grief was acute, and overflowed in manifold questions and
exclamations of regret. But with his characteristic strength
of mind he had soon mastered his feelings, postponing for
a later date the indulgence of his grief and anger. He turned
all his attention to the work in hand, leaving to the next day
all thought of combat, for night had fallen. But a little later
the prospect of battle filled him with uncontrollable excitement, and daybreak found him on the battlefield of Valoutina.

Ney's soldiers, and the remnants of Gudin's divisions now
without a general, were drawn up for review, on top of
Russian and French corpses, in the midst of mutilated trees.
The earth was beaten hard by the feet of the combatants,
plowed by cannon balls, and littered with broken weapons,
torn clothing, military equipment, overturned wagons, and
human limbs. These were the trophies of war! Such is the
beauty of a field of victory!

Gudin's battalions seemed to be reduced to several platoons who looked all the prouder for being few in number.
Near them, you could breathe the smell of burnt cartridges
and powder, with which the earth and their clothing were
impregnated and their faces still blackened. The Emperor
was unable to pass before them without stepping over or
walking on corpses and bayonets twisted by the violence of
the encounter.

But he covered all these horrors with glory. His review
transformed this field of death into a field of triumph over
which honor and satisfied ambition reigned supreme for a

few hours. Napoleon felt that the time had come for him to buoy up his soldiers' spirits by words and rewards. Never had his look been more affectionate, or his words warmer: "This battle has been the most brilliant exploit in all our military history," he said. "You soldiers who are listening to me are men with whom one could conquer the world. The dead here have earned immortal names for themselves." He spoke in this manner — knowing that it is in the midst of such destruction that men are most inclined to think of immortality.

He was magnificent in his awards. The 12th, 21st and 127th of the line, and the 7th Light Horse received eighty-seven decorations and promotions. These were Gudin's regiments. Until then the 127th had marched without an eagle, for at that time a regiment had to win its standard on a battlefield, and prove that it would be able to keep it. The Emperor presented one with his own hand; nor did he, of course, forget Ney's troops.

The favors were important in themselves, but Napoleon enhanced the value of the gift by his manner of giving. One after another he gathered the regiments about him, like so many families. He questioned the officers and soldiers, asking for the bravest among all these brave men (or for the luckiest) and rewarding them immediately. The officers selected, the soldiers confirmed, the Emperor approved. The choice was made right there, with each regiment in a circle around him, and sanctioned by the applause of the troops.

Everyone was carried away by his paternal manner that made the simple soldier a companion in arms of the master of Europe, as well as by his mode of procedure, which revived the defunct customs of the Republic. He was a monarch, but the monarch of the Revolution; and they loved this self-made man who also made others. Everything about him was admirable; there was nothing to criticize.

Never has a field of victory presented a more exalting spectacle. The gift of the well-deserved eagle, the ceremony of the promotions, the shouts of joy, the glory of the warriors receiving awards on the very spot where they had earned them, their bravery proclaimed by a voice whose every word echoed through an attentive Europe, the fact that their names would be famous over the whole world, especially among their fellow townsmen and families — so many favors at one time made the soldiers drunk with excitement and Napoleon seemed to warm himself at the fire of their enthusiasm.

But when, out of the soldiers' sight, he had been sobered by the attitude of Ney and Murat and had listened to the words of Poniatowski who was as frank and wise in counsel as he was brave in battle; when he learned that scouts had advanced twenty miles without overtaking the enemy, when the suffocating heat began to press down on him — then his disillusionment began.

On the way back to Smolensk his disenchantment was completed by the jolting of his carriage over the tragic reminders of battle and the obstruction of the road by the long line of wounded men dragging themselves along or carried on stretchers. In the city he passed carts loaded with amputated limbs which were going to be thrown away. Here was the loathsome reverse of the field of glory. Smolensk had become one vast hospital, and the great moan rising from it silenced in his ears the shouts of victory on the field of Valoutina.

The surgeons' reports were terrifying. In that country a brandy made of grain,* containing narcotic plants, supple-

* Vodka. — J.D.T.

mented wine and grape brandy. Our young soldiers, weakened by hunger and fatigue, had an idea that this drink
would restore their energy, but its deceptive heat made them
spend all their remaining vitality in one burst, after which
they fell completely exhausted, and were too sick to rise.

There were others, even more intoxicated, or weaker, who
were overcome by dizziness, stupor, or drowsiness, and sank
down in ditches or on the road. Their eyes, dim, half closed,
watery, seemed to look on with indifference as death finally
took control of all their being, and they died dully, without
even a whimper.

At Vilna we had been able to establish hospitals for only
six thousand patients. Convents, churches, synagogues, and
barns had been requisitioned to house this multitude of
sufferers. In these wretched quarters, often unwholesome,
always overcrowded, the sick commonly went without food,
bed, blankets, straw, and medicine. There were soon not
enough surgeons, so that everything, even the hospitals
themselves, tended to breed disease, and nothing to cure it.

At Vitebsk four hundred wounded Russians were left on
the battlefield, and three hundred more were abandoned in
the city when the army evacuated. As the inhabitants had
followed the army, these unfortunate men lay for three days
forgotten, without care, piled up pell-mell, the dead and the
dying together, in unmentionable stench and filth. They
were finally rescued and put with our wounded, also numbering seven hundred. Our surgeons used their own shirts as
well as those of the wretched patients to bandage the wounds,
for clean dressings were already lacking.

When the wounds of these poor fellows finally began to
heal, and all that was needed to complete the cure was wholesome food, they died of starvation. French or Russian, few
survived. Those whom extreme weakness or loss of limbs

prevented from going out to forage for food were the first to succumb. Such disasters as these occurred everywhere when Napoleon was not on the scene, for his orders were never scrupulously carried out except when he was present.

There was no lack of hospitals in Smolensk where fifteen large brick buildings had been spared by the fire. We even found stocks of brandy and wine and some medicine. Our reserve ambulances had finally caught up with us, but even all this was insufficient. The surgeons, who worked around the clock, were unable to cope with the situation. At the end of the second day they were already out of dressings, and were having to substitute paper found in the archives for linen. Parchment was used for splints and bandages, and tow and birchbark fibers replaced lint. There was such an overwhelming amount of work for our doctors that for three days a hospital containing a hundred patients was completely forgotten, and it was only by chance that it was rediscovered. General Rapp paid a visit to that house of death. I will spare my readers an account of the horrors he saw. Rapp, however, did not spare Napoleon's ears, and the Emperor had his own wine and a number of gold coins distributed among the unfortunate inmates who had kept alive by a tenacious hold on life and some revolting food.

To the strong emotions aroused in the Emperor by these reports was added another frightening realization: the burning of Smolensk could no longer be looked upon as an inevitable, unpredictable accident of war or an act of desperation. It was the fruit of cool determination. The Russians had done their destructive work with the care, order, and thought that are usually employed in attempts to preserve.

That same day the courageous replies of a pope of the Russian church, the only one remaining in Smolensk, enabled Napoleon to see more clearly the blind rage we had inspired in the people of Russia. The interpreter for the priest, frightened by this hatred, had brought him to Napoleon. With quiet resolution the old man reproached the Emperor for his sacrilege. He did not know then that it was the Russian general himself who had given the order to burn the shops and churches, and had accused us of these atrocities in order that the merchants and peasants should not separate their cause from that of the nobility.

The Emperor listened attentively. "But your church," he asked after a while. "Was it burned?"

"No, sire," the pope replied. "God is more powerful than you. He will protect it, for I have opened its doors to all the poor folk whom the fire has made homeless."

"You are right," the Emperor said, deeply moved. "Yes, God will watch over the innocent victims of war. He will reward you for your courage. Go back to your post, good priest. If all your popes had followed your example, if they had not basely betrayed the mission of peace which they received from heaven, if they had not abandoned their temples when their mere presence made them inviolable, my soldiers would have respected your sanctuaries; for we are Christians, and your *Bog* is our God."

After this speech, Napoleon sent the priest back to his church with a protective escort. A horrified cry arose when our soldiers were seen entering the sanctuary, and a crowd of women and children crowded around the altar, but the priest called out to them, "Set your minds at rest. I have seen Napoleon . . . I have spoken with him. Oh, how we have been deceived, my children! The Emperor of France is not at all as he had been described to you. Be assured that he and his soldiers worship the same God we do. The war he is waging is not a religious one. It is a political quarrel with our Emperor. His soldiers are fighting only our soldiers. They are not cutting the throats of old people, women, and children, as you have been told. Therefore set your minds at ease, and thank God for having delivered you from the necessity of hating the French as heathens and incendiaries." Then he struck up a hymn of thanksgiving in which the people joined, tears streaming down their cheeks.

The words of this priest showed to what extent the Russian people had been deceived. The rest of the inhabitants of Smolensk had fled; and from now on, it was not merely the army that retreated before us but all Russia. Napoleon felt that with the going of the civilian population one of his most powerful means of conquest was slipping from his grasp.

Already, at Vitebsk, the Emperor had delegated two of his men to find out what these people were thinking. His idea was to convert them to the doctrine of Liberty, so that they might get themselves involved in our cause by a more or less general uprising. But we had been able to communicate with only a few stupid peasants whom the army had probably left behind as spies. Our attempt had had no other result than to expose our plan and put the Russians on their guard against us.

Actually, this procedure was repugnant to Napoleon, who was by nature more inclined to sympathize with kings than with the people. Therefore he did not persist in it. Later on, in Moscow, he received petitions from the heads of several different families, in which they complained of being treated like cattle by the nobles, who bought and exchanged them at will. They requested Napoleon to decree the abolition of serfdom. They offered to be leaders of several partial insurrections which they promised soon to make general. These offers were rejected. With a race of barbarians, this would have resulted in a savage abuse of freedom, and in unbridled license. Several minor rebellions of earlier days gave an idea of what this might be like. The Russian nobles, like the colonists of San Domingo, would have been ruined. This fear was uppermost in Napoleon's mind and prompted him to stop trying to incite a disturbance which he would have been unable to control.

Besides, the masters themselves were distrustful of their slaves. Among the many dangers that threatened them, they recognized this as the most urgent, and therefore set out to influence the minds of the unfortunate serfs, brutalized by all sorts of hard labor. Their priests, in whom they had entire confidence, deceived them with lying speeches. They convinced these peasants that we were a legion of devils commanded by the Anti-Christ, infernal spirits, horrible to look upon, and whose very touch defiled. Our prisoners noticed that their jailors did not dare to use the dishes out of which they (the French) had eaten, but put them aside for the use of their most unclean animals.

Still, we were advancing, and we thought that these crude fabrications would disappear with our coming. But the nobles retreated into the interior with their serfs, as if at the approach of a deadly plague, sacrificing riches, homes, everything that might detain them or be of use to us. They put hunger, fire, and the desert between themselves and us; for it was as much in fear of their serfs as of Napoleon that this high resolution was carried out. It was no longer a war of kings that we were fighting, but a class war, a party war, a religious war, a national war — all sorts of wars rolled into one.

The Emperor by now was fully aware of the enormity of his undertaking. The farther he advanced, the greater it grew. So long as he had encountered only kings, their defeat had been child's play. But all the kings were beaten, and now he had to deal with the people. This was another Spain, but a Spain remote, barren, endless, that he had found at the opposite end of Europe. He hesitated, uncertain as how to proceed, and came to a halt.

At Vitebsk — no matter what decision he made — Smolensk was necessary to him; and he seemed to have put off any definite course until he had reached that city. But now he was as uncertain as before. His perplexity was aggravated by the flames, the epidemic, the victims all around him. Possessed by a fever of hesitation, he turned his eyes toward Kiev, St. Petersburg, Moscow.

At Kiev he could surround Tchitchakov and his army, thus freeing the right flank and rear of the Grand Army. He could overrun the Polish provinces most productive in men, provisions, and horses, while the fortified cantonments — Mohilef, Smolensk, Vitebsk, Polotsk, Dunabourg, and Riga — would defend the rest of the country. Behind this line during the winter months he could arouse and organize all Old Poland, so that when spring came he would be able to hurl this force against Russia, opposing one nation to another, equalizing the balance of the war.

But here at Smolensk, he was at the junction of the main roads to St. Petersburg and Moscow — twenty-nine days' march from the first of these capitals, fifteen from the second. St. Petersburg was the seat of government, the knot tying all the threads of the administration together, the brain of Russia. It was the arsenal for both land and sea forces, and, last but not least, the only point of communication between Russia and England. The victory at Polotsk, of which he had just learned, seemed to urge him in that direction. By marching with Saint Cyr upon St. Petersburg he would surround Wittgenstein and give Riga to MacDonald.

On the other hand, in attacking Moscow he would attack the nobility of the nation in their stronghold, in their age-old honor. The road to this capital was shorter, presented fewer obstacles, and promised more resources. The main army of Russia, which could not be ignored and which must be destroyed, was there with the chance of a battle and the hope of unsettling the nation by striking at its heart.

Of these three objectives the last alone seemed feasible, despite the advanced season. Yet the history of Charles XII was before his eyes, not the one written by Voltaire which he had just laid aside with impatience, judging it over-romantic and inaccurate, but Adlerfeld's * journal which he was reading at that time. In his comparison of the two expeditions he found a thousand significant differences; for who can be the judge of his own case? And of what use is the example of the past in a world where no two men, no two things, or no two situations are ever exactly alike?

Nevertheless at this critical time the name of Charles XII was constantly on his lips.

*

## Viazma

By the twenty-eighth of August our army was crossing the broad plains of the province of Viazma, marching at top speed across the fields, several regiments abreast, each one forming a short, compact column. The main road was reserved for the artillery, baggage wagons, and ambulances. The Emperor, on horseback, could be seen everywhere. Certain letters from Murat and the proximity of Viazma

---

* Gustave Adlerfeld, Swedish historian: aide-de-camp of Charles XII, killed at the battle of Poltava, 1709. — J.D.T.

deceived him once more with the hope of a battle. As he
rode along he could be heard reckoning up numbers, like a
storekeeper. He was counting the thousands of cannon
blasts which would be needed to crush the enemy.

But Barclay did not give battle except with our advance
guard, and then no more than was required to slow up our
march, without bringing us to a full stop. Barclay's determination, the weakening of our army, the quarrels of our
generals, and the approach of the decisive moment worried
Napoleon. At Dresden, at Vitebsk, again at Smolensk, he
had waited in vain for some communication from Alexander.
At Ribky, about the twenty-eighth of August, he seemed to
solicit it. A letter from Berthier to Barclay concluded with
these words: "The Emperor wishes me to beg you to present
his compliments to the Emperor Alexander. Tell him that
neither the vicissitudes of war nor any other circumstances
will ever affect the friendship he has for him."

On the twenty-eighth our vanguard drove the Russians
back into Viazma. Our men, terribly thirsty from the march,
the heat, and the dust, were out of water. They quarreled
over puddles, fought for the springs and drained them down
to the mud. The Emperor himself had to be satisfied with a
cupful of liquid mud. During the night the enemy destroyed
the bridges over the Viazma, sacked the town and set fire to
it. Murat and Davout rushed in to extinguish the fire, which
the Russians defended; but we were able to ford the river
at a point near the ruins of the bridges, and a part of our
vanguard fought the incendiaries while the others fought
the fire, soon bringing it under control.

Our advance guard in this case was made up of picked
men. They were ordered to close in on the Russian soldiers
in Viazma, and to find out whether it was really they, or our
own soldiers who had set the fire. The report they brought

back dispelled any doubts the Emperor might have concerning the Russians' deadly intentions.

In Viazma we found some provisions, but these were soon squandered by plunderers. In crossing the city Napoleon witnessed this disorder. Furiously angry, he drove his horse into the groups of pillaging soldiers, striking them and knocking them down. He had a sutler seized, and ordered him to be tried and shot immediately. But we all knew how much importance to attach to these words, and knew also that the more violent his fits of temper were, the more promptly they were followed by indulgence. Therefore, a moment later, this wretch was placed kneeling in Napoleon's path, with a woman and several children who were passed off as his, beside him. Napoleon, already cooled off, inquired what he wanted, and had him set free.

He was still on his horse when he was surprised to see Belliard, Murat's companion in arms for fifteen years, now his chief of staff, hurrying toward him. Astonished, he thought there had been a disaster, but Belliard reassured him, then gave his news.

"Just beyond the Viazma, the enemy suddenly appeared in full force, in a favorable position on the edge of a ravine, ready for battle. Immediately the cavalry went into action on all sides, and as the infantry was also required, the King put himself at the head of one of Davout's divisions, and set it in motion against the Russians. But Davout dashed up at that instant, calling to his men to halt, openly criticizing this maneuver, harshly reproaching the King, and forbidding his generals to obey him. The moment was critical. Murat reminded him in vain of his rank . . . He has sent me to say that he is disgusted by this challenge to his authority, and that you must choose between him and Davout!"

At this news Napoleon exploded. "Davout has forgotten

discipline completely. He has refused to recognize my
brother-in-law whom I made my lieutenant!" He immediately dispatched Berthier with the order to place Compans'
division, the subject of the dispute, under Murat's command from that time forward. Davout made no attempt to
excuse his action, but upheld his motives, claiming that he
had acted to forestall Murat's habitual recklessness, and that
he was a better judge of the terrain and the sort of action
best suited to it, which was quite possible.

When the fighting was over and the enemy no longer held
his attention, Murat gave himself up entirely to the recollection of his quarrel. Shut up in his tent with Belliard, as
if in hiding, his blood grew hotter from shame and rage as
the expressions the marshal had used returned to his
memory.

"I have been slighted, publicly insulted!" he said. "And
Davout still lives! But we shall meet again . . . What difference do the Emperor's anger and decision make to me? It's
up to me to avenge this wrong. Who cares for his noble
blood? My sword made me king, and I call upon my sword
now!" And he was in the act of seizing his arms to attack
Davout when Belliard stopped him, reminding him of the
example he must always set his troops, of the enemy that had
to be overtaken, of the sorrow that such an outburst would
cause his family, and the delight it would give the Russians.
Belliard declares that the King then cursed his crown, and
tried hard to swallow the insult, but tears of vexation rolled
down his cheeks and fell on his uniform. While he was
suffering in this way, Davout, seated quietly in his headquarters, stubbornly stuck to his opinion, and insisted that
the Emperor had made a mistake.

Napoleon returned to Viazma, where he was to stay until
he had studied his new conquest and decided upon the best

use he could make of it. The reports received from the interior indicated that the Russian government was appropriating our successes and trying to make the people believe that the loss of so many provinces was the result of a general plan of retreat, worked out in advance. Papers seized in Viazma stated that *Te Deums* were being sung in St. Petersburg to celebrate the alleged victories at Vitebsk and Smolensk. Shocked by the news, Napoleon exclaimed, "What! *Te Deums?* Then they dare to lie to God as they lie to men!"

By noon on the first of September only a grove of young firs stood between Murat and Gzhatsk. In that town, as at Smolensk and Viazma, the Bazaar, either by chance or in accord with a Tartar custom, was on the farther side of the river, the side toward Asia. The Russian rear guard, protected by the river, had the time to burn all that quarter; only Murat's prompt action saved the rest of the city.

We crossed the Gzhatsk as we could, on girders, in small boats, or by fording. Our front-line troops were following the Russians into the flames behind which they had disappeared when they saw one of the inhabitants running toward them, shouting that he was French. His joy and accent confirming his statement, he was taken to Davout who questioned him. According to this man's story, the Russian army had undergone a complete change. A general outcry had gone up from the ranks against Barclay; and in Moscow, the nobles, the merchants, and the people had echoed the dissatisfaction.

"They are saying that this general, this minister is a traitor," he told them. "That he is having all their divisions shot to pieces, and dishonors the army with his endless flight. The people are suffering the shame of invasion, and their

cities are going up in flames. If they had felt it necessary to
go to such ruinous extremes, they would have made the
sacrifice themselves. Then they would have kept some
honor, while to let themselves be sacrificed by a foreigner
means that they will lose everything, even the honor of the
sacrifice."

"They are asking," the Frenchman went on, "why they
must have this foreigner. Doesn't there still exist a contem-
porary, a companion in arms, a pupil of the great Suvarov? *
To save Russia, it will take a Russian!"

Everybody was clamoring for Kutuzov and a decisive
battle. The Frenchman informed us that Alexander had
yielded to persuasion. Bagration's insubordination and the
general outcry had gained the desired result — Kutuzov
and a battle. The Russian Emperor himself had judged an
encounter indispensable, now that they had drawn the
French army so far into their country.

On the twenty-ninth of August, Kutuzov had arrived at
Tsarevo-Zamische, between Viazma and Gzhatsk, and his
announcement of a battle had made the Russian army thrill
with a double joy. Immediately all the corps had marched
toward Borodino, no longer in flight but to take their stand
on the frontier of the region of Moscow, to entrench themselves for a combat to the death.

A minor incident, the arrival of a Russian envoy bearing
a flag of truce, seemed to confirm the Frenchman's words.
This Russian officer had so little to say that it was at once
evident that he had come as an observer. His bearing displeased Davout in particular, who found him overconfident.
One of our generals, having thoughtlessly asked him what
we should find between Viazma and Moscow, got the arro-

* Count Alexander Suvarov, famous Russian military leader, who distinguished himself particularly in the war with the Turks. — J.D.T.

gant reply, "Poltava!" * This answer promised a battle and
pleased our generals, who appreciated a ready rejoinder and
were always happy to encounter opponents worthy of them.

This envoy was escorted away without precaution, as he
had been admitted and saw that anyone could get into the
imperial headquarters without any difficulty. He passed our
outposts without being challenged by a single sentry. Everywhere he found the same carelessness, that boldness natural
to the French, and to victors. Everybody was asleep, there
was no password, no patrol. Our soldiers seemed to neglect
these precautions as being beneath their notice. Why worry
about security? They were attacking, they were victorious.
Let the Russians be on the defensive. This same officer said
later that he was tempted to take advantage of our imprudence that night, but there was no Russian force at hand.

In their haste to burn the bridges over the Gzhatsk the
enemy had left a number of Cossacks behind. They were
sent to Napoleon, who was approaching on horseback, and
he insisted on questioning them himself. He called his
interpreter, and had two of these Scythians with their strange
uniforms and savage appearance placed one on either side
of him. It was in this company that he rode through Gzhatsk.
The replies of these barbarians agreed with what the Frenchman had told us; and other news that came in from the outposts on the nights of the first and second of September
confirmed them.

Barclay, up to the very last minute, alone against everybody, had been faithful to the plan of constant retreat which,
as early as 1807, he had outlined to one of our generals as
the only hope of salvation for Russia. Among us he was
praised for having persisted in this wise defensive, before so

---

* Site of the battle in which Charles XII of Sweden was defeated by Peter
the Great of Russia. — J.D.T.

aggressive an adversary and despite the outcry of a proud
nation infuriated by disaster.

Doubtless he had made a mistake in allowing himself to be
taken by surprise at Vilna, and in not recognizing the marshy
meanderings of the Berezina as the real frontier of Lithuania.
But it must be noted that from Vitebsk to Smolensk he
anticipated Napoleon's moves; on the Luczissa, the
Dnieper, and at Valoutina his resistance had been equal to
the time and place. This war of details and the losses it en-
tailed had been to his advantage, each backward step he
took carrying us farther from our base of supplies while
bringing him closer to his. Whether he had risked, defended,
or surrendered, he had always acted for the best.

Yet he had somehow managed to incur universal disfavor.
In our eyes this was the highest praise. We approved of him
for having scorned public opinion when it was in the wrong,
and to have been satisfied to spy on all our movements in
order to turn them to his advantage, and thus to have discovered that, more often than not, nations are saved in spite
of themselves.

Barclay showed himself even greater during the rest of
the campaign. This commander-in-chief and minister of war,
from whom the command had been taken that it might be
given to Kutuzov, was willing to serve under him; and he
obeyed as zealously as he had commanded.

# CHAPTER III

********

## *Borodino * : The Fifth of September*

THE RUSSIAN ARMY had come to a stop at last! Miloradovich, with sixteen thousand recruits, and a multitude
of peasants carrying crosses and shouting *God wills it,*
swarmed up to join the ranks. We were told that they were
turning up the whole plain of Borodino, throwing up breastworks and digging in with the evident intention of not retreating another inch.

Napoleon announced to his army that there would be a
battle. He allowed them two days to rest, prepare their
arms, and requisition food, warning the detachments sent
out to gather supplies, "If you haven't returned by tomorrow,
you'll be depriving yourselves of the honor of fighting."

He wanted to know everything about his new adversary.
Kutuzov was described to him as an old man whose reputation dated from the time, long ago, when he had received an
unusual wound. Since then he had always managed to take
skillful advantage of events. Even the defeat at Austerlitz
— which he had predicted — had increased his standing,
and his last campaigns against the Turks had added to his
stature. His courage was beyond question; but people reproached him with regulating its movements to suit his
personal interests, for he calculated everything. His slow,

* Ségur calls this the Battle of the Moskva. — J.D.T.

52

vindictive, and crafty nature was characteristic of the Tartar, and he could prepare for implacable warfare with a policy of gentleness, flexibility, and patience.

On the whole he was a more able courtier than general. But he was a power to be reckoned with, because of his reputation and his ability to make everything and everybody contribute to it. He was able to please an entire nation and every individual citizen, from the general to the soldier.

Furthermore, in his outward appearance, his language, his clothing, his superstitious practices, there was much that reminded one of Suvarov — something of the ancient Muscovite, a strong national identity which endeared him to the Russians. In Moscow the people, completely carried away in their elation, kissed each other in the streets and believed that they were saved.

When Napoleon had gathered this information and issued his orders, he awaited events with that tranquillity of spirit peculiar to superior men, limiting his activity to the inspection of the vicinity of his headquarters. Since the arrival of Kutuzov, bands of Cossacks had been worrying the heads of our columns. Murat, who had preceded the Emperor by several miles, was exasperated at the sight of his cavalry being forced to deploy before so insignificant an adversary. It is claimed that in an impulsive movement, worthy of the days of chivalry, he finally rushed unaccompanied upon the Cossacks, and halting only a short distance from their front line, sword in hand, ordered the barbarians to withdraw with such an imperious gesture that they obeyed and retreated in amazement.

This incident, which was immediately related to us, was received without question. The martial air of that monarch, the magnificence of his uniform, his reputation, and the novelty of such an action made his momentary influence over these savages seem true, despite its improbability. For such was Murat: a stage king in the studied elegance of his attire, a real king in his bravery and inexhaustible activity, equal to any attack and always armed with an air of superiority and menacing assurance — the most dangerous of all offensive weapons.

We immediately occupied the villages and woods. At the left and center were placed the army of Italy, Compans' divisions, and Murat; at the right, Poniatowski. These combined forces, in a sudden attack on the two wings of the imperial column, forced the Russian rear guard back toward Borodino, so that the combat was concentrated at one point. The screen of troops being removed, the first Russian redoubt came into view. Placed too far in advance of their left flank, this redoubt defended the front lines without being defended itself, the irregularity of the terrain making this isolated position necessary.

Compans skillfully took advantage of the rolling nature of the ground; the hillocks provided platforms from which his cannon could batter the redoubt, and sheltered the infantry as they formed their columns for attack. The 61st Regiment was the first to advance; the redoubt was captured by a single bayonet charge, but Bagration sent reinforcements, and it was regained. Three times the 61st wrested it from the Russians, and three times they were driven out. Finally they held the position, bleeding and half destroyed.

The next day when the Emperor reviewed this regiment he asked where the third battalion was. "It is in the redoubt, sire," the colonel answered. But that was not the end of the engagement. The neighboring woods were still swarming with Russian sharpshooters who were continuously coming out of cover to renew their attacks, in which they were supported by three divisions. In the end the combined attack on Shevardino by Morand and on the Elnia wood by Ponia-towski proved too much for Bagration's troops, and Murat's cavalry cleared the plain. It was the exceptional tenacity of one Spanish regiment that discouraged the enemy, who finally yielded, and this redoubt, their most advanced post, became ours.

While this was taking place the Emperor was assigning a position to each corps. The rest of the army fell into line, and a general fusillade, interspersed with volleys of cannon fire, was ordered and kept up until the limits of each division had been established and night had blotted out the targets.

One of Davout's regiments, trying to find their place in the first line, went beyond it in the dark and blundered into the midst of a company of Russian cuirassiers, who fell upon them and scattered them, capturing three guns and taking or killing three hundred men. The survivors immediately gathered themselves up in a compact mass, bristling with steel and firearms. The enemy were unable to penetrate them further, and the greatly weakened troop managed to find its way back into the battle line.

The Emperor camped behind the army of Italy, at the right of the main road, with the Old Guard drawn up in a square round his tents. As soon as the shooting had stopped, the campfires were lit. On the Russian side they blazed in a vast semicircle, but on our side they burned with a faint irregular light and in no particular order, our troops arriving late and in great haste on an unfamiliar terrain, with nothing prepared and wood very scarce, especially in the center and on the left flank.

The Emperor slept little. General Caulaincourt returned from the captured redoubt and reported that not a single prisoner had fallen into our hands, and Napoleon, astonished, questioned him over and over. "Didn't my cavalry charge in time? . . . Are those Russians determined to win or die?" He was told that the Russians, spurred into a fanatic state by their officers and accustomed to fighting with the Turks who put their prisoners to death, preferred being killed to being taken alive. The Emperor was lost in thought for a considerable time; then, having decided that an artillery battle was the most certain to succeed, he issued immediate orders to hasten the arrival of the trains that had not yet caught up with us.

That very night a fine cold rain began to fall, and a high wind heralded the coming of autumn. This was one more enemy to be reckoned with. This season corresponded to the age into which Napoleon was entering; and the influence of the seasons of the year on the corresponding ages of man is well known.

The night was a troubled one for all of us. The soldiers and officers were busy getting their arms ready, mending their uniforms, and fighting cold and hunger — their life was one continual struggle. The generals as well as the Emperor were worried lest the Russians, discouraged by the day's losses, might slip away under cover of the night. Murat had warned us of that possibility; and several times it seemed to us that their campfires were growing fainter, and we imagined we could hear the noise of their departure. But it was the morning sun that put their fires out.

*

## The Sixth of September

This time we did not have to go far to seek the enemy. The sun of the sixth of September rose on the two armies, and showed them to each other in the same positions they had occupied at sunset. There was general rejoicing. This incoherent, sluggish, shifting war in which our best efforts had been fruitless and in which we seemed to be hopelessly, endlessly sinking, was at last centered in one spot. Here we touched bottom, here was the end, here everything would be decided!

The Emperor took advantage of the first light of day to ride up between the two battle lines and inspect the Russian front from one end to the other; and when he had finished the reconnaissance to his satisfaction, his mind was made up. He could be heard giving orders: "Eugène * will be the pivot . . . The right will bring on the action . . . They will advance under cover of the wood, and as soon as they have entered the redoubt facing them, they will turn to the left and march on the Russian flank, driving the whole army to the right and into the Kolocha."

The main line of attack being planned, Napoleon took up the details. During the night three batteries of sixty guns each would be set up to act against the Russian redoubts, two in front of their left, the other trained on their center. As soon as it was light, Poniatowski and his troops, now reduced to five thousand men, were to advance on the old Smolensk road; and passing round the wood against which both the French right flank and the Russian left flank were resting, they would defend the former and impede the latter. We were to wait until we heard the sound of their first volley.

Our artillery was then to open fire immediately on the Russian left flank. This would split their ranks and expose the redoubts; and Davout and Ney would rush into the breach supported by Junot and his Westphalians, Murat's cavalry, and then by the Emperor himself with his Old Guard,

* Eugène de Beauharnais, Viceroy of Italy. — J.D.T.

twenty thousand strong. Our first efforts would be directed against the two redoubts. Through them we would penetrate to the heart of the Russian army, which would be badly mutilated by then, with the center and right unmasked and almost entirely surrounded.

However, the Russians seemed to be massing their forces at the center and right, thus threatening the Moscow road, the sole line of operation and retreat for the Grand Army. As Napoleon would put the Kolocha River between himself and that road by moving the main body of his troops against the enemy's left, he decided to reinforce the army of Italy, occupying the road, by the addition of two of Davout's divisions and General Grouchy's cavalry. He judged that one Italian division, the Bavarian cavalry, and Ornano's battalions, in all about ten thousand men, would be sufficient to cover his own left flank. Such were Napoleon's plans.

Never was there a quieter day than the one before the great battle. It was like something agreed upon. And why should anyone stir or make any needless trouble? Would the next day not decide everything? Besides, there were preparations to be made by everyone: the different corps had to get their weapons, their men, their ammunition ready, and re-form their lines which had been disorganized by the march. The generals had to study their reciprocal preparations for attack, defense, and retreat in order to bring them into conformity with each other and the terrain, and so leave as little as possible to chance.

And now, before engaging in the terrible struggle, these two giants were looking each other over carefully, measuring each other's strength and preparing in silence for the deadly encounter.

The Emperor, no longer able to doubt that the battle would take place, retired to his tent to dictate his orders; and there he pondered the gravity of the situation. He had seen that the two armies were equal — about a hundred and twenty thousand men and six hundred cannon on either side. The Russians had the advantage of familiarity with the terrain, a common language and uniform, of being one nation fighting for one cause; but their army included many irregular troops and raw recruits. The French had the same number of men, but more soldiers. Napoleon had just been handed a report of the situation of his corps, giving the numerical account of his divisions. As this was not a matter of review or distribution of awards, but of combat, the muster roll was not padded. It was true that his army was reduced; but it was still healthy, flexible, vigorous, like those virile bodies which, having lost the soft curves of youth, exhibit the firmer lines of full manhood.

During the past few days that he had been marching in their midst he had found them silent with the silence of great expectation or great awe; like nature just before a hurricane, or crowds in the presence of imminent danger.

He felt that the army urgently needed a rest, of whatever kind, and there was no rest in store for his troops save in death or victory. He had them in a position where it was so desperately urgent for them to conquer that conquer they must at any cost. The rashness of that position was evident; but he knew that, of all faults, rashness was the one the French condoned most willingly. At bottom he had no fear for them, for himself, or for the final outcome, no matter what individual misfortunes they might suffer.

In the course of the day Napoleon noticed an extraordinary activity in the enemy's camp. In fact the entire army seemed to be armed and on foot. In the midst of the troops Kutuzov was seen advancing, surrounded by all religious and

military pomp. The commander-in-chief had had the popes
and archimandrates put on their richest, most majestic vest-
ments — a heritage from the Greeks. They preceded him,
bearing their precious religious symbols, in particular the
beloved icon from Smolensk, which, they claimed, had been
miraculously saved from the profanation of the sacrilegious
French.

When the Russian general saw his soldiers deeply moved
by this imposing spectacle, he addressed them, speaking
chiefly of heaven — the only country left to the enslaved. In
the name of religion and equality he sought to incite the
serfs to defend their masters' possessions. Holding up the
icon that had taken refuge in their ranks, he appealed to
their courage and fanned their indignation. He spoke of
Napoleon as "a universal despot, a tyrannical disturber of
the peace of the world, a worm, an arch-rebel who over-
threw their altars and defiled them with blood; who exposed
the Ark of the Lord, represented by the Smolensk icon, to the
profanation of men and to the ravages of the seasons."

He went on to show the Russians their cities in ashes, reminded them of their wives and children, paid a short tribute to their emperor, and ended by appealing to their piety
and patriotism. Thus he flattered the instinctive virtues of
this people, whose very coarseness and primitive emotions
made them all the more to be feared as soldiers as they were
not likely to be distracted from discipline by reasoning.
Shut up within a narrow circle by slavery, they were reduced
to a limited number of sensations which became the only
source of their needs, their desires, or their ideas. Moreover,
they were proud through lack of comparison, and credulous
through lack of knowledge, worshiping images, as idolatrous
as Christians can be; for, in order to bring their faith within
the reach of the most brutal understanding, they had trans-

formed a religion of the spirit, purely intellectual and moral, into something physical and material.

This solemn spectacle, the exhortations of the officers, the benedictions of the priests, finally aroused the courage of the spectators to a fanatical heat. Down to the simplest soldier, they believed themselves consecrated by God to the defense of heaven and the sacred soil of Russia.

On the French side there was no religious or military display, no review of troops, nothing was done to arouse the men. The Emperor's proclamation was distributed very late and read the next morning just before the battle, so that several corps went into action without having an opportunity to hear it. While the Russians, excited by the most powerful stimuli, were invoking the sword of Saint Michael and borrowing strength from all the heavenly powers, the French were seeking it within themselves, convinced that all true strength is in the heart, that there the heavenly host is found.

It chanced that that very day the Emperor received from Paris a portrait of the King of Rome,* the child whom the Empire had welcomed with as much joy as had the Emperor himself. Every day since the birth of his son Napoleon had been seen at his side in the palace, expressing the most tender of sentiments: and when on such far-removed fields, in the midst of such threatening preparations, he looked on the image of that gentle face again, his soldier's heart was strangely softened. He set up the picture outside his tent and called his officers, even the soldiers of the Old Guard, wishing to share his feelings with those seasoned troopers, to show his private family to his military family, and display this symbol of hope in the presence of grave danger.

* Napoleon II, son of Marie Louise, born in 1811, and given the title of *King of Rome.* — J.D.T.

That evening General Fabvier, an aide-de-camp of Marmont, whose name was to figure later in our domestic affairs, arrived on the field of Borodino, fresh from the battlefields of Spain. The Emperor received the aide-de-camp of a defeated leader cordially. On the eve of this uncertain battle he was disposed to make allowances for defeat, and listened to all Fabvier had to say concerning the scattering of his forces in Spain and the multiplicity of generals-in-chief. Napoleon seemed to approve, but explained his motives, which we need not mention here.

Night came, and with it the old fear that under cover of darkness the Russians might escape from the field of battle. This apprehension disturbed Napoleon's sleep. He kept waking up and calling out, asking what time it was, and if anybody had heard a noise, and each time dispatched someone to see if the enemy was still there. He was so doubtful that he had his proclamation distributed with the order that it should not be read until morning, and then only in case there should be a battle.

Reassured on that score for a while, he would then be assailed by fears of a different nature. The miserable condition of his soldiers appalled him. Weak and starved as they were, how could they stand up under a prolonged and violent encounter? In the presence of such danger he looked upon his Old Guard as his only resource, and it seemed to him that they must answer now for the two armies. Several times he summoned Bessières, the marshal in whom he had the greatest confidence as commander of his chosen troops, and asked him whether the needs of the guards were all provided for. He had a three-day ration of biscuit and rice, taken out of their own reserve supplies, distributed to these men. Then, fearing that he might not have been obeyed, he went out and inquired of the grenadiers on guard before his tent whether they had got their rations. Satisfied with their reply, he went back and fell into a doze, only to call out again in a few minutes.

This time his aide-de-camp found him sitting with his head in his hands reflecting on the vanity of glory. "What is war? A barbarous profession whose art consists in being stronger than the enemy at a given moment." Then he went on to complain of the inconstancy of Fortune from which, he said, he was beginning to suffer. A little later, appearing to return to more reassuring thoughts, he recalled what had been told him concerning Kutuzov's slowness and negligence, remarking that he was surprised that the Russians should have preferred him to Bennigsen. Then, thinking of the critical position in which he had got himself, he exclaimed: "A great day is in the making! It will be a terrible battle." He asked Rapp if he expected a victory. "Without any doubt," Rapp replied. "But a bloody one." Then Napoleon went on: "I know; but I have eighty thousand men. I shall enter Moscow with sixty thousand. The stragglers will join us there, then the makeshift battalions, and we shall be even stronger than before the battle." He appeared not to have included in his enumeration either the Guard or the cavalry.

Then his first fears overwhelmed him again, and he sent out to ascertain the Russian position. He was told that their fires were burning as bright as ever and that, judging by the great number of shadows moving about them, it was not merely a rear guard that was keeping them burning, but a whole army. The presence of the enemy soothed the Emperor, and he lay down again.

But the long marches with the army, the fatigue of the preceding days and nights, so many worries, so much waiting and hoping had exhausted him. The sudden drop in temperature having brought on a heavy cold, he was tormented by a high fever, a dry cough, and a burning thirst, which he spent the rest of the night trying to quench. This fresh indisposition was aggravated by a chronic ailment; for a day or so he had been suffering from a painful attack of a cruel disease with which he had been afflicted for a long time — dysuresis.*

Five o'clock came at last. One of Ney's officers hurried in to report that the Russians were still there, and the marshal wished to attack. This news appeared to restore to the Emperor the energy of which his fever had deprived him. He rose, called his retinue about him, and left his tent shouting, "At least we have them! Forward march! We're going to open the gates of Moscow!"

*

## The Seventh of September

It was half past five in the morning when Napoleon reached the redoubt we had taken two days before, where he awaited daylight and the first shots from Poniatowski. As the sun rose the Emperor pointed it out to his men, crying, "There is the sun of Austerlitz!" But it was against us: it rose on the side of the Russians, making easy targets of our men, while shining full in our eyes. We found that in the darkness our batteries had been placed beyond cannon range, and would have to be pushed forward; but the enemy did not interfere with this maneuver. They seemed not to want to be the first to break the terrible silence.

The Emperor's attention was centered on the right flank, when suddenly, at about seven o'clock, fighting broke out on

* Retention of urine. — J.D.T.

his left. He soon learned that one of Prince Eugène's regiments, the 106th, had taken the village of Borodino and its bridge. They should have destroyed the latter at once; but, carried away by their success, some troops had crossed it, in spite of the warning cries of their general, and attacked the heights of Gorki. The Russians on these ridges had mowed them down with a cannonade from front and flank. The commander of the brigade had already been killed, and the entire 106th would have been wiped out, if the 92nd had not of its own initiative rushed to their assistance and brought the miserable remainder back within our lines.

It was Napoleon who had ordered the left wing to attack violently, perhaps thinking that he would be only half obeyed, or merely wanting to draw the enemy's attention to that side. He now issued order after order, at the highest pitch of excitement. His attack would have to be from the front, instead of in an oblique line, as he had planned.

During this action the Emperor, believing that Poniatowski was engaged on the old Moscow road, had given the signal for attack in that direction. Suddenly puffs and columns of smoke and fire sprang up above the peaceful plains and silent hills, followed almost instantaneously by numberless explosions and the whistling of bullets in all directions. In the midst of this dreadful uproar Davout with General Compans' divisions, General Desaix, and thirty cannon moved rapidly against the first fortifications.

Then the Russians opened fire. The French replied with cannon only, as their infantry was advancing without firing, hurrying to fall upon the enemy's battery and silence it. But Compans, commander of this column, fell wounded along with the bravest of his soldiers: the rest of the men, bewildered, halted under the hail of bullets to reply by a volley of musketry, but at that moment Rapp galloped up to replace Compans and led them at a run with leveled bayonets against the redoubt. Just as he reached it he, too, fell — this was the twenty-second time he had been wounded. A third general succeeded him, only to fall in his turn, and Davout himself was wounded. Rapp was carried to the Emperor who exclaimed on seeing him, "What, Rapp, again! . . . But what's going on up there?" The aide-de-camp replied that the Guard would be required to bring the encounter to a successful end.

"No," said the Emperor. "I will take good care to see that the Guard is not used. I will not have them knocked to bits! I'll win the battle without them."

Then Ney with his three divisions, now reduced to six thousand men, galloped out on the plain to support Davout. The Russians turned half their fire on him, without slowing him up. Compans' 57th Regiment, finding themselves reinforced, rallied to make a final dash against the enemy's intrenchments, scaled them, swarmed over the Russians and routed them with their bayonets. Those who were not killed or wounded fled, leaving the 57th in full command. At the same time Ney was charging the other two redoubts, and with such violence that he snatched them from the enemy.

It was noon. The left of the Russian line having been disorganized and the plain opened up, the Emperor ordered Murat to rush in with his cavalry and complete the victory. In a very few minutes the King could be seen on the heights in the midst of Russian troops — the second line and reinforcements led by Bagawout that had come to the assistance of the first line. They all rushed together upon the redoubts to reconquer them. The French, still in the disorder of victory, were stunned and fell back.

The Westphalians whom Napoleon had sent to help Poniatowski were crossing the wood that separated this general from the rest of the army when through clouds of dust and smoke they saw our fleeing troops. From the direction of their march they believed them to be Russians, and opened fire on them. This mistake, in which they persisted, increased the chaos.

The enemy's cavalry, vigorously pressing their success, surrounded Murat, who had forgotten his own safety in an attempt to rally his men. Hands were already reaching out to seize him when he escaped by leaping into the redoubt, where he found only a few distracted soldiers, completely out of control and racing wildly around the parapet. The only thing that prevented them from running away was the lack of an exit.

The presence of the King and his shouts restored the courage of some of the men. He seized a weapon himself, and fighting with one hand, held his plumed hat up with the other and waved it as a sign to his men who rallied to the authority of his example. Meanwhile Ney had re-formed his divisions, stopped the Russian cuirassiers with his fire and spread disorder in their ranks. They fell back: Murat was finally rescued, and the knoll retaken.

No sooner had the King got himself out of this danger than he rushed into another. He charged the enemy with the cavalry of Bruyères and Nansouty, and by a series of stubbornly repeated attacks succeeded in breaking their line and pushing them back toward the center, concluding within an hour the defeat of the entire left flank.

But the high ground of the ruined village of Semenovsk, marking the extreme left of the Russian center, was still not taken. The reinforcements that Kutuzov was continually drawing from his right were using this as a vantage post. From it their fire swept Ney and Murat on the plain below, checking their victory. It was evident that this position must be seized. First came Maubourg with his cavalry who cleared the front, then Friant, one of Davout's generals, brought in the infantry; but it was Dufour at the head of the 15th Light Horse who scaled the steep slope first, and drove the Russians out of the ruined village, which was badly fortified. Friant, though wounded, backed up this effort and helped to make it a definite success.

We should have taken immediate advantage of this vigorous action which opened the way to victory; but both Ney and Murat were fought out. They halted; and while they were re-forming their troops they sent a demand for reinforcements. It was then that Napoleon gave his first signs of indecision. He reflected for a long time, and finally, after a series of orders and counterorders issued to the Young Guard, decided that the combined forces of Friant and Maubourg were adequate to hold the knoll, as the decisive moment — in his opinion — had not yet come.

Kutuzov, meanwhile, was taking advantage of this respite, which he had certainly not anticipated, by calling all his reserve, even the Russian Guard, to the assistance of his unprotected left flank. Bagration re-formed his line with all available reinforcements, the right supported by the powerful battery that Prince Eugène was attacking, the left by the wood which bounded the battlefield on the side toward Psarevo. Their fire decimated our ranks. Their attack was violent, impetuous, with infantry, artillery, and cavalry all joining in one great effort. Ney and Murat, whose concern now was not to complete the victory, but just to hold what they had gained, braced themselves against this onslaught.

Friant's soldiers drawn up before Semenovsk repulsed the first charge; but under the burning hail of shells and grapeshot they began to give way. One of the officers, who could take no more, had given the order to retreat when Murat rushed up to him, seized him by the collar, and shouted, "What are you doing?" The colonel pointed to the ground littered with his dead — half his troops — and answered, "Surely you can see we can't hold out here any longer."

"Well," cried the King, "I'm staying!"

Stung by these words, the officer stared at Murat coldly and said, "All right . . . Soldiers, about face! Let's go get ourselves killed!"

Then Murat dispatched Borelli to the Emperor to ask for relief. To convince Napoleon that the enemy was drawing nearer, this officer pointed out the clouds of dust stirred up by the Russian cavalry on the ridge, which had been quiet since we had taken it, and called attention to the occasional cannon balls which for the first time were landing almost at the Emperor's feet. Borelli insisted, and Napoleon reluctantly promised his Young Guard; yet they had advanced only a few paces when he himself called out to them to halt. Count Lobau, under pretense of straightening the line, continued to advance them little by little, until Napoleon noticed his action and repeated his order.

Fortunately our reserve artillery rolled out at that moment to take its position on the knoll. Lauriston had received the Emperor's consent to this maneuver. But this very move, which he allowed rather than ordered, soon seemed to Napoleon of such importance that he urged its execution with the only sign of impatience he had shown the entire day.

One cannot say whether it was the doubtful outcome of the action of Poniatowski on the right and of Prince Eugène on the left that shook his confidence. One thing is certain, the idea of the extreme Russian left breaking away from the Poles and seizing the field behind Ney and Murat worried him, and may have been one of the reasons for his keeping

his Guard on the lookout at that point. To all who urged
him he replied, "I want to see more clearly . . . My battle
hasn't begun yet . . . The day will be long. You have to know
how to wait. Time always has to be considered: it's the element of which all things are made. Nothing is clear yet."
Then he asked what time it was and remarked, "The time
for my battle hasn't come yet. It will begin in two hours."

But *his* battle never began. Almost all that day he sat or
paced slowly up and down, in front of and a little to the left
of the redoubt we had taken on the fifth, on the edge of a
ravine far removed from the battle, of which he could see but
little since the action had moved on over the hills. When he
did catch a glimpse of the fighting he was without alarm or
impatience with either his own troops or the enemy's. He
made a sorrowful gesture of resignation when, as frequently
happened, he was informed of the loss of one of his best generals. He rose from time to time, took a few steps, and sat
down again.

The members of his staff stared at him with amazement.
Until then, during all important encounters he had displayed a calm unruffled activity; but here he was sluggish,
apathetic, and inactive. Some thought his depression was
the normal aftermath of violent emotions, others, that he was
so jaded that even battle failed to arouse any feeling in him.
The most devoted ascribed his immobility to the necessity
for a commander covering a wide field not to move about too
much, in order that he might be reached at all times. Then
there were others who with more good sense laid the blame
on his weakened condition, a hidden ailment, the beginning
of a serious illness.

The commanders of the artillery, who also had been won-
dering at their inaction, promptly took advantage of the
permission to fight which had just been transmitted to them,

and were soon masters of the ridges. Eighty pieces of cannon were fired all together. The Russian cavalry, first to receive the terrible impact, took shelter behind the infantry. The latter advanced in compact masses in which our cannon balls cut wide and deep swaths; yet they continued to come on until our batteries increased their violence by the addition of grapeshot. Then whole platoons fell together. We could see the soldiers struggling to re-form their lines under the murderous fire. Continually separated by the dead, they closed their ranks over them, trampling them under foot.

They stopped at last, not daring to advance any farther, either because they were petrified with horror in the midst of such awful destruction, or because Bagration was wounded at that moment; or perhaps because their generals, unlike Napoleon who possessed the art of moving great masses without stress or confusion, did not know how to change an order once the initial movement had failed.

Those inert masses simply let themselves be mowed down for two long hours, without any other motion than that of falling. The massacre was frightful; and our artillerymen, knowing the value of bravery, admired the blind, motionless, resigned courage of their enemies.

It was the victors who tired first. The slowness of this uncontested artillery attack tried their patience, and their ammunition was giving out: they ceased fire. Ney then sent his right flank ahead at top speed to pass around the new left front drawn up to oppose him. Supported by Davout and Murat, the wreck of his army was victorious over the remains of Bagration's.

With that the fighting on the plain ceased, and the action was concentrated on the ridges remaining in the enemy's hands, in the direction of the main redoubt which Barclay with his center and right was obstinately defending against

Prince Eugène. Thus in the middle of the day the entire French right wing under Ney, Davout, and Murat, after defeating Bagration and half the Russian line, appeared before a gap in the flank of what was left of the enemy's army, through which they could see the interior, with the reserve, the deserted rear, and the beginning of a retreat. But feeling themselves too weak to venture into this opening behind a line still formidably strong, they called for the Guard: "The Young Guard! Let them follow us at a distance. Let them just show themselves! Have them replace us on the ridges! They are all we need to win!"

They sent Belliard to the Emperor. "From our present position we have an unobstructed view up to the Mozhaysk road, at the rear of the Russian army," he told Napoleon. "We can see a disorganized mass of soldiers, ambulances, and baggage wagons in full retreat. It is true that a ravine and a thicket still separate them from us; but the disheartened Russian generals have not thought of taking advantage of them. At this point one quick dash will carry us into the midst of this disorder and decide the fate of the enemy's army and the war."

Still the Emperor hesitated, doubted, and ordered Belliard to go and take another look, and then come back to report to him. Belliard, surprised, hurried off and returned almost immediately. "The Russians seem to be changing their mind," he said. "Already the thicket is filling up with their skirmishers. We are going to miss the opportunity. There is not a minute to lose, unless we want to fight a second battle to finish the first!"

Bessières, returning from the knoll where he had been posted by Napoleon to examine the Russian position, told him, "They're not retreating at all! They have drawn up a second line, and appear to be preparing for a fresh attack," and the Emperor said to Belliard, "Nothing is clear as yet. Before I send my reserve, *I want to see my chessboard more clearly.*" That was the expression he used, and he repeated it several times, pointing out on one hand the old Moscow road which Poniatowski had not yet been able to take, and on the other an attack by Russian cavalry behind our left flank; and, lastly, the strong redoubt against which the best efforts of Prince Eugène were proving fruitless.

Belliard returned to the King in consternation. "It's impossible to get the Emperor to send his reserve!" said he. "I found him sitting on the same spot, looking sick and depressed, his face sagging, his eyes dull, giving orders languidly in the midst of the horrible din of war which he doesn't even seem to hear."

When Ney, fiery and impatient by nature, was informed of this, he flared up and shouted, "Have we come all this distance to be satisfied with one battlefield? What's the Emperor doing *behind* his army? He doesn't see any of our successes there — only our reverses. Since he isn't fighting the war himself any longer and isn't the general any more, but wants to play the Emperor everywhere, why doesn't he go back to the Tuileries and let us be generals for him?"

Murat was more composed. He remembered having seen Napoleon, as they were riding along the enemy's line the evening before, stop several times to get down from his horse and lean his head against a cannon, showing evidence of extreme suffering. He knew what a restless night the Emperor had spent, his breathing made very difficult by a persistent cough. The King understood how his weakened constitution had been adversely affected by fatigue and the first signs of the equinox, and realized that at this critical moment his genius was chained down, as it were, by his body, overwhelmed by the triple weight of fatigue, fever, and an ailment which perhaps more than any other drains a man of physical and moral strength.

The Emperor, however, was not to be left in peace. Immediately after Belliard had left, Daru, incited by Dumas and Berthier, informed him in a low voice that the Old Guard was being clamored for on all parts of the field. Napoleon replied, "And if there is a second battle tomorrow, what shall I fight it with?" The minister did not insist, amazed to see the Emperor for the first time put something off till another day, and postpone success.

Meanwhile the Russian right flank under Barclay was holding out against Prince Eugène, who after taking Borodino had crossed the Kolocha and attacked the strongest redoubt. There the Russians had counted on the steep, rugged hills surrounded by deep, miry ravines, on their intrenchments armed with heavy field pieces, on eighty guns placed along the ridges literally bristling with steel and fire, and also on our weakened condition. But these formidable means of defense — military art and nature — all failed them at the same time. Overcome by a sudden spurt of the famous battle ardor of the French, seeing Morand's soldiers suddenly in their midst, they fled in disorderly confusion.

Eighteen hundred men of the 30th Regiment, with General Bonnamy at their head, had accomplished this feat of arms. In this encounter Fabvier, Marmont's aide-de-camp who had arrived from Spain the evening before, distinguished himself. On foot, he voluntarily took his place at the head of the most advanced skirmishers, as if he had come to represent the army of Spain in the midst of the Grand Army, and, full of the spirit of rivalry which produces heroes, wanted to be the first to meet the enemy.

But the victory was short-lived, and Fabvier fell wounded

on that famous redoubt. The attack was lacking in co-ordination, because of either the undue haste of the assailants or the slowness of those behind them. Some of our forces were stopped while crossing a ravine whose depth made the enemy fire certain and deadly. Morand, therefore, found himself unsupported facing several Russian lines. It was then only ten o'clock. On his right, Friant had not yet attacked Semenovsk; on his left, the divisions of Gérard and Broussier and the Italian Guard were not even in battle formation.

This attack should not have been started so abruptly, since our intention was merely to confine Barclay on that side, while the battle was really to begin on the right and then pivot to the left. Such had been Napoleon's plan; and no one knows why he failed to carry it out at the moment of execution. In fact it was he himself who at the first sound of firing sent one officer after another to Prince Eugène, to urge him to attack.

The Russians, recovering from their first shock, rushed up from all sides, led by Kutuzov and Yermolov themselves with a resolution equal to the crucial emergency. Our 30th, facing this army alone, was reckless enough to charge them with the bayonet. They were surrounded, overwhelmed, and thrown out of the redoubt, leaving behind a third of their men and their dauntless general, Bonnamy, wounded in twenty places. The Russians, greatly encouraged, were no longer satisfied to defend themselves, but attacked; and all the efforts, skills and fury of war were concentrated on this one point. The French held out for four hours on the slope of this volcano, under a rain of steel and lead. Each division changed generals several times. The Viceroy went from one division to another, mingling prayers with re-proaches, and reminding them of previous victories. He had

Napoleon informed of his critical situation, but the Emperor replied, "I can do nothing. It is up to him to win. He has only to make a greater effort. The battle is on!"

Prince Eugène had rallied all his forces for a general assault, when his attention was attracted by a furious shouting coming from the left. Ouvarov, with two regiments of cavalry and several thousand Cossacks, had fallen upon his reserve, spreading general disorder; but this horde whose noise was worse than its blows was soon scattered by the Prince, seconded by Generals Delzons and Ornano. Eugène then galloped back to put himself at the head of the decisive attack.

It was at this juncture that Murat, condemned to inaction on the plain of which he had made himself master, sent a fourth messenger to his brother-in-law to complain of the losses that the Russians, protected by the redoubts opposing Prince Eugène, were inflicting on his cavalry. "I ask for no other reinforcements than the Old Guard," he wrote. "Supported by them I will pass round the entrenched ridges, and capture them along with the troops defending them."

Napoleon appeared to consent to this, and sent for Bessières, general in command of this mounted guard. Unfortunately, the marshal could not be found, he having gone, at Napoleon's order, to have a closer look at the battle. The Emperor waited nearly an hour, without impatience and without repeating his order! When Bessières finally returned he received him with an air of satisfaction, listened quietly to his report, and gave him permission to advance as far as he might think fit.

But it was already too late. We could no longer think of taking the entire Russian army or all Russia, but merely this battlefield. We had given Kutuzov time enough to collect himself, and he had fortified his position at all the inaccessible points he still held, and covered the plain with his cavalry.

For the third time the Russians re-formed their left flank before Ney and Murat. The latter called for Montbrun's cavalry. This general having been killed, Caulaincourt went to replace him, and found the aides-de-camp of the unfortunate Montbrun weeping over their loss. "Follow me!" he shouted. "Don't weep, but come and take your revenge!"

The King pointed out to Caulaincourt the enemy's new flank which he must break through till he was abreast of the defile where the principal battery was stationed. While the light cavalry was carrying the charge to a successful issue he, Caulaincourt, would suddenly swing to the left with his cuirassiers and take the rear of the terrible redoubt which was still raining death on Prince Eugène's troops.

Caulaincourt replied, "You'll see me up there very soon — dead or alive!" With that he dashed off and mowed down everything that stood in his way. Then, having led his cuirassiers around to the left, he was the first to enter this gory redoubt, but a bullet struck and killed him. His conquest became his grave!

A messenger raced to the Emperor to announce both the victory and the loss. The grand equerry, brother of the slain general, was listening. At first he was shocked, but immediately braced himself against the cruel loss; and had it not been for the tears that ran silently down his cheeks, one would have thought him unmoved. The Emperor said to him, "You have heard: do you wish to withdraw?" accompanying his words by an exclamation of grief. But at that time we were advancing against the enemy. The equerry neither answered nor moved, but simply touched his hat, as a sign of thanks and refusal.

While the decisive cavalry charge was taking place, the

Viceroy with his infantry had come within a short distance
of the mouth of the volcano. Suddenly he saw its fires go
out, its smoke drift away; and there on the crest were the
shining brass helmets of our cuirassiers. At last those hills,
until then Russian, had become French! The Viceroy rushed
up to have his part in the victory, to complete it, and
establish himself in that position.

But the Russians would not give it up. Stubbornly re-
newing their efforts, they gathered into small groups in front
of our troops. Beaten time and time again, they were forced
back into the fight by their generals, and they found death
at the foot of the fortifications they themselves had thrown
up.

Fortunately, their last column of attack which moved
against Semenovsk and the strong redoubt was without the
artillery, whose march had been doubtless slowed up by the
numerous ravines. Belliard had just time enough to assemble
thirty guns against this infantry. They advanced to the very
mouths of the cannon, which pounded them so effectively
that they whirled about and withdrew without being able to
deploy. Murat and Belliard claimed that if they had had
ten thousand foot soldiers of the reserve, at that juncture,
their victory would have been decisive; but that having only
their cavalry they considered themselves fortunate to have
held the field.

General Grouchy, by repeated attacks at the left of the
strong redoubt, had made the victory sure on that side, and
swept the plain clean, but was unable to pursue the remnant of the Russian army whose retreat was protected by a
series of ravines and a second line of redoubts. These troops
defended themselves with fury until nightfall, blocking the
main road to Moscow — their holy city, their storehouse,
their refuge.

From the second ridges they fired on the first which had surrendered to us. The Viceroy was forced to conceal his troops, now winded, weary, and greatly reduced in number, behind rises in the ground and half-destroyed trenches. His soldiers had to be kept on their knees, bent double, in the shelter of these miserable breastworks, remaining in this uncomfortable position for several hours, held in check by the enemy they were holding in check.

It was about half past three when the last victory — one of several that day — was won. Each corps had successively defeated the adversary opposing it, yet without once following up the success with a decisive action. Not being reinforced by the reserve in time, they had halted through exhaustion. Still, all the obstacles of first importance had been overcome, and now the noise of firing was dying away. From all sides officers came pouring into the imperial headquarters. Poniatowski and Sebastiani, after a stubborn struggle, had finally won. The enemy had halted and were entrenching themselves in a new position, it was getting late in the day, our ammunition was used up, *the battle was over*.

Then Belliard for the third time that day approached the Emperor, whose suffering seemed to have increased. He could hardly mount his horse, and rode slowly up to the hills around Semenovsk, where he found a field only incompletely occupied, as Russians bullets and shells were still trying to wrest it from us.

Surrounded by the clamors of war and in sharp contrast to the hot-headed activity of Ney and Murat, he remained apathetic, hardly able to speak above a whisper, dragging his feet like an old man. However, the sight of the Russians and the whistling of their bullets animated him a little; and upon riding closer to their position, he suddenly declared that he was going to drive them out. But Murat reminded him of the poor condition of our much reduced troops and insisted that the Old Guard would be required for that action. Bessières, thoroughly convinced that this crack corps should be preserved at all costs, objected to this, saying, "We are too far away from our reinforcements. All Europe lies between Napoleon and France, and we must preserve at least this handful of men to be answerable for his safe return."

Since it was already nearly five o'clock, Berthier said, "It's too late now. The enemy are strengthening their present position, and we would sacrifice several thousand men and get little in return."

The Emperor now seemed to have only one thought in mind — that the victors should exercise prudence. Then he rode slowly back to his tents set up behind the high battery we had won on the fifth, and in front of which, since early morning, he had been sitting, an almost motionless witness of the vicissitudes of that terrible day.

As he rode along he summoned Mortier * and ordered him to lead the Young Guard forward. "But take care not to go beyond the ravine separating us from the enemy," he said. "I entrust you with the responsibility of guarding the battlefield. That's all I ask of you, so do what is required for that, and no more."

He called him back in a few minutes to inquire if he had understood him. "You are not to get involved in any action — just guard the battlefield."

In his tent he was overcome by painful dejection, mental as well as physical. He had seen the battlefield, and it had spoken more eloquently than any human voice. The victory, so long and ardently sought, so dearly purchased, was in-

---

* Marshal Adolphe Mortier, Duke of Trévise, killed in 1835 by a bomb intended for King Louis-Philippe. — J.D.T.

complete. Was it indeed he, he who had always pursued success to the farthest possible limit, whom Fortune had found cold and inactive when she had come to offer him her highest favors?

The losses had been enormous and without proportionate results. The chances of war had dealt hardest with the high-ranking officers, and every man around him was mourning the loss of some friend, relative, or brother. Forty-three generals had been killed or wounded. What mourning there would be in Paris! What rejoicing among the enemy! And what matter for dangerous reflections for the Germans!

In his army, in his tent, the victory was silent, dismal, personal, without anyone to speak even a word of praise. Dumas, Daru — all whom he called in — listened without speaking; but their attitude, their downcast eyes, their silence, was more eloquent than words.

It was ten o'clock at night when Murat, whose ardor had not entirely abated after twelve hours of fighting, rushed in to demand the Old Guard for the last time. "The Russian army is crossing the Moskva in great haste and disorder!" he cried. "I could make a surprise attack and finish them off!" The Emperor brushed this wild proposal aside angrily; then he proceeded to dictate the report of the day's happenings.

We who had not left his side all day understood that this conqueror of many nations had been himself conquered by a burning fever added to an attack of that painful chronic disease which always flared up after any prolonged activity and violent emotion. We recalled his own words written in Italy fifteen years before: "Good health is indispensable in war, and nothing can take its place." Also that prophetic exclamation uttered on the field of Austerlitz: "To command is to wear out! There is only one age for war. I am good for six years more. After that, I myself shall have to stop!"

\*

## *Epilogue*

During the night the Russians made their presence known by several unwelcome outbursts. The next morning an alert was sounded in the very tent of the Emperor, and the guard rushed to arms, which, coming after a victory, seemed to us somewhat of an affront. The army was motionless until noon — or rather, one might have said there was no army, but only an advance guard. The rest of the troops were scattered over the battlefield picking up the wounded, of whom there were more than twenty thousand. These were carried five miles in the rear, to the great abbey of Kolotskoi.

Larrey, the surgeon-general, drafted assistants from every regiment, and the ambulances had rejoined the army, yet there were shortages of everything. Larrey has since stated in a printed report that he was never given any troops for the purpose of requisitioning badly needed supplies.

Napoleon rode over the battlefield; there was never such a ghastly sight. Everything contributed to the horror of it: the gloomy sky, the cold rain, the violent gale, the houses in ashes, the plain torn up, littered with ruins and debris. On the horizon the melancholy foliage of the northern trees; soldiers wandering among the corpses, looking for food in the very knapsacks of their fallen comrades; dreadful wounds (Russian bullets were larger than ours); cold campfires without song or tale; a tragic silence!

Clustered round the standards were the few remaining officers, noncommissioned officers, and soldiers — barely enough to guard the eagle. Their clothing was torn by the violence of the struggle, black with powder, stained with blood. Yet, despite the rags, the misery and disaster, they still looked proud and let out shouts of triumph at the sight of the Emperor. The shouts, though, were rare and excited; for in this army, capable of self-analysis as well as enthusiasm, each individual was aware of the total situation. French soldiers are not easily deceived; and these wondered why, with so many Russians killed and wounded, there should be only eight hundred prisoners. It was by the number of prisoners that they judged success, since the dead attested to the courage of the defeated, rather than to a victory. If the survivors were able to retreat in such good order, proud and undaunted, what did the winning of one field matter? In this vast country, would the Russians ever lack for space on which to fight?

As Napoleon and his retinue were riding on ground so littered with corpses that it was impossible to avoid stepping on them, one of the horses trod on a dying soldier and drew a last moan of pain from him. The Emperor, until then as silent as his victory, terribly depressed by the sight of so many victims, suddenly exploded and relieved his feelings by cries of indignation and an exaggerated solicitude for the poor soldier. Someone, to appease him, remarked that after all *it was only a Russian.* To which Napoleon replied, "There are no enemies after a victory, but only men!" Then he scattered the officers who were following him over the field to succor the wounded whose cries could be heard on all sides.

The dead and dying were particularly numerous at the bottom of the ravines, where so many of our troops had been hurled and others had dragged themselves to seek shelter from the enemy or the storm. The youngest of them moaned out the name of their country or their mother. The older men awaited death with either an impassive or a sardonic air, without condescending to beg or complain. Some of the men asked to be killed at once, but we quickly passed these poor wretches by, knowing that they were beyond all hope, yet not having the heart to put them out of their misery. One man, the most horribly mutilated of all (he had only his trunk and one arm left), looked so lively, so full of hope, even gaiety, that we undertook to save his life. As he was being carried off the field he complained of pain in his missing limbs, a common occurrence among people who have had arms or legs amputated. This seems to be a fresh proof that the spirit remains whole, and that feeling belongs to it alone, and not to the body which can no more feel than think.

We saw Russians crawling to spots where heaps of corpses provided horrible shelters. It has been said on good authority that one of these miserable creatures lived several days in the carcass of a horse split open by a shell, feeding on its insides! We saw men who were setting their broken legs by tying branches tightly against them, then limping off to the nearest village on crutches made of larger branches; and not a groan passed their lips. Because they were so far from their own people, they evidently did not expect pity. One thing is certain, they endured pain better than the French. Not that they suffered more courageously, but that they suffered less; for they are less sensitive in both body and mind, as a result of living in a more primitive civilization and having their constitutions hardened by a harsh climate.

In the course of this dreary review the Emperor vainly sought to recapture a shred of illusion by having the handful of prisoners counted again, and collecting a few disabled guns. Seven or eight hundred prisoners and a score of broken cannon — these were the trophies of this incomplete victory!

Meanwhile Murat had driven the Russian rear guard as far as Mozhaysk. He found the road behind them absolutely free from debris, carts, and clothing; and all their dead had been buried; for they have a religious respect for the dead. When Murat came in sight of Mozhaysk he fancied himself already master of it, and sent to tell Napoleon that he could come and lodge there; but the Russian rear guard had taken their stand before the city, and beyond, on a range of hills, the rest of the army could be seen. Thus they protected the roads to Moscow and Kaluga, in an attitude as firm and commanding as before the great battle. Yet Murat, with his usual rashness, chose to pounce upon them.

This engagement was serious enough to add to the losses of the day before, and Belliard was wounded. This general, whom Murat was to miss greatly in the days to come, had been reconnoitering the left of the enemy's position, which he had found easily accessible. It was on that side that the action should have begun, but Murat thought only of rushing upon whatever lay in front of him.

As for the Emperor, he did not reach the scene of battle till nightfall, and then accompanied by insufficient forces. He advanced toward Mozhaysk at a pace even slower than the day before, absorbed so deeply in his own thoughts that he seemed unconscious of the noise of battle and the bullets whistling around him. Someone stopped him to point out the Russian rear guard between the city and himself, and beyond the town the fires of fifty thousand men. This sight proved both the incompleteness of his victory, and the enemy's unshaken courage, but Napoleon seemed oblivious to it. He listened to the reports with an absent air and issued no orders, then turned back and slept in a nearby village, within the range of the enemy's fire.

He had been overwhelmed by the Russian autumn! It is

possible that, without this ally, Russia might have yielded to us on the fields of Moskva. The premature inclemency had come to the help of the enemy at a singularly timely moment. It was ushered in on the sixth of September, the eve of the all-important battle, by a high wind which all but froze Napoleon. The cold he caught paralyzed his movements and shackled his genius for five days, not only preserving Kutuzov from total ruin at Borodino, but giving him the time to re-form his army and escape from our pursuit.

The ninth of September found Mozhaysk still standing and open, with the Russian rear guard occupying the hills on the farther side where the whole army had been the evening before. Our troops entered the city, some to cross it in pursuit of the enemy, others bent on pillage or seeking lodgings. The latter found neither inhabitants nor provisions, only the dead whom they had to throw out of the windows so they could take their places, and the dying, whom they brought together in one building. The wounded were everywhere, and in such numbers that the Russians had not dared to set fire to the dwellings. However, their humanity, which had not always been so scrupulous, gave way before the necessity of firing on the first French troops they saw marching in. Using explosive shells, they set fire to the city, entirely built of wood, and roasted many of their own wounded.

While we were doing our best to save these poor wretches, fifty light-infantrymen of the 33rd climbed the slope of the hill occupied by the Russian cavalry and artillery. The French army, from their station under the walls of Mozhaysk, watched with amazement this handful of men on the steep, unprotected slope, taunting thousands of Russians with their fire. Suddenly, as we had anticipated, several squadrons moved forward. In an instant they had surrounded the

reckless Frenchmen who drew together in a compact group
and opened fire on all sides; but there were so few of them,
on so wide a surface, in the midst of so many horses, that
they soon disappeared from sight.

A tremendous groan rose from our ranks. The soldiers
craned their necks and glued their eyes on the enemy, trying
to make out what was happening to their companions in
arms. Some cursed the distance, and wanted to go to help
them. Some automatically loaded their muskets or leveled
their bayonets, as if they were near enough to be of some
assistance. Others shouted words of encouragement or advice, forgetting they could not be heard.

A few puffs of smoke rising from the center of this mass
prolonged the uncertainty, and the watchers exclaimed, "It's
our men firing! They're still defending themselves! There's
still hope!" In fact, the officer commanding our light-
infantrymen had just killed a Russian officer in reply to a
summons to surrender. Our anxiety had lasted several
minutes when suddenly a shout of joy and admiration went
up from our army as the Russians, surprised at such bold
resistance, drew back from the brisk fire and scattered in all
directions, disclosing to our sight this handful of brave men,
masters of the wide field on which they occupied only a few
square feet!

As soon as the Russians saw that we were making serious
preparations for a general attack, they disappeared without
leaving a trace behind them, as they had done at Vitebsk
and Smolensk, except that it was more remarkable this time,
coming as it did the second day after so great a disaster. We
were not sure at first whether they had taken the road to
Kaluga or the one to Moscow, but finally Murat and Mortier
took the risk and marched toward Moscow.

On the eleventh of September the enemy's army came in

sight again, in a strong position near Krymskoie. They had
resumed their old way of retreating which consisted in paying more attention to the terrain than to the enemy. At the
outset the Duke of Trévise made Murat admit the impossi-
bility of attack; but the smell of powder soon intoxicated
the King who committed a serious blunder, forcing Dufour
and Mortier to advance with their infantry — all that remained of Friand's division and the Young Guard. There
we lost to no purpose whatever two thousand men of that
reserve which had been so foolishly hoarded the day of the
battle. Mortier, furiously angry, wrote to inform the
Emperor that he would no longer obey Murat.

At that point, it was by letter that the front-line generals
communicated with Napoleon who had remained behind
these three days, shut up in his room at Mozhaysk, still burning with fever, overburdened with affairs of state and consumed with apprehension, besides having lost his voice as a
result of his cold. Since he had to dictate to seven people at
the same time, and was unable to make himself heard, he
wrote summaries of his dispatches on different sheets of
paper. If difficulties arose, he tried to make his meaning
clear by signs.

At one time Bessières was enumerating the generals
wounded the day of the great battle. The tragic roll call
affected Napoleon so deeply that, finding his voice for a
moment, he interrupted the marshal with the exclamation,
"One week of Moscow, and this will not matter any more!"

Nevertheless, though he had until then staked all his
future on this capital, the bloody and uncertain victory of
Borodino had lessened his hopes. His instructions given to
Berthier on the eleventh to be transmitted to General
Victor * gave proof of his distress: "The enemy, struck to the

---

* Claude Victor, Duke of Belluno, who had remained behind in Polish
territory with a line of reinforcements. — J.D.T.

heart, no longer busy themselves with the extremities . . .
Tell the Duke of Belluno to send everything, battalions,
squadrons, artillery, detached men to Smolensk, whence
they can come to Moscow."

Though the Emperor was concealing his physical and
mental suffering from the eyes of his army, Davout was able
to get in to see him. Despite his wound, this marshal offered
to take command of the advance guard, promising that he
would march day and night until he had overtaken the
enemy and forced them to wage a battle, without squander-
ing, as Murat had done, the strength and lives of his soldiers.
Napoleon's only answer was to praise, a trifle too enthusi-
astically, the audacious, inexhaustible ardor of his brother-
in-law.

Napoleon had just learned that the Russian army had been
found again, that they had not withdrawn in the direction of
Kaluga as he had feared, but were still retreating, and that
we were now only two days' march from Moscow. This
great name and the high hopes he associated with it revived his strength, and on the twelfth of September he was
well enough to set out in a carriage to catch up with the front
lines.

# CHAPTER IV

************

## *The Army Enters Moscow*

THE RUSSIAN CAPITAL, rightly called by the poets *City of Golden Domes,* was a vast and fantastic jumble of some two hundred and ninety-five churches and fifteen hundred palaces with their gardens and dependencies. These great brick mansions and their grounds, interspersed with attractive wooden houses and even thatched cottages, were scattered over several square miles of hilly ground. They were grouped around a lofty, triangular fortress with double walls over a mile in circumference, the first of which enclosed several palaces and churches and some rock-strewn vacant lots; the second, an immense bazaar, or merchant city, where the riches of the four corners of the earth formed a brilliant display.

All these buildings, shops as well as palaces, were roofed with sheet iron, burnished or painted. The churches, with their flat roofs and numerous steeples and towers topped by golden cupolas bearing aloft crosses set over crescents, epitomized the history of this people: here was Asia with its religion, at first victorious, then vanquished, and after that the crescent of Mohammed, with the cross of Christ triumphant over all.

A single ray of sunshine set this superb city glowing with a thousand variegated colors. At the sight of it the enchanted traveler stopped short in wonder, reminded of the marvels with which the Eastern poets had amused his childhood. When he passed through the gates his astonishment was heightened by a nearer view. He noted that the nobles had adopted the customs, the manners, and the different languages of modern Europe, along with the easy elegance of its clothing. He beheld with surprise the luxury and Asiatic form of the dress of the merchants, the Greek costumes and long beards of the common people. He was struck with a similar diversity in the buildings; yet everything was tinged with a definite local color — harsh, severe, as befitting Muscovy.

The noblemen of the most illustrious lineage lived there in the midst of their families, as if beyond the reach of the court. They were less courtiers than citizens. Their princes were not at all anxious to return to this vast warehouse of glory and commerce, in the midst of nobles who escaped from their authority because of age and reputation for independence, and whom they were forced to handle with kid gloves.

Necessity brought Czar Alexander there: he came by the way of Polotsk, preceded by his proclamations and eagerly awaited.

He appeared first to the assembled nobility. There everything was on a grand scale — the circumstance, the company, the orator, and the resolutions he inspired. His voice trembled. He had scarcely ceased speaking when one cry, simultaneous, unanimous, broke from all breasts. Everywhere was heard, "Sire, ask anything! We offer you everything! Take our all!"

Alexander then spoke to the merchants, but more briefly. He had that proclamation read to them in which Napoleon was represented as a "betrayer, a Moloch who, with treachery in his heart and loyalty on his lips, had come to wipe Russia from the face of the earth." It is said that at these words a great fury lit up all those manly, ruddy countenances to which long beards lent an antique, imposing, savage appearance. Their eyes glittered, a convulsive rage seized them; their twitching stiffened arms, their doubled fists, their stifled cries, the grinding of their teeth attested to the violence of their feelings. The effect was as might be expected. Their leader, who had been elected by themselves, showed himself worthy of his station by making the first subscription of fifty thousand rubles, two thirds of his fortune, which he paid the very next day.

These merchants were divided into three classes. It was proposed that each should make a fixed contribution; but one man belonging to the lowest class declared that his patriotism would brook no limit, and on the spot he obligated himself far beyond the proposed amount. The others followed his example, in varying degrees. It is said that this patriotic tribute amounted to two million rubles. The other provinces were to repeat, like so many echoes, the national cry from Moscow.

Nevertheless, Smolensk had been reduced, Napoleon had reached Viazma, consternation reigned in Moscow. The great battle had not yet been lost, and the people were already beginning to abandon their capital.

Meanwhile, not far from Moscow, on the order of Alexander, the construction of a gigantic balloon was going forward under the direction of a German pyrotechnician. This aerial machine was to fly over the French army, single out its leader, and crush him with a rain of fire and steel! Several unsuccessful attempts to raise it had been made, the wings breaking off each time.

Governor Rostopchin, making a pretense of working on

this scheme, was supervising the manufacture of an immense quantity of explosives and combustibles; but Moscow herself was to be the great infernal machine whose sudden explosion by night would destroy the Emperor and his army.* If the invaders survived this danger, they would at least be left shelterless and without supplies. It would be only too easy to lay the blame for the holocaust on Napoleon's army, as the enemy had done before when they burned their own cities; and the horror of so great a disaster would arouse all Russia.

Such was the terrible plan of this noble descendent of one of the greatest conquerors of Asia. It was conceived without effort, ripened with care, and coolly carried out. Later I saw this Russian gentleman in Paris. He is a steady man, a good husband and father; his mind is superior and cultivated, his manners gentle and attractive. But, like many of his compatriots, he combines the civilization of modern times with the energy of the ancients. Henceforth his name belongs to history. It must be said, though, that he should have only a part — the greatest part — of the credit for the sacrifice. It was really begun at Smolensk: he completed it. This resolution, like all that is born of a singleness of purpose, was wholly admirable; the motive was sufficient and justified by success; the devotion so unprecedented that the historian must pause to examine it and to attempt to fathom it.

One man alone in the midst of an empire now almost overthrown, faced the danger without faltering. He measured it, estimated it, and dared to evaluate the public and private interests he must sacrifice to it. A mere subject, he decided the fate of the state without the approval of his

---

* Tolstoy in *War and Peace* absolves Rostopchin of all guilt in this matter of the burning of Moscow. It is quite possible that Ségur had had firsthand information, his nephew having married Rostopchin's daughter. — J.D.T.

sovereign. A nobleman, he pronounced the destruction of the palaces of all the nobles, without their consent. By virtue of his office the protector of a whole population, a multitude of rich merchants, and one of the greatest capitals of Europe, he sacrificed its fortunes, its industries, the city itself. He gave to the flames the finest of his own palaces; and proud, satisfied, and calm he stood in the midst of all those shocked and devastated interests.

In this grave crisis Rostopchin saw two particular dangers: the first, which threatened the national honor, was that of a shameful peace in Moscow, wrung from the Czar. The second was a political rather than a military danger. In the latter he feared the seduction of the enemy more than their arms, and a revolution more than a conquest.

The governor did not desire any treaty; for he foresaw that in this populous capital, which the Russians themselves considered the oracle, the mouthpiece of the empire, Napoleon would have recourse to the weapon of *revolution,* the only one remaining to him, to complete his victory. For that reason he decided to erect a barrier of fire between this great captain and all weaknesses, from whatever source they might proceed, from the throne or from his own class, either nobles or senators; between a population of serfs and the soldiers of a nation of free landowners; more particularly, between the latter and the mass of artisans and merchants in Moscow who formed the beginning of an intermediate class, that class for and by whom the French Revolution had been made.

The silence of Alexander leaves some doubt as to whether he approved this momentous decision or not. The part he played in the catastrophe is still a mystery for the Russians, who either do not know or do not say — the consequence of despotism, which enjoins ignorance or silence.

Two weeks before the invasion the removal of the records of the banking houses, the treasury, and of the noblemen and richest merchants, along with their most valuable possessions, indicated to the rest of the inhabitants what was expected of them. The governor, in his anxiety to see the city completely emptied, hastened the evacuation.

On the third of September a Frenchwoman living in the capital ventured to come out of hiding, at the risk of being massacred by the infuriated Muscovites. She had wandered for some time through the more spacious quarters, puzzled by their absolute emptiness, when a far-off mournful wailing fell on her terrified ears. It was like the death chant of this great city. Unable to move, she looked and saw an immense multitude of afflicted men and women coming toward her carrying their poor belongings and their icons, and leading their children by the hands. Their priests, loaded down with the sacred symbols of their religion, went before them, calling upon heaven with hymns of lamentation that were echoed by the weeping crowd.

These unfortunate creatures hesitated an instant before passing through the city gates, looking backward sadly on Moscow and seeming to bid farewell to their holy city. But by degrees their sorrowful chants and weeping died away in the encircling plains.

The Russian army drawn up at Fili before Moscow numbered about ninety-one thousand men — six thousand Cossacks, sixty-five thousand veteran troops (all that remained of the one hundred and twenty thousand that had answered the call at the Moskva) and twenty thousand recruits, half of whom were armed with muskets, half with pikes.

The French army, one hundred and thirty thousand strong on the eve of the great battle, had lost about forty thousand at Borodino, leaving only ninety thousand. Several makeshift regiments and the divisions of Laborde and Pino joined them later, so that the army numbered altogether about a hundred thousand men on reaching Moscow. Its march was slowed down by six hundred and seven pieces of cannon, twenty-five hundred artillery wagons, and five thousand supply wagons. There remained only enough ammunition for one day's fighting.

Perhaps Kutuzov took into account the disproportion of his effective forces with ours. This, however, is a matter of conjecture, as he gave purely strategic reasons for his re-treat. One thing is certain, the old general deceived the governor up to the last minute. He was still swearing "on his white hair" that he would "perish with him before Moscow" when Rostopchin learned that that night, at a council of war held in the camp, they had decided to sur-render the capital without a struggle.

At this news, the governor, furious but unshaken, gave himself up to the task that lay before him. He must work fast, as time was running out. No further attempt was made to conceal from Moscow the fate that was in store for her. It was not worth the trouble to conceal the situation from the few remaining inhabitants; besides, they must be induced to seek safety in flight.

That night, therefore, secret agents went about knocking at every door, giving warning of the conflagration. Bombs were slipped into every available opening, especially in the iron-roofed shops in the mercantile districts, and all fire engines were removed. Disaster was imminent, and every civilian, according to his disposition, either became totally paralyzed by terror or made a move toward escape. The majority gathered in the public squares, crowding, pushing, asking each other what they should do, seeking counsel. Others wandered aimlessly up and down, some numb with fear, some in a dreadful state of excitement. Then the army, the last hope of these doomed people, deserted them. As the troops flowed through the city streets they drew along with them the not inconsiderable remnant of the inhabitants.

They went out through the Koloma gate, the army and this mob of hopeless women, children, and old people. The plains were covered with them. They fled in every direction, by every path, across the fields — without provisions, but all carrying some prized possession, the first thing, possibly, they had been able to put their hands on in their confusion. There were some who, for want of horses, had hitched themselves to carts and were pulling their small children, their sick wives, their invalid fathers, or whatever they valued most. The woods afforded them shelter, and they lived off the charity of their fellows in misery.

That day a terrible scene brought this melancholy drama to an end. When the last day of Moscow had dawned, Rostopchin mustered as many men as he could seize and arm. The prisons were opened, and a dirty, disgusting mob poured out. These miserable creatures rushed into the streets with ferocious joy. Two men, a Russian and a Frenchman, one accused of treason, the other of political imprudence, were picked up in the midst of this horde and taken before Rostopchin, who reproached the Russian with his betrayal. He, the son of a merchant, had been arrested while inciting the people to revolt. The alarming aspect of the case was that the young man had been found to belong to a sect of German religious and political fanatics called Martinists. His audacity had not failed him in prison. It seemed for a moment that the spirit of "égalité" had entered into Russia. He could not, however, be made to disclose any accomplices.

At the last moment his father rushed in. All expected to

hear him plead for his son's life; but it was his death he demanded. The governor granted him a few minutes in which
to speak with his son and give him a blessing. "I bless a
traitor!" he cried, and turning upon him, cursed him in a
terrible voice, with threatening gestures.

This was the signal for his execution. The unfortunate
lad was cut down with a badly aimed blow of a saber. He
fell, but only wounded; and perhaps the arrival of the
French might have saved him if the people had not noticed
he was still alive. The wild mob forced the barrier, threw
themselves upon him, and tore him to pieces.

The Frenchman stood frozen with terror when Rostopchin
turned to him and said, "As for you, being a Frenchman, you
can but wish for the arrival of the French. You are free: go
tell your friends that Russia has had only one traitor, and he
has been punished." Then addressing the miserable crew,
calling them *sons of Russia,* he ordered them to make atone-
ment for their crimes by serving their country. He, the last
to leave the doomed city, then rejoined the Russian army.

From that moment mighty Moscow belonged neither to
the Russians nor to the French, but to that foul mob whose
fury was directed by a few officers and soldiers of the police
force. They were organized, each one was allotted a post, and
they were scattered in order that pillage, devastation, and fire
might break out everywhere at the same time.

On the fourteenth of September Napoleon mounted his
horse a few miles from Moscow. He rode slowly, with precaution, sending scouts before him to examine the woods
and ravines and climb all the hills to look for the enemy's
army. It was expected that there would be a battle: indeed,
the position was favorable, and earthworks had been begun;
but everything had been abandoned, and we did not encounter the least resistance.

One last height remained to be scaled. This was close to and overlooking Moscow — the *Mount of Greetings* * it was called, because from its top, at the sight of the holy city, the inhabitants always knelt and crossed themselves. Our scouts were soon at the top. It was two o'clock, and the sun made the magnificent city twinkle and shine with a thousand colors. Struck with amazement at the sight, the man came to a stop, exclaiming, "Moscow! Moscow!" They all quickened their step to a disorderly run, and the entire army, clapping their hands, took up the delirious cry, "Moscow! Moscow!" as sailors shout "Land! Land!" after a long and perilous crossing.

At the sight of this gilded city, this brilliant capital uniting Europe and Asia, this majestic meetingplace of the opulence, the customs, and the arts of the two fairest divisions of the earth, we stood still in proud contemplation. Our day of glory had come! Would it not become the greatest, the most wonderful memory of our whole lives? We felt that at that moment the eyes of an astonished universe were fixed upon our movements, and that the least of our actions would be recorded by history.

On our long awaited return to France, with what respectful consideration, what enthusiasm would we be received by our wives, our fellow countrymen, our own fathers! For the remainder of our lives we would be set apart from ordinary human beings — never beheld but with amazement, never listened to but with fond admiration. Wherever we went people would flock around us, our least word would be treasured. This marvelous conquest would surround us with a halo of glory; henceforth we should move in an atmosphere of wonder and miracle.

When these wild thoughts had given place to more rational

* Poklonny Hill. — J.D.T.

sentiments, we reminded ourselves that this was the long-promised end to our labors; that at last we were going to stop, since we could not now be surpassed by ourselves, after an expedition worthy to be compared with that of Egypt, a successful rival of all the great and glorious wars of antiquity.

At that moment all our dangers and suffering were forgotten. Was it possible to purchase too dearly the ineffable happiness of being able to say for the rest of our lives, "I belonged to the army of Moscow!" On this immense and imposing stage we had the sensation of marching in the midst of the acclamations of all the peoples of the world. Proud at being able to exalt our century above all other centuries, we already saw it great with our greatness and shining with our glory.

Napoleon himself hastened up. He stopped short in rapture, an exclamation of delight breaking from his lips. Since the great battle, the discontented marshals had avoided him; but at the sight of captive Moscow, at the news of the impending arrival of a flag of truce, they forgot all their grievances. Impressed with so important a result, intoxicated with the enthusiasm of glory, they now crowded around the Emperor, paying homage to his good fortune and feeling inclined to attribute his failure to complete his victory to the foresight of his genius.

But first impulses were of short duration with Napoleon. He had too much to think of to indulge his sensations for any considerable time. His first exclamation had been, "So here at last is that famous city!" His second was, "It was high time!"

His eyes already expressed impatience as they dwelt on the city in which he fancied he saw the whole Russian empire, its walls enclosing all his hopes — peace, the cost of the war, immortal glory. Therefore he kept his eyes glued on all its points of egress. When would those gates open to let out the deputation coming to offer him the city's wealth, its population, its senate, and the cream of Russian nobility? . . . His imagination soared. Henceforth this enterprise upon which he had so rashly ventured, but which had been brought to a successful termination by his daring, would be considered the result of a shrewd combination, and his imprudence would pass for greatness. Henceforth his victory at the Moskva, incomplete as it was, would become his finest feat of arms. Thus all that might have contributed to his ruin would contribute to his glory. The next few days would decide whether he was the greatest man in the world or the most foolhardy; in short, whether he had raised himself an altar, or dug himself a grave.

But he was beginning to feel uneasy. On his right and left he saw that Prince Eugène and Poniatowski had already outflanked the enemy's city. In front, Murat with his scouts had reached the suburbs, but still no deputation appeared. Only one of Miloradovich's officers had come out to inform them that this general would set fire to the city if his rear guard were not given the time to evacuate it.

Napoleon granted all that was asked, and the troops of the two armies mingled for a short time. Murat was recognized by the Cossacks who, as uninhibited as nomads and demonstrative as Latins, crowded around him, extolling his valor by gestures and exclamations, and intoxicating him with their admiration. The King took the watches of his officers and distributed them among these barbarians, one of whom called him his *Hetman*.

Murat was momentarily tempted to believe that among their officers he might find a new Mazeppa, or that he would become one himself, and imagined he had completely won them over. This brief armistice under such circumstances fed Napoleon's hope, so greatly did he need to preserve his illusions, and for two hours afforded him a little amusement.

But day was drawing to its close, and Moscow remained silent, gloomy, apparently lifeless. The Emperor's anxiety increased, and it was becoming more and more difficult to repress the impatience of the solders. Some officers who had ventured within the city walls returned with the news, "Moscow is empty!"

At this intelligence, which he brushed aside with annoyance, Napoleon descended the Mount of Greetings and approached the river and the Dorogomilov gate, where he paused a moment. But Murat urged him to allow his soldiers to enter the city. "Very well," he said. "Go on in, if that's what they want." But he enjoined the strictest discipline, not yet having lost all hope. Perhaps, he thought, these people do not even know how to surrender. Everything is new here, they to us, and we to them.

But similar reports followed each other in rapid succession. Some French citizens, residents of Moscow, venturing out of hiding places which for several days had concealed them from the fury of the mob, confirmed the dread news. The Emperor summoned Daru. "Moscow deserted!" he shouted. "An unlikely story! We shall get to the bottom of this. Go, bring the Boyars to me!" He imagined that those men, either stiffened with pride or paralyzed with terror, were sitting helpless by their firesides; and he who had until then always been met by the submission of the vanquished now elicited their confidence and anticipated their petitions.

How, indeed, could he bring himself to believe that so many sumptuous palaces, glittering temples, and rich shops had been abandoned by their owners, like the mean hamlets he had recently passed through? Nevertheless, Daru's mission had failed, and not a single Muscovite appeared. Not a trace of smoke hung over the poorest chimney, not the faintest sound rose from the vast, populous city: its three hundred thousand inhabitants seemed to have been struck dumb and motionless by enchantment. This was the silence of the desert!

But such was the persistence of Napoleon that he stubbornly continued to wait. At length an officer, determined to please him, or persuaded that everything the Emperor wanted must come to pass, went into the city, caught five or six vagabonds, and drove them in front of his horse back to Napoleon, fondly imagining he had brought a deputation. At their first words the Emperor perceived that they were just poor laborers.

Only then did he cease to doubt the complete evacuation of Moscow, and lost the last shred of the hope he had built on it. With a shrug of his shoulders and that contemptuous look with which he dismissed everything that opposed his wishes, he cried, "Ah, the Russians do not yet know the effect that the fall of their capital will have on them!"

For an hour Murat and his long compact column of cavalry had been marching into the city, penetrating to the very heart of the gigantic body as yet unharmed, but lifeless. Filled with wonder at the sight of such complete solitude, they responded to the awe-inspiring silence of this modern Thebes by a silence equally solemn. These warriors shivered inwardly at the lonely echo of their horses' hoofs among the deserted palaces, amazed to hear no other sound in the midst of so many dwellings than those made by themselves. No one thought of stopping or of looting, either from prudence or because civilized peoples respect themselves in the capitals of their enemies, in the presence of great centers of civilization.

Riding in silence, they admired this mighty city which would have been remarkable if they had come upon it in a fertile, thickly populated country, but was all the more astonishing in this desert region. It was like a rich and dazzling oasis! They had been struck at first by the unexpected sight of so many magnificent mansions, but they soon noticed that there were hovels scattered among them, a condition which indicated the lack of any graduation of the classes, and showed that here luxury was not the outgrowth of industry, as in other lands, but that it had preceded it; whereas in the natural order it should have been the more or less inevitable consequence.

Here *inequality* prevailed — that curse of human society which produces the arrogance of some, the degradation of others, and the corruption of all. However, the willingness with which all this opulence had been sacrificed proved that excessive luxury, only recently acquired, had not made the nobility completely spineless.

And so our troops advanced, now swayed by pity, now by surprise, now by a noble enthusiasm. Several, in a spirit of boasting, mentioned the outstanding conquests of history, though not as a warning; for they, having left all the conquerors of antiquity far behind them, felt they were above comparison with anybody else. They were exalted by that which comes next after virtue — glory . . . Then came a feeling of melancholy, the result of exhaustion brought on by so many experiences, or the effect of loneliness produced by immeasurable elevation and the void in which they were moving on those heights; for the higher one climbs, the wider grows the horizon, and the more clearly does one perceive one's nothingness.

These reflections, which were favored by the slow pace of the horses, were suddenly interrupted by the sound of shooting, and the column halted. Its last horses were still out in the fields, its center was engaged in one of the city's longest streets, its head had reached the Kremlin. The gates of that citadel* seemed tightly bolted, but from within came a prodigious roaring. A band of armed men and women of revolting appearance sprang up on the walls, giving vent to horrible drunken curses. Murat sent them peaceful proposals which were without effect, and in the end it was necessary to use cannon to batter down the gate.

We made our way without too much opposition into the midst of those ruffians, one of whom rushed toward Murat and endeavored to kill one of his officers. We thought we had done enough in disarming him, but he fell upon his victim again, threw him to the ground, and began to strangle him. Even when his arms were seized from behind, he tried to tear him with his teeth. These were the only Muscovites that had awaited our coming, and they had been left behind, possibly, as an inhuman token of the national hatred.

There was no sign, however, of concerted action in this patriotic fury. Five hundred recruits, who had been overlooked in the withdrawal of the troops from the Kremlin, witnessed this scene without apparent emotion, and dispersed at the first summons. When, a little later, we came upon a convoy of provisions, the escort promptly threw down their arms. Several thousand stragglers and deserters surrendered without a struggle to our advance guard, who left the responsibility of rounding them up to the corps that followed. These left it to others, and so on; with the result that they remained at liberty in our midst, until fire and pillage had shown them where their duty lay and united them in a common hate, then went and joined up with Kutuzov.

Murat halted just long enough at the Kremlin to dis-

* Ségur on several occasions mistakenly refers to the Kremlin as a citadel or fortress. — J.D.T.

perse the mob, for whom he felt only loathing. As fiery and indefatigable as he had been in Italy and Egypt, after a march of two thousand miles and sixty battles fought to reach Moscow, he crossed that superb city without deigning to stop, and in hot pursuit of the Russian rear guard, boldly and without hesitation, took the road to Vladimir and Asia.

Several thousand Cossacks with four pieces of cannon were retreating in the same direction. There the armistice came to an end. Murat, tired of this half-day's peace, promptly ordered it to be broken by a discharge of carbines. But our cavalry, to whom Moscow was the ultimate goal, believed that the war was over. The outposts of both armies seemed reluctant to renew hostilities. A second order was given, but a similar hesitation followed. At length Murat in a great rage gave the order in person; and the firing with which he seemed to be threatening Asia, but which was to cease only at the banks of the Seine, was resumed.

*

## Moscow Burns

Napoleon did not enter Moscow till nightfall. He lodged in one of the houses in the Dorogomilov suburb, where he appointed Mortier governor of the capital. "Above all," he told him. "No looting. You shall answer for it with your life. Defend Moscow against both friend and foe!"

That was a gloomy night, with sinister reports following one another. Some Frenchmen living in that country, and even a Russian police officer, came to warn us of a conflagration, giving all the particulars of the preparations for it. The Emperor, distressed, tried in vain to get a little rest. Every few minutes he called out and had the fatal news repeated to him. Still he persisted in his incredulity, till at about two in the morning he learned that the fire had broken out.

It was in the Bazaar, the richest quarter, in the very center of the city. He immediately issued order upon order, and as soon as it was daylight hurried there himself. He threatened the Young Guard and Mortier, who pointed out to him several of the iron-roofed houses still tightly closed, still intact, with no trace of having been broken into, but from which thick black smoke was already pouring. Napoleon entered the Kremlin, lost in thought.

His earlier hopes revived at the sight of the palace — part Gothic, part modern — of the Romanovs and of the Ruricks, with their throne still in place, and the cross of Ivan the Great soaring over everything. From there he had a view of the finest part of the city which the fire, still confined to the Bazaar, seemed disposed to spare. His ambition was flattered by such a conquest, and he was heard to exclaim, "At last I am in Moscow, in the ancient palace of the Czars, in the Kremlin!" He examined every detail of it with curiosity and satisfied pride.

He demanded a statement of the resources of the city, and in that brief moment, flushed with hope, wrote a proposal of peace to Emperor Alexander. A superior Russian officer who had just been found in the great hospital was entrusted with this letter. It was by the sinister light from the blaze in the Bazaar that Napoleon finished it and the Russian set out. He must have borne the news of the disaster to his sovereign, whose only answer was that conflagration.

Daylight came to Mortier's assistance, and he was able to get the fire under control. The incendiaries kept themselves so well hidden that their very existence was questioned. At length, strict orders having been given, order restored, and

panic temporarily quieted, each man took possession of a
comfortable house or a sumptuous mansion, hoping to enjoy
a season of ease and repose purchased by long and excessive
privations.

Two officers who had found quarters in one of the buildings of the Kremlin, from where they could see all the north
and west of the city, were awakened about midnight by an
extraordinary light. They looked and saw that flames were
sweeping through the palaces, whose noble and elegant archi-
tecture they illuminated at first, and soon brought crashing
down. The men observed that the north wind was driving
the flames toward the Kremlin and grew alarmed for the
safety of the fortress in which the flower of the army and its
commander were resting. They were apprehensive also for
all the surrounding houses where our soldiers, attendants,
and horses, tired out and glutted with food and drink, were
doubtless buried in deepest sleep. Sparks and glowing embers
were already falling on the roof of the Kremlin when the
wind, suddenly shifting from north to west, blew them in another direction.

Then one of the officers, his mind at rest concerning the
safety of his own corps, went back to sleep, exclaiming, "The
others can attend to it! It isn't any of our business!" For
such was the callousness engendered by this onslaught of
events and misfortunes, such the selfishness born of fatigue
and suffering, that each one of us had retained only the
measure of feeling and strength necessary for his service and
personal preservation.

However, they were awakened again by fresh, vivid flashes
of light, and now they saw flames rising in the new path that
the wind had taken, still in the direction of the Kremlin; and
they began to curse French imprudence and insubordination,
to which they imputed the disaster. Three times the wind

changed from north to west, and three times the hostile
fire, stubborn avenger, was quick to follow its new course,
as if bent on destroying the imperial headquarters.

Then a grave suspicion took possession of all our minds:
had the Muscovites, aware of our carelessness and negligence, conceived the plan of burning with Moscow our soldiers, besotted with wine, fatigue, and sleep? Or, rather, had
they dared to believe that they would entangle Napoleon in
this catastrophe, that the loss of this man was well worth
the loss of their capital? Did they think that the result was
of sufficient importance to justify the sacrifice of all Moscow;
that heaven, perhaps, in exchange for so great a victory,
required so great a holocaust; that this colossus deserved an
equally gigantic funeral pyre?

Whether or not this was their thought, we cannot tell;
but nothing less than the Emperor's lucky star kept it from
becoming a reality. Indeed, unknown to us, the Kremlin
not only contained a powder magazine, but that night the
guard, half asleep and carelessly posted, had allowed a whole
battery of artillery to enter and station under Napoleon's
very windows. It was now that the wild flames were blowing
with the greatest violence from all sides upon the Kremlin;
for the wind, no doubt intensified by the great combustion,
had increased to the velocity of a gale. The flower of our
army, the Emperor himself, would have been destroyed if
but one of the brands flying over our heads had fallen on a
powder wagon. Thus for several hours the fate of the entire
army depended on any one of the sparks fluttering through
the air!

At last day dawned, a lurid, dreadful day which intensified
the horror of the spectacle by dimming it and taking away
its glitter. Many of the officers sought refuge in the halls of
the palace; and the generals, Mortier himself, mastered by

the conflagration they had been battling for thirty-six hours, fell with exhaustion and discouragement.

They had nothing to say, and we accused ourselves. Most of us believed that the lack of discipline and the drunkenness of our soldiers had begun the disaster which the gale was completing. We looked upon ourselves with a sort of disgust. The cry of horror that would go up from all Europe terrified us. We were ashamed to meet each other's eyes, filled with consternation at so appalling a disaster, which sullied our glory and snatched its fruits from our hands, and threatened our very existence, both present and future. We had been reduced to an army of criminals on whom heaven and the civilized world would be avenged . . . We were diverted from our black thoughts and our fits of rage against the incendiaries only by our anxiety to obtain further information. Now accounts began to come in accusing the Russians alone of the disaster.

Indeed, officers returning from the different parts of the city all agreed: the very first night, that of the fourteenth, a ball of fire had settled on the palace of Prince Troubetskoy and burned it down. This had been a signal; for, immediately after the Bourse had been set on fire, Russian policemen had been seen there stirring up the blaze with tarred lances. Treacherously placed bombs had exploded in the stoves in several houses, wounding the soldiers crowding round them for warmth. Retiring to districts as yet untouched, they had selected other lodgings; but as they were about to enter those houses, closed and apparently abandoned, faint explosions had come from within, followed by light smoke which soon became thick and black, then reddish, then fire-colored, until in a short time the buildings were wrapped in swirling flames.

All the officers had seen wild-looking women and men in

rags with hideous faces wandering about in the flames, completing an awful image of hell. These wretched creatures, drunk with wine and the success of their crimes, no longer attempted to conceal themselves, but raced in triumph through the blazing streets. They were caught in the act of spreading the fire with torches they were carrying, and our men actually had to cut off their hands with sabers to make them loose their hold. People were saying that these criminals had been let out of the prisons by the Russian leaders to burn Moscow, and indeed so grave, so extreme a decision could only have been made through patriotism and executed by crime.

An order was immediately issued to judge and shoot all the incendiaries on the spot. The army was ready to move, and the Old Guard, lodged in its entirety in one section of the Kremlin, was under arms. The courtyard was filled with baggage and horses, ready loaded. We were benumbed with surprise, fatigue, and despair at witnessing the destruction of such a rich cantonment. Though masters of Moscow, we were to be forced to go and bivouac, without provisions, outside the city gates!

While our soldiers continued fighting the conflagration and the army was doing its best to cheat the flames of their prey, Napoleon, whose sleep none had dared to disturb during the night, was awakened by the double light of day and the fire. His first impulse was to wrathfully command this element to cease; but he soon gave way and drew back before the impossible. After striking at the heart of an empire, he was surprised to discover there another reaction besides submission and terror, and he felt himself defeated and surpassed in determination.

The conquest for which he had sacrificed everything was like a phantom he had been pursuing, which had vanished into the air in a whirlwind of smoke and flame as he thought he was about to seize it. Then an extreme agitation took hold of him, so that one would have thought he was being consumed by the fires around him. He jumped up every minute, walked a few paces, suddenly sat down again. He crossed and recrossed his chambers with hurried step, his nervous, choppy gestures betraying a tortured perplexity. He laid aside, took up, and laid aside again some urgent piece of business, to run to the windows and watch the progress of the conflagration. Short, violent exclamations broke from his burdened bosom: "What a horrible sight! To do it themselves! All those palaces! What extraordinary resolution! Why, they are Scythians!"

Between the fire and the spot where he stood lay a wide vacant space and the Moskva with its two embankments, yet the panes of the window against which he was leaning were burning hot, and the incessant labor of the sweepers on the iron roofs of the palace did not suffice to clear away the countless flakes of fire as they rained down.

At that juncture the rumor spread that the Kremlin had been mined: the Russians had said so, and there were documents to prove it. Some of the attendants went wild with terror, the army awaited impassively whatever Fate and the Emperor's order might decide, and the Emperor's only reply to the alarm was a smile of incredulity. But back and forth, back and forth he went, stopping at every window to gaze on the terrible victorious element which was furiously devouring his brilliant conquest, seizing on all the bridges and streets leading from his fortress, encircling him, besieging him, invading one after another the surrounding houses, confining him to narrower and still narrower limits, finally leaving him only the walled enclosure of the Kremlin.

We were already breathing nothing but smoke and ashes.

Night was coming on, about to add darkness to our dangers, and the equinoctial gale, as if in alliance with the Russians, was increasing in violence. It was then that Murat and Prince Eugène appeared on the scene and, with the Prince of Neu-châtel, made their way into the Emperor's apartments and entreated him on their knees to leave that place of desola-tion — but in vain.

Master at last of the palace of the Czars, Napoleon ob-stinately refused to yield his conquest, even to the flames. Suddenly the cry, "The Kremlin is on fire!" ran from mouth to mouth, rousing us from the contemplative stupor into which we had fallen. The Emperor went out to take stock of the danger. Twice fire had been detected in the building in which he was standing, and put out, but the arsenal tower was still burning. A Russian police officer found in it was brought to Napoleon to be questioned. This man was the incendiary, and he had executed his mission at a signal given by his superior. So everything was doomed to be destroyed, even the ancient and sacred Kremlin! The Em-peror made a gesture of contemptuous ill-humor, and the wretch was hustled into the courtyard, where the angry grenadiers dispatched him with their bayonets.

This incident decided Napoleon. He hurried down the northern staircase, made famous by the massacre of the Strelitz,* and gave the order that he should be conducted out of the city to the imperial palace of Petrovski, a couple of miles away, on the road to St. Petersburg. But we were be-sieged by an ocean of fire which blocked every outlet from the citadel, and defeated our first attempt to break through. After considerable groping we discovered a postern gate in

---

* Strelitz, old Muscovite infantry corps instituted in 1545 by Ivan IV. De-stroyed in 1705 by Peter the Great who had become fearful of their power. — J.D.T.

the rocks on the side toward the river. It was through this narrow passage that Napoleon, his officers, and the guard managed to escape from the Kremlin. But what had they gained by this movement? Even nearer the fire than before, they could neither retreat nor remain where they were. Yet how were they to advance, how force a way through the billows of that sea of fire? Even those who were familiar with the city, deafened by the tempest and blinded by ashes, could no longer tell where they were, as the streets had disappeared in smoke and ruins.

But we had to get on. The roaring of the flames around us was growing louder every minute. Only one way was open — a narrow winding street already afire from one end to the other, which seemed more like an entrance to that hell than an escape from it. But the Emperor without hesitation rushed into this dangerous passage, and forced his way ahead in the roar and crackling of flames, the crash of floors and ceilings, and the fall of burning beams and red-hot sheets of iron roofing. This fiery rubble blocked our way. The flames that were noisily consuming the buildings on both sides of the street rose high above the roofs and were caught by the wind and curled downward over our heads. Thus we were walking on a floor of fire, under a sky of fire, between walls of fire. The intense heat burned our eyes, but we had to keep them open and fixed on the danger. The consuming air, the glowing ashes, the leaping tongues of fire reduced our breathing to short, painful gasps, and we were almost suffocated by the smoke. Our hands were scorched as we sought to shield our faces from the insupportable heat, or brushed away the embers that burned through our clothing.

In this unspeakable distress, when rapid progress seemed our only salvation, our guide stopped, confused, uncertain. Here our adventurous existence would probably have come to an end if some looters from the first corps had not recognized the Emperor in the midst of the tempest of flames, and run to him and guided him toward the smoking ruins of a quarter reduced to ashes that morning.

It was there we came upon Davout, who, though wounded at Borodino, had had himself carried back into the conflagration to rescue Napoleon or to perish with him. He flew into his arms in extreme joy. Napoleon received him kindly, but with that composure which never deserted him in moments of peril.

In order to escape from this vast region of suffering we were forced to pass a long convoy of powder wagons trailing through the fiery streets. This was the last, though not the least of our dangers; and by nightfall we reached Petrovski.

On awaking the next morning, the seventeenth of September, Napoleon looked anxiously toward Moscow, hoping to find that the conflagration had subsided; but he saw it still raging as violently as ever. The whole city seemed one vast swirling column of fire, towering into the sky and dyeing it with lurid colors. Sunk in gloomy contemplation, he kept a long, mournful silence, which he broke at length by the exclamation, "This forbodes great misfortune for us!"

*

## Napoleon Returns to Moscow

Nevertheless, Napoleon tried to preserve an appearance of victory, declaring that he was going to march on St. Petersburg. He had already sketched this campaign on his maps, until then so prophetic, and given the order to the various corps to hold themselves in readiness. His decision, however, was only apparent — a good face he was trying to put on, a distraction from his intense suffering at seeing Moscow lost — so that Berthier and Bessières had little difficulty convincing him that time, supplies, and roads were lacking for the safe execution of such an important expedition.

At the same time he learned that Kutuzov's westward flight had suddenly been changed to a southern one, and that he was now somewhere between Moscow and Kaluga, which was one more reason for giving up the St. Petersburg project; whereas there were three reasons why he should march against the disorganized army and definitely defeat it: he would preserve his right flank and line of operation; take Kaluga and Tula, the storehouse and arsenal of Russia; and open a new, safe, short, and untried line of retreat toward Smolensk and Lithuania.

Someone proposed that he should turn back and march against Wittgenstein and Vitebsk. Napoleon vacillated between these various projects, of which the conquest of St. Petersburg was the one that naturally appealed to him most. The others seemed to him as nothing more than ways of retreat, avowals of blunders; and either through pride or his policy of being above making mistakes, he rejected them all.

Little more than a third of his army or of the Russian capital was in existence. But he and the Kremlin still stood! His renown was still intact; and he was persuaded that these two great names, *Napoleon* and *Moscow*, taken together would suffice to finish everything successfully. He therefore decided to return to the Kremlin which a battalion of his guard had unfortunately preserved.

The terrain he had to cross to reach Moscow presented a strange appearance. Enormous fires had been lit in the middle of the fields, in thick, cold mud, and were being fed with mahogany furniture and gilded windows and doors.

Around these fires, on litters of damp straw, ill protected by a few boards, soldiers and their officers, mud-stained and smoke-blackened, were seated in splendid armchairs or lying on silk sofas. At their feet were heaped or spread out cashmere shawls, the rarest of Siberian furs, cloth of gold from Persia, and silver dishes in which they were eating coarse black bread, baked in the ashes, and half-cooked, bloody horseflesh — strange combination of abundance and famine, wealth and filth, luxury and poverty!

Between the camps and the city we met flocks of soldiers dragging their own plunder or driving moujiks before them like beasts of burden, bowed under the weight of plunder from their capital, for the fire had forced out into the open some twenty thousand inhabitants who had until then remained under cover in the great city. Some of the Muscovites, both men and women, were well dressed. These were merchants. Carrying the remains of their wordly goods, they sought refuge round our fires, and lived for some time with our troops, actually protected by some, tolerated by others.

It was the same with ten thousand Russian soldiers, who for several days wandered freely about our camps, a few of them still bearing arms. Our soldiers accepted these defeated men without animosity, without thinking of taking them prisoners, either because they believed the war was over, or through indifference or pity; for off the battlefield your Frenchman is only too happy not to have any enemies. They allowed them to share their fires, even tolerated them as looting companions. When the disorder had diminished, or rather when the marshals had organized the pillage into a general forage, then the great number of Russian stragglers was noticed. An order was issued for their arrest, but seven or eight thousand of them had already escaped. These we were soon to be fighting again.

On entering Moscow the Emperor was met with an even more extraordinary sight. Of the entire great city he found only a few scattered houses standing in the midst of ruins. This stricken giant, scorched and blackened, exhaled a horrible stench. Heaps of ashes and an occasional section of a wall or a broken column alone indicated the existence of streets. In the poorer quarters scattered groups of men and women with their clothes almost burnt off them were wandering about like ghosts among the ruins. Some, crouched down in what had once been gardens, were digging in the earth for an occasional vegetable; others were fighting the crows for the possession of dead animals our army had left behind; and still others were diving into the Moskva to salvage grain which Rostopchin had had thrown into the water, and which they devoured without cooking, spoiled as it already was.

The Emperor saw that his entire army was scattered over the city. His progress was impeded by long lines of marauders going for plunder or returning with it, and by noisy groups of soldiers gathered around the vent holes of cellars and trying to batter down the doors of palaces, shops, and churches as yet untouched by the fire.

He stumbled over the debris of all sorts of furniture which had been thrown out of the windows to save it from the flames, or over heaps of rich plunder that had been abandoned in favor of other loot; for soldiers are like that, snatching up anything they can lay their hands on, greedily loading themselves with more than they can hope to carry, then after a few steps finding their strength unequal to the load, dropping, piece by piece, the greater part of their booty.

The thoroughfares were blocked with it, and the public squares, like the camps, had become markets where the superfluous was being exchanged for the necessary. The most precious of articles, not appreciated by their possessors, were sold for next to nothing, while other things having a deceptively rich appearance brought more than they were worth. Gold, being easier to carry, was bought at a great loss for silver, which the knapsacks would not hold. Soldiers were seated everywhere on bundles of merchandise, on heaps of coffee and sugar, in the midst of the finest wines and liquors that they were trying to trade for bread. Some of the men, overcome by drunkenness combined with exhaustion, fell too close to the flames and were burned to death.

The majority of the houses and mansions which had escaped the fire were occupied by the generals who spared their contents. We were all filled with sadness at the sight of this wholesale destruction, and the pillage which was the inevitable consequence. Some of the highest ranking officers were accused of being only too willing to keep what they could save from the flames, but such cases were so rare they could be counted. War with these energetic men was a passion that presupposed others. They were not inspired by greed, for they hoarded nothing. They availed themselves of what they came across, taking to be able to give, lavish with everything, believing they had paid in suffering for whatever they got.

It was through such disorder that Napoleon rode back into Moscow. He willingly gave it over to pillage, trusting that his soldiers, scattered everywhere over the ruins, would not search them fruitlessly. But when he saw that the disorder was increasing, that even the Old Guard was involved in it, that the Russian peasants, attracted by the prices they were able to get for their wares, were being robbed by our famished soldiers of the food they were bringing us, when he realized that all the still existing resources were being squandered by this lawless pillage — then he reined in the Guard and issued severe orders. The churches in which our cavalry had taken shelter were evacuated and reopened for worship. Each corps of the army was ordered to take its turn at pillage, like any other duty, and we finally began to arrest the Russian stragglers.

But it was too late! The soldiers had disappeared, the terrified peasants never returned, and many, many supplies had been wasted. The French army had been guilty of similar mistakes before, but in this case the fire was their excuse, as they had been compelled to act in haste to get ahead of the flames. It is remarkable enough that order was restored at the Emperor's first command.

*

## Diplomatic Moves

When Kutuzov abandoned Moscow he drew Murat after him in the direction of Kolomna, up to the point where the road crosses the Moskva. There, under cover of night, he turned sharply southward and marched toward Podol, between Moscow and Kaluga. This nocturnal march of the Russian army around Moscow, with the high wind carrying live embers and flames over them, was somber and religious. They advanced by the sinister light of the conflagration which was destroying the center of their commerce, the sanctuary of their faith, the cradle of their empire. Filled with horror and indignation, the men preserved a gloomy silence, broken only by the monotonous thud of their boots, the roar of the blaze, and the whistling of the gale. From time to time the mournful light was cut through by sudden brilliant flashes. Then the soldiers' faces were contracted by savage grief, and the dangerous fire in their eyes reflected the fire which they believed to be our work, and revealed the ferocious desire for revenge which was fermenting in their hearts and spreading through the whole empire, and of which so many Frenchmen were to be victims.

At that solemn moment Kutuzov notified his emperor of the loss of the capital, in noble, resolute terms informing him, "In order to preserve the rich provinces of the south and my communications with Tormasov and Tchitchakov, I have been forced to abandon Moscow. But the city is emptied of the people who are its life. In all the world the people are the soul of an empire. Wherever the Russian people are, there is Moscow, there the Russian empire!"

A little later, seeming to break under the weight of his grief, Kutuzov cried, "This wound will be deep and indelible!" Then, recovering his composure, he said, "Moscow lost is only one city less in an empire, the sacrifice of one part for the preservation of all. I have taken my stand on the flank of the enemy's long line of operation, holding it blocked by my detachments. From here I can keep an eye on their movements, protect the resources of the empire, and re-form my army." On the sixteenth of September he declared, "Napoleon will be forced to give up his disastrous conquest."

It is said that Alexander was struck with consternation on receiving this news. Napoleon pinned his hopes on the weakness of his rival, while the Russians feared the effect of the disaster on him, but the Czar gave the lie to both hopes and fears, showing himself in his speeches as great as the misfortune.

"This is no time for faintheartedness!" he cried. "Let us swear to be doubly courageous and persevering! The enemy is in a capital as empty as a tomb, with no way of dominating, even of existing. He entered Russia with three hundred thousand men of all races, without union, without national or religious ties. Half his forces have been destroyed by the sword, hunger, and desertion. In Moscow now there are only ruins. He is in the center of Russia, but not a Russian is at his feet . . . Meanwhile our forces are increasing and are hemming him in. He is in the heart of a thickly populated country, surrounded by troops that have halted him and are ready to pounce on him. To escape starvation he will soon have to flee through the dense ranks of our fearless soldiers. Shall we draw back now, when all Europe is following us with encouraging eyes? Let us be an example to them, and welcome the Hand which has chosen us to be the first nation in the cause of truth and liberty!" He ended with an invocation to the Almighty.

The Russians have different opinions of their general and their emperor. We, as enemies, can only judge our adversaries by their acts, and certainly their actions were in keeping with their words. Comrades, we must do them justice. Their sacrifice was complete, without reservation or tardy regrets; and since that time they have never made any demands on us, even in our capital,* which they left unharmed. Their reputation has remained high and spotless. They have known true glory; and when a higher civilization has pervaded their masses, this great people will have its great century, and in their turn wield the sceptre of power which, it seems, the nations of the earth must successively surrender to each other.

The devious route that Kutuzov took, whether because of indecision or as a ruse, succeeded so well that Murat lost all trace of him for three days. The Russian took advantage of

---

* On March 30, 1814, Paris fell before the armies of the Sixth Coalition and the Russians occupied the city with the others. — J.D.T.

this respite to study the terrain and entrench himself. The head of his army was approaching Vorovno, one of Rostopchin's finest estates, when the governor of Moscow rode ahead of them. The soldiers believed that he wished to be alone to see his home for the last time; but suddenly the building disappeared in a cloud of smoke. They rushed to put the fire out; but it was Rostopchin himself who opposed them. They saw him in the midst of the fire he had set, smiling as the superb mansion crumbled around him, then in a firm hand tracing these words on the door of the chapel that was still standing — words which the French were to read with a shudder: "For eight years I have been improving this property, and have lived here happily with my family. The seventeen hundred tenants of my domain left their homes as you drew near, and I have set fire to my own house to save it from being defiled by your presence. Frenchmen, I abandoned to you my two homes in Moscow, with furnishings worth half a million rubles. Here you will find nothing but ashes!"

It was on the twentieth of September that Napoleon returned to the palace of the Czars from which he had been driven by the fire on the evening of the sixteenth. With the eyes of all Europe upon him, he waited for the supply trains, reinforcements, and the stragglers, confident that all his forces would be rallied by his victory, by the tempting bait of such rich booty, by the amazing spectacle of a subjugated Moscow, and particularly by himself whose glory dominated those noble ruins, shining and beckoning like a signal light on a reef!

Twice, however, on the twenty-second and the twenty-eighth of September letters from Murat, who had overtaken Kutuzov near Czarikovo, almost succeeded in tearing the

Emperor away from the fatal conquest. They announced a
battle, but two orders for a movement of troops were written
and burned. It seemed that, as far as our Emperor was concerned, the war was over, and that he was only waiting for a
reply from St. Petersburg. This hope was fed by memories
of Tilsit and Erfurt. Would he, then, have less influence
with Alexander at Moscow? Like all men who have been
fortunate for a very long time, he expected whatever he desired.

His genius, moreover, possessed the precious faculty which
consisted in being able to interrupt his most serious pre-
occupations at will, either to change them or to rest his
mind; for with him will was stronger than imagination, in
which respect he ruled himself as firmly as others.

But eleven days passed, and still Alexander had not broken
his silence. Napoleon, hoping to outdo his rival in stubbornness, lost time which he should have gained, thus
strengthening the defense to the detriment of the attack.

His behavior now, even more than at Vitebsk, warned the
Russians that he intended to remain indefinitely in the heart
of their empire. The ashes of Moscow were given a governor
and divided into wards, and the order to lay in sufficient
supplies for the winter was issued. A theater took shape in
the midst of the ruins, and word went around that the greatest actors in Paris had been sent for. An Italian singer was
imported in an attempt to bring the *soirées* of the Tuileries
to life in the Kremlin. In so doing Napoleon believed he was
deceiving a government that had become past master in deception through the practice of encouraging the errors and
ignorance of the people.

Napoleon was conscious of the insufficiency of the means
at his disposal. Yet September slipped away and October
began, and Alexander had not deigned to reply, which Na-

poleon, exasperated, considered an indignity. On the third
of October, after a restless, wrathful night, he summoned his
marshals.

"Come in," he cried as soon as he saw them. "And listen
to the new plan I have just conceived . . . Read, Prince
Eugène."

The Prince read, and the marshals listened: "All that is
left of Moscow must be burned . . . We shall march on St.
Petersburg where MacDonald will join us. Murat and
Davout will be the rear guard."

The Emperor, highly excited, turned his burning eyes on
his generals, whose faces betrayed only amazement. Then,
getting more excited in order to arouse them, he cried,
"What! You, you are not inflamed by this idea! Has there
ever been a greater military exploit? Henceforth nothing
short of that conquest will be worthy of us. We shall be overwhelmed with praise! What will the world say when it
learns that in three months' time we have conquered the two
greatest capitals of the North?"

But both Davout and Daru pointed out to him the obstacles lying in the way of such an expedition — the season of
the year, shortage of food, a barren, deserted road. The
officers of his staff have since declared that they suggested
several other projects, which was a waste of time and energy
with a sovereign whose genius outdistanced their imagina-
tions, and who would not have been stopped by their objections if he had really decided to march on St. Petersburg. But
this idea with him was only the fruit of a fit of anger, an
inspiration of despair at seeing himself obliged to yield, to
abandon a conquest and retreat before the eyes of Europe.

It was primarily a threat intended to frighten his own generals as well as his enemies, and pave the way for negotiations
with the Czar. The man designated for this mission was

Caulaincourt,* a high-ranking officer who had found favor with Alexander. He alone, among all the eminent men of Napoleon's court, had had any influence with his rival; but for some months he had denied him access to his intimate circle, as he had been unable to make him approve of his expedition.

It was to Caulaincourt, however, that he was finally forced to have recourse and to lay bare his anxiety. He summoned him, but when they were alone together he did not know how to begin, pacing nervously up and down for some time before his pride would let him break the painful silence. Finally, after a few indistinctly pronounced words, he began: "I'm going to march on St. Petersburg. I know that the destruction of that city will distress you; but then Russia will rise up against Alexander, there will be a conspiracy, and he will be assassinated — which will be a great calamity. I esteem this sovereign highly, and will regret him, as much for my own sake as for France. His nature suits our interests, and no other prince could replace him advantageously for us. Therefore, in order to prevent this catastrophe, I have thought of sending you to him."

But the Duke of Vicenza, as stubborn as he was deaf to flattery, could not be swayed. "These overtures will be useless," he said. "As long as Russian territory is not entirely evacuated, Alexander will not listen to any proposal. At this season of the year Russia is fully aware of her advantages. I believe, further, that this course would be harmful to you, as it would disclose your need for peace and expose the awkwardness of our position. Besides, the more conspicuous your choice of a negotiator, the more it would indicate your

---

* Marquis Louis de Caulaincourt (Duke of Vicenza), grand equerry and ambassador to the Russian court under the Empire, whose brother was killed at Borodino. — J.D.T.

anxiety. I, more than any other, would be sure to fail, particularly as I should set out with the certainty of failure."

The Emperor brought this interview to an abrupt close
with the exclamation, "All right! Then I'll send Lauriston!" *

Lauriston declares that he added his objections to Caulaincourt's and that, provoked by the Emperor, he even volun-
teered the opinion that they should begin the retreat that
very day by marching toward Kaluga. Napoleon, highly incensed, replied bitterly, "I like simple plans, the roads with
the fewest turns, the main roads, the ones we took to reach
here; but I will not return over them till peace has been
made!" Then showing him, as he had done to Caulaincourt, the letter he had just written to Alexander, he ordered
him to go to Kutuzov and demand a safe conduct to St.
Petersburg. The Emperor's parting words to Lauriston
were, "I want peace! I must have peace! I want it absolutely.
Only preserve our honor."

Lauriston set out at once and reached the outposts of the
Russian army on the fifth of October. Hostilities were immediately suspended, the interview granted; but Volkonsky,
Alexander's aide-de-camp, and Bennigsen appeared without
Kutuzov. Wilson has since said that these generals and
and other Russian officers, suspicious of their commander and
accusing him of weakness, protested that treason was afoot,
and Kutuzov did not dare to leave his camp.

Now, as Lauriston's instructions stated that he was to deal
with Kutuzov, and no other, he haughtily rejected any intermediary communication, and, taking advantage of this opportunity to break off negotiations of which he disapproved,
withdrew, despite Volkonsky's entreaties. He declared his

* Jacques-Law Lauriston, Marquis, and Marshal of France, great-nephew
of the Scotch financier, John Law. — J.D.T.

intention of returning to Moscow, which would doubtless have angered Napoleon, and he would have fallen upon Kutuzov, defeated him, destroyed his still incomplete army, and forced him to make peace. In the case of a less decisive success, he would at least have been able to withdraw toward his reinforcements without a disaster.

Unfortunately Bennigsen made haste to demand an interview with Murat, while Lauriston waited. The Russian chief of staff, more skillful at negotiating than fighting, endeavored to charm the newmade King by his polished and respectful manners, to seduce him with flattery, and deceive him with gentle words breathing distrust of war and hope of peace. And Murat, weary of battles, uncertain of the outcome of this war, homesick for his own throne since he no longer expected a richer one, let himself be charmed, seduced, and deceived.

Having persuaded both his own commander and Murat, Bennigsen sent for Lauriston and had him conducted at midnight to the Russian camp where Kutuzov was waiting for him. The interview began badly. Konownitzin and Volkonsky wished to remain as witnesses, which displeased the French general. They finally withdrew, on his insistence.

As soon as Lauriston was alone with Kutuzov he stated his errand and demanded a safe conduct for St. Petersburg. The Russian general replied that this demand exceeded his powers, but proposed to entrust Volkonsky with Napoleon's letter to the Czar, and offered an armistice until the return of the Russian aide-de-camp. He accompanied his words with professions of good will which were echoed by his generals.

It was shortly demonstrated that they were all together in a scheme to deceive Murat and the Emperor — and they succeeded in doing so. Napoleon was delighted with the detailed account of Lauriston's mission. Made credulous by hope — or by hopelessness — he was elated by appearances for a short time. Eager to free himself from a profound depression, he seemed to be trying to forget by giving himself up to unreserved joy. He summoned all his generals and triumphantly announced an imminent peace.

Nevertheless, Kutuzov's proposed armistice displeased him, and he ordered Murat to break it without delay. Yet it was none the less observed, no one knows why.

That armistice was an unusual one. All that was necessary to break it was a reciprocal three-hour notice, and it applied only to the fronts of the two camps, and not to their flanks. At least, that is the way the Russians interpreted it. We could neither bring in a convoy nor send out a foraging party without a struggle, so that fighting continued on every hand, except where it might be favorable to us.

During the next few days Murat took great pleasure in showing himself at the enemy's outposts, reveling in the flattering looks which his fine appearance, his reputation for bravery, and his high rank won for him; and the Russian generals were careful not to do anything that would put him out of conceit. They showered him with proofs of deference likely to preserve his illusions. He ordered their mounted sentries about as if they were French, and when the portion of the field they were occupying suited him, they immediately surrendered it to him.

Some of the Cossack officers went so far as to feign enthusiasm, and to declare that they no longer recognized any other emperor than the one reigning in Moscow. For a time Murat foolishly believed that they would never fight him again. He went even further . . . Napoleon was heard to exclaim as he read one of his letters, "Murat, King of the Cossacks! What foolishness!" All sorts of ideas occurred to those men to whom everything imaginable had happened.

The Emperor, who was not often deceived, was to have only a few minutes of trumped-up joy. Two more important convoys had fallen into the enemy's hands — one through the carelessness of its leader, who killed himself in despair; the other through the cowardice of an officer, who was about to be shot when our retreat began: the loss of an army saved his life!

Every morning our soldiers, our cavalry in particular, had to go out to forage provisions for the evening and next day. As the vicinity of Moscow and Vinkovo was rapidly growing leaner and leaner, each day they went farther afield. The men and horses returned exhausted — those who did return; for every measure of rye, every bale of hay had to be fought for, had to be snatched away from the enemy. It was one continual fight, loss, surprise. The peasants took a hand in it by punishing with death anyone whom the love of money tempted into our camps with a little food. Others set fire to their own villages to drive our foragers out and deliver them into the hands of the Cossacks, whom they had warned beforehand and who had encircled us. It was also the peasants who took Vereia, a small town in the neighborhood of Moscow, though one of their priests, it is said, conceived and carried out this bold project. He armed the inhabitants and obtained some troops from Kutuzov, then, before dawn on the tenth of October, had a false alarm given on one side while he charged the palisades on the other, demolished them, rushed into the town, and cut the throats of the whole garrison.

So war was all around us — in front, on our flanks, and behind us. Our army was growing weaker, while the enemy was daily becoming more daring. It was going to be with this conquest as with so many others, that are won in the mass and lost in detail!

Finally Murat himself grew alarmed, realizing that half his cavalry had perished in daily skirmishes. When the Russian officers encountered ours at the outposts — inspired by fatigue, vanity, or military frankness carried to the point of indiscretion — they exclaimed in commiseration at the misfortunes lying in wait for us. They showed us * horses that still looked wild, scarcely broken, with long tails sweeping the dust of the plain. This indicated that important cavalry reinforcements were coming in from all sides, while our own corps was being lost; and the noise of continuous firing behind their lines warned us that a multitude of recruits were exercising under the protection of the armistice.

Though Napoleon was not ignorant of these warnings, he thrust them aside, not meaning to have his resolution shaken; but his uneasiness which had come back showed itself in the violent orders he gave. It was then that he had the churches of Moscow despoiled of everything that could serve as a trophy for the Grand Army. He pretended that these objects, doomed to destruction by the Russians themselves, belonged to the conqueror by the double right conferred by victory and the fire.

It required all our efforts to remove the gigantic cross from the tower of Ivan the Great.† The Emperor intended that this should grace the dome of the Invalides in Paris. There was a Russian superstition that the welfare of the nation depended on the possession of this precious object. As our men toiled, flocks of ravens circled in the air above the cross, until Napoleon, weary of their melancholy cawing, exclaimed, "It looks as if these birds of ill omen wanted to protect it!" It is not known just what his thoughts were at that critical

* From this point on the author encloses the paragraph in quotation marks, though he does not indicate the source of the quotation. — J.D.T.

† This tower was 320 feet high. The cross, made of wood, was 32 feet long, covered with gilded silver plates. — J.D.T.

moment, but we did know that he was open to all sorts of presentiments.

His daily rides, with an unfailing sun shining in the sky, a sun in which he tried to see his lucky star and to make others see it, failed to distract his mind from his problems. To the gloomy silence of a dead Moscow was added that of the surrounding wastes, and the still more threatening silence of Alexander. The faint tramp of his soldiers' feet wandering through this immense tomb was not sufficient to awaken the Emperor from his revery and tear him away from his cruel memories or even crueler premonitions. His nights had become particularly wearisome. He spent a part of them with Count Daru, to whom alone he acknowledged the gravity of his situation.

Fully aware of the power he reaped from the prestige of his infallibility, he shuddered at the thought of dealing it its first wound.

"What a frightful succession of perilous conflicts will begin with my first backward step!" he argued. "You must no longer find fault with my inaction. Oh, don't I know that from a purely military point of view Moscow is worthless! But Moscow is not a military position, it is a political position. You think I am a general, while I am really an Emperor." Then he cried, "In affairs of state one must never retreat, never retrace one's steps, never admit an error — that brings disrepute. When one makes a mistake, one must stick to it — that makes it right!"

This explains why he clung to his position with such tenacity: stubbornness, his finest quality elsewhere, became his worst defect here. But his distress was increasing. He knew that he must not count on the Prussian army, and a document from an unquestionable source, addressed to Berthier, made him lose confidence in the support of the

Austrians. He felt that Kutuzov was making a fool of him, but he had gone ahead so far now that he could neither advance nor stand still, neither retreat nor fight with honor or success. So, alternately urged forward and held back, he remained with the ashes of his conquest, with little to hope for, yet still wishing.

His letter, delivered by Lauriston, must have left on the sixth of October. He could not expect an answer before the twentieth, yet, despite so many threats of danger, Napoleon's pride, his policy, or perhaps his bad health, led him to adopt the most hazardous of all courses — that of waiting for a reply. Daru, like the other generals, was amazed to find him so lacking in his old ability to make quick decisions. Still, in this critical situation it was not logical to expect a character of such unshakable perseverance to renounce so easily the aims he had set for himself at Vitebsk.

The attitude of the army encouraged him in his stand. The majority of the officers were steadfast in their confidence; and the simple soldiers, who lived only in the present moment and looked forward to little in the future, showed no sign of uneasiness, preserving their unconcern, their most precious quality. However, the rewards that the Emperor distributed so generously in his daily reviews were now received with a more restrained joy, even with a shade of sadness. The vacant posts he had to offer were still bloody: his were dangerous favors.

Upon entering Russia many of the soldiers had thrown away their winter uniforms in order to be able to carry a heavier load of provisions; the road had worn their boots out; the rest of their clothing was torn and threadbare from repeated battles. But, in spite of everything, they still put on a brave front. They carefully hid their destitute condition from their Emperor and appeared before him with their weapons dazzlingly clean and well repaired. In the first courtyard of the palace of the Czars, two thousand miles from their base of supplies, and after so many battles and bivouacs, they made it a point of honor to look clean, ready, and shining.

The Emperor willingly lent himself to this deception, snatching at every straw to keep his hope alive. Then, without warning, came the first snowfall. With it perished all the illusions with which he had sought to surround himself; and from that moment he thought only of retreat, though he neither pronounced the word nor issued any order positively proclaiming it. He simply said that within twenty days the army must be in its winter quarters, and hastened the evacuation of the wounded. There, as everywhere else, his pride would not consent to any voluntary relinquishment. He found that there were not enough horses for his artillery, which was now too large for our shrunken army. He seemed not to care, and grew angry when it was proposed that he leave a part of it in Moscow. "Oh no," he said. "The enemy would make a trophy out of it!" and insisted that everything should go along with him.

In that deserted region he gave an order for the purchase of twenty thousand horses, and wanted us to gather a two months' supply of forage in fields where it had become increasingly difficult for us to find food enough for a single day. Some of his generals expressed astonishment at hearing these inpractical orders; but we knew that he sometimes gave such orders to deceive the enemy, or to acquaint his own army with the extent of our needs and suggest the effort that should be made to meet them.

And still Napoleon could not make up his mind whether to remain or to flee. Defeated in this trial of stubbornness, he put off acknowledging his defeat from one day to another. In the midst of the terrible confusion of men and the elements that was building up around him, under the eyes of his ministers and aides-de-camp, he spent those last days discussing the merits of a book of verse he had just received, or settling the accounts of the Comédie Française in Paris, which took three whole evenings. As we were well aware of his anxiety, we admired the force of his genius and the ease with which he was able to change at will the object of his attention.

We noticed, however, that he was prolonging his meals, which until then had been simple and brief, as if trying to forget his cares. Then, dull and heavy, he would slump down in his armchair and sit for hours as if benumbed, with a novel in his hands, waiting for the end of his terrible adventure. We said among ourselves as we watched this stubborn, unbending giant wrestle with the impossible, that there on the pinnacle of his glory he had the presentiment that the first downward step would mark the beginning of his ruin, and was therefore clinging motionless to that summit for a few last minutes.

But finally, after several days of self-deception, the charm was broken — by the intervention of a Cossack. This barbarian had shot at Murat just as he appeared at his outpost. Murat was furious, and notified Miloradovich that an armistice which was constantly being broken no longer existed, and that consequently each adversary must look to himself in the future.

At the same time he informed the Emperor that a wooded region on his left flank invited an attack from that direction; that his front line was perilously situated on a ravine into which it might be forced; that, in short, his position in front of a defile was a dangerous one, and called for immediate withdrawal. But Napoleon would not consent to this,

though he had at first referred to Voronovo as a safer position. In this conflict, which he still considered more political than military, he dreaded above all to appear to be giving
way. Any risk was preferable to that!

Still, on the thirteenth of October Lauriston was sent back
to Murat to examine the position of the front line. It was
evident that the Emperor was thinking of departure, though
he seemed to be neglecting the necessary preparations for it.
That same day he sketched a plan of retreat. Then a few
minutes later he proposed another in the direction of Smolensk. Junot received an order to burn all the guns of the
wounded at Kolotskoi on the twenty-first and to blow up the
ammunition wagons. D'Hilliers was to occupy Elnia, and
would build storehouses there. It was not till the seventeenth that Berthier first thought of distributing leather to
the soldiers in Moscow.

The chief of staff was of little assistance to his superior in
this critical situation. Though in a strange land, with an unfamiliar climate, he took no unusual precautions; and he expected the most insignificant details to be dictated to him by
the Emperor, then they were forgotten. This negligence or
lack of foresight had fatal consequences. In an army whose
component parts were commanded by marshals, princes, or
even kings, each one, perhaps, counted too much on the
others. Berthier of himself gave no orders, but was satisfied
with faithfully repeating the letter of the Emperor's wishes.
As for the spirit, he was constantly confusing the positive part
of his instructions with the purely conjectural.

Nevertheless, Napoleon began to rally the corps of his
army, and his reviews in the Kremlin became more frequent.
He formed the unhorsed cavalry into a battalion, and distributed rewards and promotions right and left. The trophies,
and the wounded who could be moved were put on the road

to Mozhaysk; the rest were assembled in the great Foundling Hospital and put in the care of French surgeons. The Russian wounded were mixed with ours to act as safeguards.

But it was too late. In the midst of these preparations, while Napoleon was reviewing Ney's division in the courtyard of the Kremlin, the news went around that the boom of guns had been heard in the direction of Vinkovo. For a while no one dared to inform the Emperor of it. Some were restrained by unbelief or uncertainty, and the dread of his first reaction; others, by weakness or the fear of being sent on a tiring journey to verify the report.

Finally Duroc told him. The Emperor's expression changed, but he soon recovered his calm and went on with the review. But just then Béranger, a young aide-de-camp, galloped up with the news that Murat's first line had been surprised and routed; his left had been outflanked under cover of the wood; his right attacked, and his retreat cut off. Twelve guns, twenty ammunition wagons, and thirty baggage wagons had been captured, two generals killed, from three to four thousand men lost, and the King himself wounded. He had been able to save only the remnant of his men by repeated attacks on the powerful body of troops that now occupied the main road behind him, cutting off his retreat.

Nevertheless, our honor was saved. Kutuzov's frontal attack had been weak; Poniatowski, several miles away on the right, had resisted gloriously; Murat and his carabineers by a supernatural effort had checked Bagawout as he was about to drive into our left flank, and regained the upper hand. Claparède and Latour-Maubourg had cleared the Spas-Kaplia pass five miles behind our lines, already occupied by Platov. Two Russian generals had been killed and several others wounded, and the enemy's losses in men had been serious. Yet to them belonged the advantage of the attack, our cannon, our position — in short, the victory.

Murat had no vanguard left; the armistice had cost him half his cavalry, this battle had completed its destruction. The wreck of his army, enfeebled by hunger, had scarcely enough strength left for a single charge . . . And so the war had begun again! It was the eighteenth of October.

At this news Napoleon recovered the fire of his earlier years. A thousand orders bearing on great and minor matters, all different, all logical, all necessary, issued in a flood from his quick mind. By nightfall all the immense army was in motion. The Emperor himself left Moscow before daybreak on the nineteenth. "Forward toward Kaluga!" he cried. "And woe to all who cross my path!"

# CHAPTER V

**✶✶✶✶✶✶✶✶**

## *Malo-Yaroslavetz*

A T THE SOUTHERN end of Moscow, near one of the gates, a wide avenue divides into two main highways, both leading to Kaluga: the one on the left is called the Old Road, the one on the right, the New. It was along the former that Kutuzov had just defeated Murat, and it was by this same road that Napoleon left Moscow on the nineteenth of October, having informed his staff that he would return to the Polish frontier by the route passing through Kaluga and Smolensk. He pointed upward to the clear blue sky and asked his attendants if they did not recognize his star in the bright sun. But this appeal to his lucky star and the apprehensive expression on his face gave the lie to his pretense of security.

Napoleon had entered Moscow with ninety thousand combatants and twenty thousand sick and wounded. He went out of it with more than a hundred thousand combatants, and left only twelve hundred behind in the hospitals. His brief stay there, despite certain losses, had permitted him to rest his infantry, replenish his ammunition, and increase his active force by ten thousand men, and also to provide for the recovery or removal of a good part of the sick. Still, the very first day on the road he could not help but notice that both the artillery and the cavalry were crawling rather than marching.

A sorry spectacle added to his gloomy foreboding. Since the evening before, the army had been marching out of Moscow without interruption. In this column of a hundred and forty thousand human beings and fifty thousand horses, a hundred thousand, marching at the head with their knapsacks and arms, with some five hundred cannon and two thousand artillery wagons, still bore some resemblance to the tremendous military organization which had conquered the world. But the rest — a frightening proportion of the whole — looked like a horde of Tartars after a successful raid: a jumble of carriages, wagons, rich coaches, and carts of all sorts, four or five abreast, and seeming to stretch on forever. Here were the trophies — Russian, Turkish, and Persian flags — and the gigantic cross of Ivan the Great; there, a flock of long-bearded Russian peasants driving or carrying our plunder, of which they were a part, and soldiers wheeling barrows loaded with everything they had been able to pile on them. These foolish creatures would not be able to hold out to the end of the first day, but their senseless greed had closed their eyes to the fact that two thousand miles and many battles lay between them and their destination.

Marching in the train of the army were crowds of men of all nations, without weapons or uniforms, and lackeys swearing in a Babel of tongues and urging on with threats and blows tiny ponies that were harnessed with rope to elegant carriages loaded with food or plunder that had been saved from the fire. They also carried a number of Frenchwomen with their children. These ladies had previously been contented residents of Moscow; now they were fleeing the hatred of the Muscovites, and the army was their only refuge. A few Russian women of easy virtue, voluntary captives, also followed in our train.

One could have taken it for a caravan, a nomadic horde, or one of those armies of antiquity laden with spoils and slaves, returning from some dreadful destruction. It was inconceivable that the head of this column could drag along after them such a mass of vehicles and baggage for so long a distance.

Despite the width of the road and the warning shouts of his escorts, Napoleon had trouble making his way through this formless mob. All that was needed to free us of the weight of this train was one difficult pass, two or three forced marches, or a skirmish with the Cossacks; but only fate or the enemy had the right to lighten us in this manner. The Emperor did not feel that he could reproach his soldiers or deprive them of the fruits of their labors. Besides, the plunder was hidden under supplies; and he, who was unable to provide sufficient food for his men, could not very well forbid them to carry their own rations. Then too, as there was a shortage of ambulances, the carriages were the only means of transportation for the sick and wounded.

Without breaking his silence, Napoleon extricated himself from the chaotic mob and moved forward on the old Kaluga road. He pushed on in this direction for several hours, with the avowed intention of giving battle to Kutuzov on the very field he had won from Murat. But in the middle of the day, after a halt at the castle of Krasnopachra, Napoleon turned suddenly to the right with his army, and in three stages, marching across the fields, reached the new Kaluga road. In the midst of this maneuver it began to rain, the side roads became impassable, and we were forced to halt. This was a real calamity, as we pulled our cannon from the mud only with the greatest difficulty.

Napoleon had masked his operation behind Ney's corps

and the remains of Murat's cavalry, which was still on the other side of the Mótscha River and at Voronovo. Kutuzov, deceived by this stratagem, was waiting for the Grand Army on the old road, whereas since the twenty-third of October our troops had been on the new road, and had only one day's march to go before quietly passing him and reaching Kaluga ahead of him.

A letter from Berthier, written on the day of this flank march, was our last attempt at a settlement, as well as a stratagem of war. It was never satisfactorily answered.

On the twenty-third, the Emperor spent a peaceful night in the imperial headquarters at Borovsk. He had been informed that at six o'clock in the evening, Delzons with his division had found Malo-Yaroslavetz, ten miles away, and the woods above it unoccupied. This position was a strong one, conveniently near Kutuzov, and the only point at which he could join the new Kaluga road.

The Emperor wanted to make sure of success by being present himself. An order to advance was even given; we have no idea why he later retracted it. He spent all that evening on his horse on the main road near Borovsk, on the side where he supposed Kutuzov to be. In a pouring rain he examined the terrain, as if it were to be the scene of a battle. The next morning, the twenty-fourth, he learned that the Russians were fighting Delzons for the possession of Malo-Yaroslavetz. The news did not trouble him, either because he was overconfident, or because he was still uncertain of his plans.

He left Borovsk late and at a leisurely pace, but had gone only a short distance when sounds of firing reached his ears. Then he became alarmed, and galloped to the top of a hill where he stood listening. Have the Russians got the start of me? he asked himself. Has my maneuver failed? Didn't we march fast enough when we were supposed to be outflanking Kutuzov?

As a matter of fact, during the whole movement the troops had exhibited the sort of torpor which follows a prolonged rest. Malo-Yaroslavetz was only seventy-odd miles from Moscow, which distance should have been covered in four days, whereas it had taken us six; but the army was overloaded with food and plunder, and the roads were marshy. We had lost an entire day crossing the Nara and the surrounding swamps, and another, rallying the different corps. Besides, passing so close to the enemy we had been forced to compress our ranks in order not to expose a drawn-out flank to their fire. Be that as it may, we can date all our subsequent disasters from that halt.

The Emperor heard the noise of combat grow louder and louder. "Can it be a battle?" he cried. Every volley seemed to tear through him; for it was no longer a question of conquering with him, but of preserving. He dispatched Davout to the scene of the battle, but that marshal did not reach the field till nightfall, when the firing was almost over and the outcome was certain. The Emperor witnessed the end of the encounter without being able to help the Viceroy. A band of Cossacks very nearly captured one of his officers standing a short distance from him. When night had fallen Prince Eugène sent a general to give the Emperor a complete report of the affair.

The encounter had been a bloody one. The same points had been successively won and lost four times over. The town of Malo-Yaroslavetz, built of wood, had been set on fire and completely destroyed. Many men, both Russian and French, had been burned to death. Napoleon sadly surveyed the field where seven generals and four thousand

French and Italian soldiers had just been killed or wounded. The sight of the enemy's great losses did not console him: they were not twice as heavy as ours, and *their* wounded would be saved. He recalled how Peter the Great in a similar situation, though he had sacrificed ten Russians for every Swede, not only believed that the losses were equal, but that he had even got the better of the terrible bargain.

The worst thing about it was the knowledge that this bloody encounter might have been avoided: the campfires burning so brightly on our left on the night of the twenty-third had given us sufficient warning of the movement of the Russians toward Malo-Yaroslavetz. Nevertheless we had not increased our pace, only one division had been sent ahead, and that was carelessly posted seven miles away from all reinforcements, and the corps of the army were out of touch with each other. Where were the rapid and decisive movements of Marengo, Ulm, Eckmuehl? Why this slow, lifeless, sluggish advance in such critical circumstances? Had our artillery and baggage sapped our strength to that extent? That seemed to be the most likely explanation.

The Emperor received the report of the battle in a filthy, tumbledown old frame house, a weaver's cabin, situated at the bottom of a ravine a few steps from the main road, near the village of Ghorodinia. Here he was about a mile from Malo-Yaroslavetz, at the first bend of the Louja River. It was in this miserable hut, in a dark, dirty room divided by a curtain, that the fate of the army and of Europe was to be decided.

The first hours of the night were spent in receiving reports. These all showed that the enemy was preparing a battle for the next day. We were all strongly against it. Bessières arrived at eleven o'clock. This marshal owed his promotion to honorable service, and also to the Emperor's liking for

him; for Napoleon clung to him as something he had created.
It was true that one could not be a favorite with Napoleon
as with any other monarch. One must have followed him,
and been of use to him; for he was not interested in mere
charm. Above all, such a one must have been more than a
witness to his many victories. The Emperor, genuinely
weary, had acquired the habit of seeing through the eyes he
believed he had trained.

Bessières had been sent to examine the enemy's position.
Now he returned, after having carefully covered the whole
of the Russian front, and announced, "It is unassailable!"

"Great God!" cried the Emperor, clasping his hands.
"Are you sure you saw rightly? Is what you say true? Are
you ready to back it up?"

Bessières repeated his statement, adding, "Three hundred
grenadiers up there would be enough to stop an army."

Then Napoleon crossed his arms in dismay, hung his head
and indulged in melancholy reflections . . . His army was
victorious, yet he was defeated; his advance was cut off, his
maneuver foiled; Kutuzov, an old man, a Scythian, had
outwitted him. Yet he could not accuse his lucky star. Did
not the sun of France appear to have followed him into
Russia? Was not the road to Malo-Yaroslavetz open only
yesterday? Fortune had not failed him; was it he, then, who
had failed Fortune?

Absorbed in such gloomy thoughts, his intense applica-
tion of mind made it impossible for anyone to extract a
word from him. We asked for orders but the most we could
get out of him was a nod. At length he decided to get a little
sleep. But he was tortured with insomnia, and all the rest of
the cruel night he kept getting up, lying down again, calling
out, though he did not utter a single word that would betray

his distress. It was only by the extreme agitation of his body that we suspected his state of mind.

At about four in the morning an orderly officer, the Prince of Arenberg, came to warn him that, under cover of the night and the woods, Cossacks were stealing between him and his outposts along several convenient gullies. The Emperor had just dispatched Poniatowski toward Kremenskoi on his right flank. Not in the least expecting the enemy on that side, he had neglected to post scouts in front of it. So now he simply scorned his orderly's warning.

As soon as the sun showed itself on the horizon on the twenty-fifth, he mounted his horse and rode out on the Kaluga road, which for him did not extend beyond Malo-Yaroslavetz. To reach the bridge into this town he had to cross a plain about a mile wide lying in a bend of the Louja. He was attended by only a few officers. His usual escort of four squadrons, not having been informed of his movement, were hastening to join him, but had not yet caught up with him. The road was thick with ambulances, artillery, wagons, and elegant carriages — the interior of the army marching along without thought of danger.

Suddenly we saw several platoons coming toward us on the right, then, behind them, long black lines of troops. Soon the noise of shouting reached our ears. A number of women and servants came running back toward us, in such terror that they were unable to answer our questions. At that moment the interminable line of wagons creaked to a stop, uncertain as to how to proceed, and great disorder resulted. The wagons behind continued to come on and piled up on those that had stopped. Some tried to go ahead, some wanted to turn around. They collided in trying to pass, and in a moment all were jammed in an inextricable jumble.

The Emperor rode on smiling, believing the panic to be the result of some false alarm. His aides-de-camp, however, suspected that the black lines were Cossacks; but they were marching in compact groups, which deceived us. If the barbarians had not yelled in attacking, as they always do, to give themselves courage, it is probable that Napoleon would not have escaped from them. What increased the danger was that at first we mistook their wild howls for cries of *Vive l'Empereur!*

It was Platov and six thousand Cossacks who had crossed the river, the flat plain, and the main road behind our victorious front line, sweeping everything before them, while the Emperor, secure in the protection of the winding river, rode calmly on in the midst of his army, unable to believe in the possibility of so bold an undertaking. Once they were started the Cossacks came on so rapidly that Rapp had just time enough to shout to the Emperor, "It's the Cossacks! Turn back!" But Napoleon, either because he did not see clearly, or because of his aversion to flight, did not move. He was on the point of being surrounded when Rapp seized the bridle of his horse and turned him around, crying, "You must!" Indeed, there was no choice left but to flee. Yet Napoleon's pride would not let him give way. He drew his sword; Berthier and Caulaincourt followed his example. Taking their stand at the side of the road, they waited for the horde to come on. They were not forty paces away when Rapp, too, swung round and faced them. The leader of the Cossacks drove his spear into Rapp's horse's chest with such force that he was unseated and thrown to the ground. The other aides-de-camp succeeded in rescuing him. This action, Lecoulteux's courage, the combined efforts of a score of officers and some light-infantrymen — but particularly the barbarians' greed for plunder — saved Napoleon's life that day.

The Cossacks had only to stretch out their hands to seize him; but at that moment they fell upon the jumble of wagons, horses, men and women on the road, in front of us. They killed or wounded the drivers of the baggage trains, whom they dragged into the woods to strip, and drove the horses hitched to cannons across the fields. But their victory was short-lived. The cavalry of the Guard galloped up, and at the sight of them the Cossacks quit the combat and fled. The torrent ebbed away leaving deplorable traces of its passage, but dropping all that it was carrying off.

Some of the barbarians had shown themselves bold to the point of insolence. We saw them calmly reloading their muskets as they left the field, walking their horses between our squadrons. They relied upon the slowness of our picked troops as much as on the swiftness of their own mounts, on which they always used the whip. Their flight was accomplished without disorder. They turned around several times and faced us, but always beyond musket range, so that they left few wounded and no prisoners. They finally led us into brush-filled ravines where their cannon halted our advance. All this made us think. Our army was fought out, and here was war being born again — fresh and undiminished!

The Emperor, amazed that the Cossacks should have dared to attack him, waited until the plain had been cleared. Then he rode back to Malo-Yaroslavetz where the Viceroy pointed out the obstacles he had overcome the day before.

The scene spoke for itself, and never had battlefield been more terribly eloquent. The smoking ruins; the streets of which all traces had disappeared except for the long lines of dead men and the skulls crushed by cannon wheels; the wounded, screaming in agony as they crawled out of the ruins with their clothing, their hair, their limbs half burnt off; the funereal sound of firing as the grenadiers rendered last honors to their slain colonels and generals — all indicated an encounter of the utmost violence. The Emperor apparently saw nothing but glory in it. "The honor of this wonderful day belongs altogether to Prince Eugène!" he said. But inwardly he was terribly shaken by the spectacle. He left the spot and rode to the high plain.

Comrades, do you remember that fatal field, on which the conquest of the world was halted, where twenty years of victories came to an end, where the final collapse of our fortune began? Can you picture to yourselves that flattened, bloody city, those deep ravines, the woods surrounding the plain so as to make a sort of arena of it? On one side — the French fleeing from the rigors of the North: on the other, at the edge of the wood, the Russians guarding the South and bent on driving us back into their terrible winter: then Napoleon in the center of the plain between the two armies, his eyes and steps wandering from south to west, from the Kaluga road to the Medyn road, both of which were closed to him. On the Kaluga road Kutuzov with twenty thousand men stood ready to oppose him over twenty miles of passes. In the direction of Medyn he saw a powerful body of cavalry — Platov and the same hordes that had ridden through our left flank and come out loaded with plunder, and were now re-forming on our right, where reinforcements and artillery were waiting for them. It was on this side that the Emperor's eyes dwelt at greatest length, and it was about this situation that he studied his maps and consulted his marshals. He was able to judge the gravity of his position by their noisy arguments which even his presence was powerless to moderate. At length, heavy with sorrow and sad forebodings, he rode slowly back to his headquarters.

Murat, Prince Eugène, Berthier, Davout, and Bessières

followed him. The mean little home of an obscure workman sheltered an emperor, two kings, and three marshals! There the fate of Europe was to be decided, as well as that of the conquering army. It was understood by all that Smolensk was their goal; but should they approach that city by Kaluga, Medyn, or Mozhaysk? They found Napoleon seated at a table, his head sunk in his hands, no doubt to hide the despair upon his face.

Everyone hesitated to break a silence charged with a sense of impending doom. Finally Murat, whose nature it was to advance by leaps and bounds, grew weary of the indecision. Springing to his feet, he began, "You may accuse me of imprudence once again, but in war everything is decided by circumstances. When there is no choice but to attack, discretion becomes valor, and valor discretion. It is impossible to stop now, and dangerous to run away. We must pursue! What do we care for the threatening attitude of the Russians or their impenetrable forests? I laugh at them all! Just give me the remainder of the cavalry and the Old Guard, and I'll go into their woods, crush their battalions, overthrow everything, and open the road to Kaluga for our army!"

At this point Napoleon raised his head and checked Murat's passion by saying, "I've had my fill of heroics! We've done far too much already for glory. The time has come now for us to turn all our thoughts to saving the remains of the army."

Then Bessières, feeling himself supported by the Emperor, spoke up. His pride rebelled at serving the King of Naples, and his one wish was to keep intact the Old Guard, which he had formed and for which he must answer to Napoleon. "The morale of the army and of the Guard itself is completely lacking for such efforts. They're already saying that there aren't enough ambulances and wagons, so that every man who falls in battle from now on will be at the mercy of the enemy; every wound will be mortal. Murat would get only feeble support — and in our position! We've just had proof of its strength. And against what enemy? Didn't you see the field of yesterday's engagement, or notice the fury with which the Russian recruits — badly armed and without uniforms — rushed up to be killed?" The marshal ended by pronouncing the word *retreat* which the Emperor approved by his silence.

Davout spoke up quickly, "Since it is decided that we are to withdraw, I demand that it be by Medyn and Smolensk."

Then Murat, either in enmity or discouragement, interrupted Davout angrily. "I'm astonished," he cried, "that anybody should dare to propose anything so imprudent to the Emperor! Has Davout sworn to ruin the army? Does he want our long, heavy column to venture without guides on an unfamiliar road, within sight of Kutuzov, our flank exposed to his fire? Will Davout defend it, perhaps? . . . When we could get to Mozhaysk through Borovsk and Vereia without any risk, why should we turn our backs on this way of escape? Provisions must have been stored there, the road is familiar, and no traitor will lead us astray!"

At these words Davout, burning with ill-repressed wrath, replied, "I'm proposing a way of retreat through a fertile region, over a road new to us, rich, and untouched, with villages still standing. This is the shortest road and one which the enemy could not cut off as they could the road from Mozhaysk to Smolensk, the one Murat suggests. And what a road that is! A desert of sand and ashes, where convoys of wounded would add to our difficulties, where we should find only ruins, blood-soaked fields, skeletons, and starvation! Moreover, it is my duty to give my advice when it is asked for. I will obey an order contrary to my opinion with as much zeal as I would execute the one I have proposed. But the Emperor alone has the right to impose silence on me, and not Murat, who is not my sovereign, and never will be!"

The quarrel was running high. Berthier and Bessières came between them. The Emperor, still in the same dejected attitude, did not seem to hear. At length he broke his silence and closed the council with these words: "All right, gentlemen, I shall decide."

The decision he made was to retreat, and by the road to Mozhaysk which would lead us from the enemy most quickly. The effort he had to make to get out an order of march was so excessively painful, it cost him so dearly that in this inner struggle he momentarily lost the use of his senses. Those who came to his assistance have since told how the news of a second skirmish with the Cossacks, a few miles behind our lines, acted as an external shock sufficient to overcome his repulsion and spur him to make the fatal resolution.

The remarkable thing here is that he gave the order for this retreat toward the north at the same time that Kutuzov and his Russians, disorganized by the encounter at Malo-Yaroslavetz, were withdrawing toward the south!

That same night, there was great agitation in the Russian camp also. During the fighting at Malo-Yaroslavetz Kutuzov had been seen approaching the scene of battle like a man feeling his way, stopping after every step and examining the ground, as if he feared it might open up beneath his feet. The successive divisions he had dispatched to the assistance of Dokhturov were literally torn from him. He did not risk crossing Napoleon's path himself until there was no longer any fear of a major battle.

Then Wilson, * burning with the zeal of combat, rushed up to him. Wilson, an active restless Englishman who had distinguished himself in Egypt and Spain, everywhere a sworn enemy of France and Napoleon, represented the allies in the Russian army, and though under Kutuzov's command, remained independent, an observer, even a judge — infallible grounds for aversion. His presence had become odious to the aged Russian leader; and since hatred never fails to engender hatred, the two detested each other.

Wilson reproached him with his incredible slowness. Five times in one day it had cost them the victory, as it had done at Vinkovo. Wilson now demanded a decisive battle for the next day. His demand was rejected; yet Kutuzov, confined on the plateau of Malo-Yaroslavetz with the French, was forced to make a show of all the troops he had at his disposal. On the twenty-fifth he deployed all his divisions and seven hundred pieces of artillery. In both armies they now believed that the great day had come. Wilson believed it himself. He had noted that there was a miry ravine in back of the Russian army with only one defective bridge across it. This sole way of retreat, in full view of the French seemed impracticable to him. Kutuzov, therefore, would have to win, or perish. The Englishman smiled at the prospect of a decisive battle. Whether it proved fatal to the French or disastrous to the Russians, it would be bloody, and England had everything to gain by it.

When night fell, Wilson, still uneasy, wandered through the ranks. He was delighted to hear Kutuzov swear at last that he intended to fight, and exulted in the sight of the generals preparing for a violent encounter. Only Bennigsen was still doubtful. The Englishman went to bed finally,

* Sir Robert Thomas Wilson, British Military Commissioner at the Russian headquarters 1812–1814. His diary was published in 1861. — J.D.T.

believing that their position would not allow them to fall
back any farther. He was sleeping soundly when, at three
o'clock in the morning, he was awakened by a general order
to retreat. All his efforts proved fruitless, as Kutuzov had
made up his mind to flee toward the south, first to Goncza-
revo, then on beyond Kaluga, and everything had been made
ready for the crossing of the Oka.

It was at that very moment that Napoleon ordered his
troops to march northward toward Mozhaysk. The two
armies, then, were standing back to back, mutually deceiving each other by their rear guard.

Wilson has described the panic which ensued on Kutuzov's
side. The Russian cavalry, cannon, wagons, and battalions
headed toward the one bridge behind the army. All the
columns from the right, the left, and the center came
together at that point and piled up in such an enormous
mass that they were unable to move. It took several
hours to clear a road and open the bridge. Several bullets
fired at random by Davout fell in the midst of the confusion.

Napoleon would only have had to advance on this disorderly mob. It was after the greatest effort, that of Malo-
Yaroslavetz, had been made and there was nothing for him
to do but to march ahead that he retreated. But such is war!
One is never enterprising, or bold enough. *L'ost ignore ce
que fait l'ost.* *

It was perhaps because Napoleon had been lacking in
prudence at Moscow that he was lacking in aggression here.
Besides, he was tired, the two engagements with the Cossacks
had disgusted him; he was touched by the suffering of the
wounded; the horrors had become repulsive to him; and, as
with all men of extreme resolutions, since he could no longer

* The army doesn't know what the army is doing.

hope for a complete victory, he determined upon a hasty retreat.

From that instant Napoleon saw nothing but Paris, as he had seen nothing but Moscow when he was leaving Paris. It was on the twenty-sixth of October that the fatal movement of our retreat really began. While Davout with the twenty-five thousand men forming the rear guard advanced a short distance, to the terror of the Russians although he did not realize it, the rest of the Grand Army turned their backs on the enemy. The soldiers marched with downcast eyes, as if ashamed and humiliated. Their Emperor in the midst of them, gloomy and silent, appeared to be anxiously estimating the length of his line of communication with the friendly cities on the Vistula.

Driven to such unpleasant conjectures, Napoleon was in a thoughtful mood when he reached Vereia, where he found Mortier . . . But I perceive that, carried along as I have been by the rapid succession of violent scenes and memorable events, I have completely overlooked a fact worthy of notice. On the twenty-third of October, at half past one in the morning, the air was shattered by a terrible explosion. The two armies wondered at this for a moment, even though nothing surprised them very much any more, as they were ready for everything.

Mortier had carried out his orders, and the Kremlin was no longer in existence.* Several tons of powder had been placed throughout the apartments in the palace of the Czars, and a hundred and eighty-three thousand kilos piled beneath the vaults supporting it. The marshal had remained with eight thousand men on top of this volcano, which one explosive Russian shell would have sufficed to set off. From

* The ancient palace of the Kremlin was not blown up. The explosion was that of the great arsenal in Moscow. — J.D.T.

that position he covered the army's march toward Kaluga and the retreat of our different convoys in the direction of Mozhaysk.

Among these eight thousand men there were hardly two thousand on whom Mortier could count. The others were unhorsed cavalrymen, soldiers from many different regiments and countries, commanded by new officers, without common customs or memories — without anything, in short, that would link them together — so that they formed a rabble rather than a corps, and soon melted away.

The command of the corps of engineers had been entrusted to Colonel Desprès, a brave and able officer, who had just come from the heart of Spain. At the beginning of September, he had witnessed the end of the retreat from Madrid to Valencia; here, one month later, he was witnessing the beginning of the retreat from Moscow to Vilna. Our armies were giving way everywhere.

We had looked upon the Duke of Trévise (Mortier) as a man sacrificed, and the other generals, his old companions in glory, had parted from him with tears in their eyes. The Emperor had said to him, "I am counting on my luck; but even so, in war somebody has to be sacrificed." Mortier had submitted without hesitation. He was ordered to defend the Kremlin, then, upon withdrawing, to blow it up and set fire to the rest of the city. It was from the castle of Krasnopachra, on the twenty-first of October, that Napoleon had sent him his last orders. After executing them, Mortier was to march toward Vereia and form the rear guard of the army. Napoleon had written, "Take particular care to load the men still in the hospitals on the wagons of the Young Guard, the light-cavalry, and any other vehicles that you can find. The Romans conferred civic crowns upon those who saved citizens' lives; you will be rewarded in a like manner, if you save soldiers. Have them carried on your horse and on those of all your men. That is what I myself did at Saint-Jean-d'Acre.* As soon as your convoy rejoins the army, I will manage to get horses, and wagons, whose teams have been killed for meat, and give them to you for saving five hundred men. Begin with the officers, then the noncommissioned officers, and favor the French. Assemble all the generals under your command and impress on them the importance of this measure, and what they may expect of their Emperor, if they save five hundred soldiers for him."

As fast as the Grand Army withdrew from Moscow, the Cossacks invaded the suburbs and the city, and Mortier retreated toward the Kremlin. The Cossacks were the scouts of a division of ten thousand Russians commanded by Wintzingerode. This foreigner, burning with hatred for Napoleon, inspired by the desire to liberate Moscow and become a naturalized Russian through this remarkable exploit, conceived the mad idea of going up to the Kremlin unaccompanied. He ran through the Georgian quarter, rushed on toward the Chinese city and the Kremlin, disregarded the sentinels he encountered, and fell into an ambush. Seeing himself captured in the city he had come to capture, he changed his tactics and, waving a handkerchief in the air, claimed that he was the bearer of a flag of truce. Conducted to Mortier, he boldly appealed to international law, which, he said, was being violated in his person. Mortier replied, "A commanding general coming as you have might be mistaken for a foolhardy soldier, but never for the bearer of a flag of truce. I shall have to ask you for your sword." Realizing that he could not hope to impress

---

* Saint-Jean-d'Acre, an ancient Syrian seaport, object of a military attack by Napoleon in 1799. — J.D.T.

Mortier, the German general gave in, and admitted his imprudence.

Finally, after four days of resistance, the French abandoned forever that accursed city, taking four hundred wounded with them. Before leaving, they lit the fuse of a cleverly made contrivance, hidden in a safe spot. The rate of progress of the fire had been calculated, and they knew exactly when the spark would reach the immense heap of powder stored in the foundations of the doomed palace.

Then Mortier fled in great haste, and as he withdrew, rapacious Cossacks and filthy moujiks, attracted by the prospect of looting, drew near. They listened, and emboldened by the apparent calm reigning inside the fortress, ventured to enter. They climbed the stairs, but as their greedy hands were reaching out to seize the booty, sudden destruction fell on everything and the walls they had come to strip were blown into the air along with thirty thousand muskets we had left behind. Mutilated limbs, mixed with the debris of the walls and broken pieces of weapons, fell back to earth in a horrible rain.

The earth quaked under Mortier's feet, and Napoleon heard the explosion at Feminskoe, twenty-five miles away!

Thus, from now on, everything was to be burned behind him. In conquering, Napoleon had preserved; in withdrawing, he would destroy, either through necessity, to ruin the enemy and slow up their march, or in reprisal, terrible consequence of wars of invasion, which in the beginning legitimize all means of defense, and later justify all means of attack.

The acts of aggression in this new and terrible sort of warfare were not on Napoleon's side. On the nineteenth of October Berthier wrote as follows to Kutuzov: "We urge you to regulate hostilities so that they will not force the

Muscovite empire to bear more hardships than those which are indispensable in a state of war. The devastation of Russia is as harmful to the people as it is painful to Napoleon." But Kutuzov replied, "It is impossible for me to repress Russian patriotism," which amounted to his sanctioning the Tartar tactics of his troops and authorized us, in a measure, to pay them in their own coin.

The same fire that destroyed Moscow later destroyed Vereia, the meeting place of Mortier and Napoleon. The former had brought Wintzingerode with him. At the sight of this German officer, Napoleon's hidden suffering came alive. His dejection turned to anger, and he vented on his enemy all the grief that had been oppressing him.

"Who are you?" he asked, crossing his arms with violence, as if to hold himself in. "Who are you? A man without a country! You've always been my personal enemy. When I was waging war against the Austrians, I found you in their ranks. Austria became my ally and you offered your services to Russia. You've been one of the most ardent abettors of the present war; yet you were born in one of the states of the Confederation of the Rhine, which makes you my subject. You are not an ordinary enemy — you're a rebel! As such I have the right to have you tried . . . Guards, lay hold of this man!"

The guards did not move, behaving like men accustomed to seeing such violent scenes come to nothing, and sure that they were obeying better by disobeying.

Napoleon went on: "Do you see the devastated country-side, sir? The villages in flame? Whom are we to blame for these disasters? Why, fifty adventurers like yourself, in the pay of England and turned loose on the continent by her. But the burden of this war will fall on those who instigated it. In six months I shall be in St. Petersburg, and I shall get satisfaction there for all this strutting and boasting!"

Then he turned to Wintzingerode's aide-de-camp, also a prisoner. "As for you, Count Narischkin," he said not unkindly, "I have nothing to reproach you with. You are a Russian, and have only done your duty. But how could you, a member of one of Russia's oldest families, ever become the aide-de-camp of a foreign mercenary? Why not become the aide-de-camp of a Russian general? That would be a more honorable post."

Up to that moment the German prisoner had stood calm and dignified, not attempting to reply to the violent words. Now he broke in: "Emperor Alexander is the benefactor of my family and myself. I owe everything I possess to his generosity. Gratitude has made me his subject. The position I occupy was assigned to me by this benefactor. Therefore, I also have been doing my duty."

Napoleon replied with threats, but he had already cooled off. His words were not followed by action, either because he had vented all his wrath in this outburst, or because he merely wanted to frighten any German who might be tempted to desert the ranks. At least, that is the way we interpreted his violence. It displeased us all, and we paid no attention to it, but gathered around the prisoner to reassure and console him. These attentions continued until we reached Lithuania, when both prisoners were rescued by the Cossacks. The Emperor had made a show of treating the young Russian nobleman with kindness, while he railed at the general, which proved that there was method in everything he did, even in his anger.

# CHAPTER VI

✶✶✶✶✶✶✶✶

## *From Mozhaysk to Gzhatsk*

ON THE TWENTY-EIGHTH of October we reached Mozhaysk, which we found still full of our wounded. Some of these we took with us; the rest were assembled in one place and abandoned, as at Moscow, to the mercy of the Russians. Napoleon had gone only a few miles beyond Mozhaysk when he had the first taste of winter. What with one bloody engagement and ten days of marching backward and forward, the army had retreated a distance equal to only three days' march; and we had brought with us from Moscow only fifteen rations of flour for each soldier. We were short of food, and winter had overtaken us!

Men were already falling along the way. On the twenty-sixth of October, the first day of the retreat, we had burned wagonloads of provisions that the horses could no longer pull. Now the order to burn everything behind us was given and unharnessed powder wagons were blown up inside the houses. Still, as the enemy had not yet given any sign of life, we fancied that we were setting out on nothing more serious than the return trip of a long journey. When Napoleon found himself on a familiar road again, he began to take heart. But that day, toward evening, a Russian prisoner was sent to him by Davout.

He questioned him casually at first; but it turned out that

this Muscovite had a good knowledge of roads, names, and distances. He let fall that the entire Russian army was marching toward Viazma by the Medyn road. At this, the Emperor became attentive. Was Kutuzov planning to forestall him at Viazma, as he had done at Malo-Yaroslavetz, and block his retreat toward Smolensk, shutting him up in this desert without shelter or provisions, in the midst of a general insurrection? . . . His first impulse, however, was to disregard this warning, for, either through vanity or experience, he was not accustomed to imputing to his enemies the cleverness he would have shown in their place.

Here, though, he had another motive. His air of security was only assumed, for it was evident now that the Russian army had taken the Medyn road, the very one that Davout had advised the French army to follow; and Davout, either inadvertently or to prove that he had been right all along, had not kept the bad news to himself. Napoleon feared its effect on the men. Therefore he pretended to attach little importance to it. But at the same time, he ordered his Guard to set out at top speed for Gzhatsk, and to march as long as there was the least daylight. He wanted his picked troops to find safe quarters and food in that town. He also hoped to ascertain Kutuzov's position more exactly, and to forestall him at that point.

But the weather had not been consulted, and it seemed to be taking its revenge. Winter was so near that only a few gusts of the north wind had been necessary to bring it on us — bleak, biting, tyrannical. Immediately, we had the distinct feeling that it was a native of this country, while we were foreigners. Everything was changed, the roads, our faces, our courage. The army became gloomy, their march was slowed up, consternation struck.

A few miles beyond Mozhaysk we had to cross the Kolocha,

which at this point was little more than a broad stream. Two tree trunks, a couple of trestles, and a few planks should have sufficed to afford us a safe crossing. But the disorder and carelessness were by now so great that the Emperor was halted. Several guns were lost in the attempt to pull them through the stream. It seemed that each corps of the army was marching independently of all others, that there was no longer a chief of staff, no general order, no common tie, nothing binding all the corps together. Indeed, the high position of all the generals made them quite independent of each other. The Emperor himself had grown so immeasurably that he was out of touch with the details of his army; and Berthier, the intermediary between himself and his generals — all kings, princes, or marshals — was obliged to be cautious. Moreover, he was unequal to his task.

The Emperor, stopped by so insignificant an obstacle as a broken bridge, did no more than make a gesture of discontent and scorn, to which Berthier replied by an air of resignation. As the details for this particular movement had not been dictated by the Emperor, he did not believe himself guilty; for Berthier was a faithful echo, a mirror, and nothing more. Always standing by, day or night, he reflected the Emperor's image, and repeated clearly and precisely exactly what he ordered, but added nothing, so that what Napoleon forgot was forever hopelessly forgotten.

Beyond the Kolocha we were plodding along, absorbed in thought, when some of the men, happening to look up, gave a cry of horrified surprise. We all stared around us, and saw a field, trampled, devastated, with every tree shorn off a few feet above the earth. In the background stood a number of hummocks with their tops blown off, the highest of which seemed the most misshapen. The spot had the appearance of a flattened, extinct volcano. Everywhere the earth was littered with battered helmets and breastplates, broken drums, fragments of weapons, shreds of uniforms, and blood-stained flags. Lying amid this desolation were thirty thousand half-devoured corpses. The scene was dominated by a number of skeletons lying on the crumbled slope of one of the hills; death seemed to have established its throne up there. This was the terrible redoubt which had been the victory and the grave of Caulaincourt. Along our lines ran the sad murmur, "The field of the Great Battle!"

The Emperor hurried by, and no one else stopped, hunger, cold, and the enemy urging us on. We only turned our heads as we marched past to cast one final backward look on the immense grave of so many of our companions in arms who had been sacrificed to no purpose, and whom we were abandoning.

On that field we had written, with the sword, in blood, one of the noblest pages of French history. Some scattered debris still marked the spot; but soon that would disappear. One day the traveler would cross the field of Borodino without knowing it, so much would it look like any other field. But when he learned that the Great Battle had been fought here,* he would retrace his steps, studying the earth with curious eyes, so that the slightest detail would be engraved on his memory, and doubtless he would exclaim, "What men! What a leader! What a fate! Who goaded them into living such a wandering, adventurous existence? They were not barbarians seeking better climates, finer homes, more seductive landscapes, greater riches. On the

* Viscount Eugène-Melchior de Vogüé, French traveler and critic, reports the following incident. "I was talking one day with the Russian priest at Borodino. The topic of our conversation was the all-important one of the approaching harvest, which promised to be mediocre that year. The priest remarked lightly, 'In my childhood the wheat crops were a great deal more abundant. You see, our earth had been well fertilized for a long time.' " (Introduction to the 1910 Nelson edition of *La Campagne de Russie*.) — J.D.T.

contrary, they already possessed these. Enjoying so many good things, they voluntarily surrendered everything to live without shelter or bread, threatened daily with death or mutilation. What necessity impelled them? What, if not a complete confidence in a leader who until now had shown himself infallible? The ambition to complete a work so gloriously begun? The intoxication of victory, the insatiable passion for glory, that powerful goad which sends men to their death in quest of immortality?"

The Grand Army was filing past this deadly field in reverent silence when a sound of moaning fell on their ears. One of the victims of that gory day was still alive! Some of our men ran in the direction of the sound and found a French soldier with both legs broken who had fallen among the dead. For fifty days he had kept himself alive by drinking the muddy water at the bottom of the ravine into which he had rolled, and eating the putrid flesh of the dead. The soldiers who claim to have found this man declare that they were able to save him.

Farther on we reached the hospital we had set up in the Abbey of Kolotskoi, where a sight even more terrible than the battlefield met our eyes. At Borodino there was death, but also peace and rest. There, at least, the struggle was over; here it was still going on. Death seemed to have pursued the victims who had escaped from the combat, and was attacking them through all their senses at the same time. They had nothing to fight it with except orders which could never be carried out in these wastes, or which came from so high or so far and passed through so many hands that they were ultimately lost.

Nevertheless, despite starvation, cold, and the most complete destitution, a considerable number of the wounded had been kept alive in this foul place of refuge by a shred of hope and the splendid devotion of the surgeons. When these poor creatures saw the army passing in a homeward direction and realized that they were going to be abandoned, that there was no longer anything to hope for, the strongest dragged themselves to the doors and lined the streets, holding out imploring hands toward us.

The Emperor ordered that one of those poor wretches should be placed on every available kind of wagon, while the weakest were to be left, as at Moscow, in the care of the wounded Russian officers who had recovered their strength under our treatment. Napoleon halted long enough to supervise the execution of this order, while he and most of his staff warmed themselves at fires fed by the wood of abandoned artillery wagons. Since early morning frequent explosions had been informing us of the great number of such sacrifices we were already forced to make.

During this halt an atrocious thing occurred. Several of the wounded had been put on the sutlers' carts. These scoundrels grumbled about the additional weight their carts, already overloaded with plunder from Moscow, would have to carry. However, they were compelled to obey, and said no more. But they had scarcely got under way when they slowed down and let the rest of the column go by. Then, taking advantage of a moment when they were alone, they threw their unfortunate charges into the ditch by the road-side. Only one of the victims, a general, lived long enough to be picked up by the first wagon of the next division that came along. Through him we learned of the crime. A shudder of horror ran through the column and finally reached the Emperor; for our suffering had not yet become keen and widespread enough to stifle all sense of pity.

In the evening of that long day, as the imperial column

was approaching Gzhatsk, we were surprised to find a number of dead Russians, still warm, on the road in front of us. We noticed that their heads had all been shattered in the same manner, and that their brains were scattered about. We knew that two thousand Russian prisoners had gone before us under the escort of Spanish, Portuguese, and Polish troops. Some of our generals greeted this with indifference, others with indignation, still others with approval. In the Emperor's presence no one expressed an opinion. Caulaincourt could no longer contain himself, and burst out, "It's an atrocity! This, then, is the civilization we are bringing to Russia! What effect will such inhumanity have on our enemies? Aren't we leaving our wounded in their care, as well as thousands of prisoners? Will they lack provocation for horrible reprisals?"

Napoleon maintained a gloomy silence; but the next day those murders had stopped. After that we simply let our unfortunate prisoners die of hunger in the enclosures where we penned them up for the night, like cattle. This was doubtless an atrocity; but what were we to do? Exchange them? The enemy refused to consider it. Set them free? They would have spread the news of our destitute condition far and wide, and soon would have joined up with others and returned to dog our steps. In this war to the death we should have sacrificed ourselves in letting them live. We were cruel by necessity. The evil lay in the fact that we had got ourselves in a position where we were faced with such a terrible alternative.

Besides, our own prisoners were certainly not treated more humanely by the Russians in their march toward the interior, though they had not the excuse of absolute necessity.

\*

## From Gzhatsk to Viazma

We reached Gzhatsk at nightfall. This first winter day had been filled with cruel experiences. The sight of the field of Borodino, the two abandoned hospitals, the great quantity of artillery wagons that had gone up in flames, the slaughtered prisoners, the interminable road, the first touch of winter — these had made the day a tragic one. Now our retreat was deteriorating into flight. Here was a novel sight — a Napoleon beaten and running away!

Some of our allied troops were enjoying it, with that secret satisfaction which inferiors feel at seeing their superiors brought low and forced to yield in their turn. But their malevolent rejoicing was soon to fade and be swallowed up in the universal misery.

Napoleon's wounded pride led him to guess their thoughts. This became evident during one of the halts we made that day. Standing on the hardened furrows of a frozen field strewn with Russian and French wreckage, he tried in the most eloquent words to exonerate himself of the unbearable responsibility for all our calamities. He held up to the horror of the whole world the author of this war he had dreaded. He accused X ——. "It is this Russian minister, sold out to the English, who fomented it! This treacherous scoundrel dragged Alexander and myself into it!"

These words, pronounced in the presence of two of his generals, were received in dead silence, inspired in part by the old respect for his rank, in part by a new sort of respect — that for misfortune. But the Duke of Vicenza, perhaps a trifle too impatient, lost his temper. With a gesture of anger and incredulity he put an end to this painful conversation by walking away.

The Emperor covered the distance from Gzhatsk to Viazma in two days. He made a halt at Viazma to wait for Prince Eugène and Davout, and to keep an eye on the road from Medyn and Yukhnov which joins the main road to Smolensk at that point. It was by this crossroad that the Russians were supposed to be marching from Malo-Yaroslavetz, but up to the first of November, after thirty-six hours of waiting, Napoleon had not seen a single forerunner of their army. He left the city, torn between the hope that Kutuzov had fallen asleep and the fear that he might have passed Viazma on the right and gone on to cut off our retreat at Dorogobuzh, two days' march farther along. Ney remained at Viazma, charged with the responsibility of assembling the 4th Corps and relieving Davout, whom Napoleon believed to be exhausted, of the command of the rear guard. The Emperor complained of the slowness of the latter, reproaching him with being five days' march in the rear, when he should have taken no more than three days. He considered him too methodical to conduct such an irregular march successfully.

The road was constantly running through swampy hollows. The wagons would slide down their ice-covered slopes and stick in the deep mud at the bottom. To get out they had to climb the opposite incline, thickly coated with ice on which the horses' hoofs, with their smooth, worn-out shoes, could find no hold. One after another they slipped back exhausted — horses and drivers on top of each other. Then the famished soldiers fell upon the fallen horses, killed them and cut them in pieces. They roasted the meat over fires made from the wrecked wagons, and devoured it half cooked and bloody.

Our crack troops, the artillerymen and their officers, all
of whom were products of the world's finest military school,
drove these poor fellows out of their way and unhitched the
teams from their own carriages and baggage wagons, which
they sacrificed willingly to save the cannon. They harnessed
their horses to the guns — they even harnessed themselves
and pulled with the horses. The Cossacks did not dare to
approach but watched our difficulties from a safe distance.
However, using fieldpieces mounted on sleds, they dropped
solid-shot into our midst, greatly increasing the disorder.

By the second of November the 1st Corps had already lost
ten thousand men. The Viceroy and Davout, after great
hardship and untold sacrifices, had reached a spot five miles
from Viazma. During the deceptively quiet night the Russian advance guard finally made its appearance, coming from
the direction of Malo-Yaroslavetz, where our retreat had put
an end to theirs. They marched up alongside the two French
corps and Poniatowski's divisions, went beyond their
bivouacs, and disposed their attacking columns at the left
side of the road in the five-mile interval between Viazma and
the French troops.

Miloradovich, known to us as the "Russian Murat," commanded these troops. According to his fellow countrymen,
he was a tireless warrior, astute, as impetuous as our own
soldier-king, as impressively tall as he, and, like him, a
favorite of Fortune. He had never been known to receive a
wound, though crowds of soldiers and officers had fallen
around him and several horses had been killed under him.
He scorned the principles of war, even showing great dex-
terity in not following the rules of this art, and claiming that
he preferred to surprise the enemy by unexpected sallies.
He never prepared a movement in advance, counting on the
place and circumstances to advise him, and acting on sudden

inspiration. But he was a leader on the battlefield only, without administrative ability of any kind, either personal or public, a notorious spendthrift, but — by contrast — honest and generous to a fault. It was against this general, seconded by Platov and twenty thousand Cossacks, that Eugène and Davout were going to have to give battle.

On the third of November Prince Eugène was approaching Viazma where his baggage trains and artillery had already preceded him. The first faint light of dawn showed him that he was in a critical position, with his retreat endangered on the left by an army, his rear guard cut off, and on the right a plain covered with stragglers and vehicles fleeing wildly from the Cossack spears. At the same time he heard firing in the direction of Viazma, which informed him that Ney, who should have come out to relieve him, was fighting for his own preservation.

Now, Prince Eugène was not one of those generals who owed their rank to favoritism alone, who foresaw nothing and were constantly being taken by surprise, through lack of experience. He perceived at once the danger and the remedy. He halted, wheeled about, deployed his divisions at the right of the high road, and on the plain checked the Russian column that was attempting to close the road to him. Their advance troops had already outflanked the right of the Italian corps and seized the highway in that one spot, and were stubbornly holding their position when Ney sent out one of his regiments from Viazma. Attacking the Russians from the rear, they forced them to fall back.

But the success of this initial maneuver had not given the French and Italian corps a chance to continue the retreat; merely the possibility of maintaining their position. They were still about thirty thousand strong; but disorder reigned in the 1st Corps — the one commanded by Davout. The sudden maneuver, the surprise, and particularly the tragic example of the crowd of unhorsed, unarmed cavalrymen running up and down in blind fright, threw this corps into utter confusion.

This spectacle encouraged the enemy, who credited themselves with a victory. Their artillery, superior in strength, galloped into position and, opening up an oblique fire on our lines, began mowing our men down, while our own guns were coming back to us at a snail's pace from Viazma. But Davout and his generals were still surrounded by their most resolute soldiers. Several of the officers who had been wounded at Borodino — one with his arm in a sling, another with his head bandaged — amazed both the enemy and our fugitives and overcame a bad example by a noble one.

Then Miloradovich, feeling that his prey was escaping from him, demanded reinforcements; and it was Wilson again, sure to be found in any place where he could be most harmful to the French, who ran to summon Kutuzov. He found the old marshal resting with his army within earshot of the clash of combat. Wilson, as fiery and insistent as the occasion demanded, tried in vain to rouse him. At length, carried away by indignation, Wilson called him a traitor, and swore that one of his English subordinates would set out that very instant for St. Petersburg to carry the news of his treason to the Czar and his allies.

This threat did not disturb Kutuzov, who persisted in his inaction, either because the chill of winter had aggravated the chill of age in his enfeebled frame, or his mind was overwhelmed with the weight of so much destruction; or perhaps, another consequence of old age, because he had become prudent where there was almost nothing to risk, and learned to procrastinate when there was no more time to lose. He still seemed to believe, as he had at Malo-Yaroslavetz, that the

Muscovite winter alone could defeat Napoleon; that this genius, this conqueror of men, had not yet been sufficiently subdued by nature; and that he could leave the honor of the victory to the freezing climate, and vengeance to the sky of Russia.

Then Miloradovich, without help, tried to break the French battle line. Only his fire managed to penetrate it, but this was frightfully destructive. Both Davout and Eugène were growing weak. Hearing the sound of fighting behind their right flank, they fancied it was the rest of the Russian army that was pouring in by the road from Yukhnov, which was covered by Ney. It was in fact only a vanguard, but the noise of combat behind their own battle line, promising a difficult retreat, alarmed them. The encounter had lasted seven hours. By now the baggage trains must have slipped away and night was falling; the two French marshals began to withdraw.

This backward movement fanned the enemy's ardor, and without a stupendous effort on the part of the 25th, 57th, and 85th Regiments, and the protection of a ravine, Davout's corps would have been split apart, outflanked on the right and destroyed. Prince Eugène, attacked less violently, was able to execute his retreat through Viazma more rapidly; but the Russians pursued him. They were still in the city when Davout, with twenty thousand men behind him, encumbered with eighty pieces of artillery, reached the gates of the town in his turn. Morand's division entered first. They were marching confidently along, believing that the fighting was over, when the Russians, hidden in the narrow, winding streets, suddenly fell upon them. Taken by surprise, they were thrown into confusion; but Morand rallied and consolidated his men, regained the upper hand, and broke his way through the assailants.

It was Compans who, bringing up the rear with his division, concluded the affair. Feeling himself too hard pressed by the boldest of Miloradovich's troops, he turned around, drove his horse into the midst of the stubbornest of them, who still held their position, and scattered them. Having thus gained their respect, he calmly continued his retreat. This engagement was glorious for each individual combatant, but the result was disastrous for the army as a whole. Order and unity were altogether lacking. There would have been enough soldiers to win, had there not been too many generals. Not until two o'clock did the latter get together to plan their maneuvers, and then these were executed haphazardly.

When at length we had put the river, the town of Viazma, night, mutual fatigue, and Marshal Ney between us and the enemy; when the immediate danger was averted and camps had been pitched — then we counted our forces. Several guns had been destroyed, considerable baggage was missing, and four thousand men had either been killed or wounded. A great many soldiers had simply wandered off. We had managed to save our honor, but there were wide gaps in our ranks. Everything had to be reduced, compressed in order to give some cohesive form to what remained. The regiments had shrunk to the size of battalions, and the battalions, to platoons. The soldiers no longer had their old positions, companions, or officers.

The dreary reorganization of the army took place by the light of the fires which were destroying Viazma, and to the sound of gunfire exchanged between Ney and Miloradovich, with the roar echoing through the combined darkness of night and the forest. Several times the brave remnant of the army, thinking themselves attacked, dragged themselves toward their weapons. The next morning when they re-formed their ranks they were surprised to find that they were so few.

However, the good example set by their generals and the hope of soon finding everything they needed at Smolensk kept their courage alive. The bright sun, universal source of life and hope, seemed to contradict and deny the scenes of despair and death that were already surrounding them on every side.

\*

## The First Snowstorm

On the sixth of November the sky became terrible; its blue disappeared. The army marched along wrapped in a cold mist. Then the mist thickened, and presently from this immense cloud great snowflakes began to sift down on us. It seemed as if the sky had come down and joined with the earth and our enemies to complete our ruin. Everything in sight became vague, unrecognizable. Objects changed their shape; we walked without knowing where we were or what lay ahead, and anything became an obstacle. While the men were struggling to make headway against the icy, cutting blast, the snow driven by the wind was piling up and filling the hollows along the way. Their smooth surfaces hid unsuspected depths which opened up treacherously under our feet. The men were swallowed up, and the weak, unable to struggle out, were buried forever.

The soldiers following them turned around, but the tempest whipped their faces with the snow falling from above or swept up from the earth, and seemed fiercely determined to oppose their progress. Russian winter in this new guise attacked them on all sides; it cut through their thin uniforms

and worn shoes, their wet clothing froze on them, and this icy
shroud molded their bodies and stiffened their limbs. The
sharp wind made them gasp for breath, and froze the moisture
from their mouths and nostrils into icicles on their beards.

Yet the poor wretches dragged themselves along, shivering,
with chattering teeth, until the snow packed under the soles
of their boots, a bit of debris, a branch, or the body of a
fallen comrade tripped them and threw them down. Then
their moans for help went unheeded. The snow soon covered
them up and only low white mounds showed where they
lay. Our road was strewn with these hummocks, like a ceme-
tery. Even the bravest or the most indifferent were deeply
moved, and looked away as they hurried by.

But in front of them, all around them, everything was
snow. The eyes of the men were lost in the immense, dreary
uniformity. To their stricken imagination it was like a
great white shroud that Nature was winding about the army.
The only objects that stood out were the tall somber firs,
graveyard trees, as we called them, with the funereal verdure,
and the gigantic immobility of their black trunks, which
completed a picture of universal mourning, a dying army in
the midst of a dead nature.

Everything turned against the men, even their muskets
which they had not used offensively since Malo-Yaroslavetz.
Now these became an unbearable load for their benumbed
arms. When they fell down, as they frequently did, their
weapons slipped from their grasp and were either broken or
lost in the snow. Though never thrown away, they were torn
from them by hunger and cold. Many other men had their
fingers frozen to the muskets they were holding and which
were depriving them of the movement necessary to maintain in their hands a remnant of heat and life.

In a short time great numbers of men could be seen wandering over the countryside, either alone or in small groups. These were not cowardly deserters: cold and starvation had detached them from their columns. In this general and individual struggle, they had got separated from the others, and now they found themselves disarmed, defeated, defenseless, without leaders, obeying only the powerful instinct of self-preservation.

Most of these stragglers, tempted by the sight of side roads, scattered over the fields in the hope of finding food and shelter for the coming night. But when they had passed that way before, they had left a swath of desolation from fifteen to twenty miles wide. Now they met only armed civilians or Cossacks who fell upon them with ferocious laughter, wounded them, stripped them of everything they had, and left them to perish naked in the snow. These guerrillas, incited by Alexander and Kutuzov, who did not then know how to avenge nobly the country they had been unable to defend, kept abreast of the army on both sides of the road, under cover of the trees. They threw back on the deadly highway the soldiers whom they did not finish off with their spears and axes.

Night came on — a night sixteen hours long! But on this waste of snow where were we to stop, where sit down or rest, where find some root to gnaw on, or dry wood for our fires? However, those who had been held together by their own moral and physical strength, and the brave efforts of their officers, were finally halted by fatigue, darkness, and repeated orders. They tried to pitch their camps, but the roaring storm played havoc with their preparations for a bivouac. The firs, coated with ice, stubbornly refused to burn. The snow falling in increased fury, and the snow on the ground, melting at the first warmth, put out our fires and dampened our strength and courage.

When at length we did get some fires burning, officers and soldiers together prepared their wretched meal around them. This consisted of scraps of tough lean meat cut off the horses we had slaughtered, and, for a very few, several spoonfuls of rye flour mixed with snow water. The next morning circular rows of soldiers stretched out stiff in death marked the spots where these fires had burned; and the fields around were strewn with thousands of dead horses.

From that day we began to count less and less on one another. Insubordination rapidly took over the high-spirited, impressionable army that had been taught to reason by an advanced civilization. Discouragement and rebellion spread quickly from one to another, imagination running unchecked in misfortune as in success. At every halt, whenever the going was particularly rough, at every instant, some body of soldiers broke off from those troops that were still in orderly formation, and fell out of line. There were, however, many who resisted this terrible contagion of unruliness and discouragement, tenacious officers, noncommissioned officers, and soldiers. These were really extraordinary men. They encouraged each other by repeating the name of Smolensk, which they were approaching and where they had been assured they would find all the supplies they needed.

From Gzhatsk to Mikalewska, a village between Dorogobuzh and Smolensk, nothing worthy of note happened in the imperial column, except that we were forced to throw all our spoils from Moscow into Lake Semlevo. The cannon, Gothic armor, works of art from the Kremlin, and the cross of Ivan the Great were sunk beneath the waters of the lake. Trophies, glory, all those things for which we had sacrificed so much, had become a burden. There was no longer any question of adorning or embellishing our lives, but merely of saving them. In this shipwreck, the army, like a great

vessel tossed by the most violent storm, was throwing over-
board on a sea of ice and snow everything that might encum-
ber it or delay its progress.

Napoleon had halted at Slavkovo from the second to the
fourth of November. This brief rest and the shame of appearing to run away inflamed his imagination. He dictated
orders according to which his rear guard, while having the
appearance of retreating in disorder, would be luring the
Russians into an ambush where he himself would be waiting for them. But this empty project vanished with the preoccupation that had given it birth. He spent the night of the
fifth at Dorogobuzh. There he found hand mills for wheat
which had been ordered for the expedition; too late and to
no purpose now, they were distributed to the men. There
also he laid plans for the cantonments in Smolensk.

The next day, the sixth of November, as we came abreast
of Mikalewska, and just as the frost-laden clouds broke over
our heads, Count Daru galloped up and a circle of cavalrymen was formed around him and Napoleon. A courier, the
first that had been able to get through to us in ten days, had
just brought the bad news of that strange conspiracy hatched
in Paris by a mysterious general confined in a prison cell.* He
had had no other support than a false report of the total destruction of the Grand Army, and false orders issued to a few
soldiers to arrest the prime minister, the police commissioner,
and the governor of Paris. All this had succeeded on account
of the rapidity of the first move, and the lack of information, and the general astonishment. But as soon as the news
of this affair had got abroad, one order had been enough to
put the leader back in prison with his accomplices and dupes.

The Emperor thus heard of the crime and its punishment

* General Claude-François de Malet. The conspiracy failed, and the in-
stigator was shot. — J.D.T.

at the same time. Those who were standing at a distance tried to read his thoughts on his face, but could see nothing. He retired within himself, his only words to Daru being, "Well, what if we had stayed in Moscow?" Then he hurried to a house protected by palisades serving as his dispatch post. As soon as he was alone with his most trusted officers he gave free vent to his feelings in exclamations of amazement, humiliation, and anger. Shortly afterward he had several other officers brought in to test the effect of this strange news on them. They showed anxiety, consternation, and a lack of confidence in the stability of his government. He gathered from them that when the officers got together they groaned over the fact that the Revolution of 1789 had evidently not yet ended, and asked each other whether they, who had grown prematurely old in the efforts to get the thing finished, were going to be forced back into it again and have to return to the terrible existence of political upheaval. So we were in the midst of strife, and it was possible that we might lose everything at the same time.

Some of the men were delighted at the news, hoping that it would hasten the Emperor's return to France and that he would remain there and never again venture abroad, since he was so little sure of matters at home. The next day, however, the sufferings of the moment had put an end to such conjectures. Still, all the Emperor's thoughts were bent on Paris as he advanced mechanically in the direction of Smolensk. But he also was awakened to the realities of the place and time by the arrival of one of Ney's aides-de-camp.

Since leaving Viazma this marshal had been protecting the retreat, providing a rear escort that proved fatal for many, while he himself seemed invulnerable. Up to Dorogobuzh we had not been molested except by some bands of Cossacks, troublesome insects attracted by our dying men and abandoned wagons, who ran off as soon as a hand was raised against them, but wearied us by continually coming back.

But this was not the subject of Ney's message . . . As he approached Dorogobuzh he had come upon abundant evidence of the disintegration of the corps preceding him, evidence which we had not been able to erase. Up to that point he had resigned himself to the necessity of leaving his gear in the hands of the enemy; but he reddened with shame at the sight of the first guns abandoned before Dorogobuzh.

Ney halted at that town. In that one horrible night, snow, wind, and hunger had driven most of his men from their fires. Dawn, always awaited so impatiently in camp, had brought with it the wild storm, the enemy, and the spectacle of the almost total defection of the army. He had vainly resisted at the head of the pitiful remnant of his forces, but had finally been forced to fall back behind the Dnieper. He had sent his aide, Colonel Dalbignac, to reveal to the Emperor the full horror of his situation, for which, he said, he refused to be held accountable.

Napoleon had seen enough around him to be able to form an opinion of the rest. Fugitives from the rear were constantly passing him. He felt that there was no alternative but to sacrifice the Grand Army piece by piece, beginning with the extremities, in order to save the head. When, therefore, the aide-de-camp began his report, he interrupted him bluntly. "Colonel, I have not asked you for those details." The messenger was silent, understanding how the Emperor, at the center of irremediable disaster, when everyone had need of all his strength, avoided complaints which could only weaken the one who indulged in them and discourage the one who listened to them.

He took note of Napoleon's attitude, which the Emperor maintained during the entire retreat. He saw him solemn, silent, resigned, suffering less in his body, perhaps, than the others, but more in his mind, and accepting his misfortune.

At this juncture General Charpentier sent him a convoy of provisions from Smolensk. Bessières wanted to get hold of them, but the Emperor sent them on without delay to the Prince of Moskva (Ney), saying, "Those who fight must eat before the others." At the same time he charged Ney to defend himself sufficiently to allow him to stay a while in Smolensk, where the army would eat, rest, and be re-formed.

Ney realized that a victim was required, and that he had been chosen. He made the sacrifice, unreservedly accepting a danger to which his courage was equal. From that moment he no longer deemed it a point of honor to save his gear, even his cannon, which winter was wresting from him. In one of the first bends of the Dnieper some of the guns got stuck at the foot of the ice-coated banks. He relinquished them without hesitation, surmounted that obstacle and faced about, using the enemy's river which barred his route as a defense.

But the Russians, pushing forward under cover of the wood and our abandoned wagons, opened fire on Ney's soldiers, half of whom, their hands numb from their icy muskets, lost heart completely. Imitating their behavior of the previous night, running away now because they had run away then, they quit the combat — a thing they would once have looked upon as impossible. Ney rushed into their midst, snatched a musket from one of them, and led them back into action by firing the first shot, exposing his life like a soldier, as he had done before he became a husband and father, rich, powerful, and esteemed. He fought as if he still had everything to gain, whereas he had everything to lose. While he became soldier again, he remained the general — availing himself of the terrain, backing up against a hill and

concealing himself behind a stockaded house. His generals
and colonels, among whom he noticed Fezensac in particular,
supported him vigorously, so that the Russians who had expected to pursue them fell back instead!

By this action Ney gave a respite of twenty-four hours to
the army, who took this opportunity to advance toward Smolensk. The next day, and the next, and the next he exhibited
the same heroism. From Viazma to Smolensk he fought for
ten whole days.

On the thirteenth of November he reached Smolensk,
which however he was not to enter until the next morning. He had wheeled about to check the enemy when the
hill against which he planned to post his left flank was suddenly covered with a horde of fugitives. In their terror these
poor fellows rushed forward and rolled down to him on the
frozen snow, which they stained with their blood. The cause
of this frenzied retreat was explained by the sight of a band of
Cossacks in their midst. The astounded marshal, having dispersed this enemy swarm, saw behind them the army of Italy,
coming back without supplies, without cannon, completely
spent!

*

## The Army of Italy Is Destroyed

Since leaving Dorogobuzh, Prince Eugène had been constantly beset by Platov. He had left the road near that town
and taken the road leading to Vitebsk — the same he had
followed two months before when marching from Smolensk.
But at that time the Wop had been a shallow stream they had
hardly noticed. Now it was a river, flowing on a wide bed of
mud, with very steep banks on either side. These ice-coated

banks had to be cut through, and the order was given to tear down the houses in the neighborhood during the night to obtain lumber for a bridge. But the Viceroy, who was more loved than feared, was not obeyed. The pontoon corps worked only halfheartedly, and when dawn brought the Cossacks back, the bridge which had collapsed twice was abandoned.

Five or six thousand soldiers still in orderly formation, twice as many disbanded men, and the sick or wounded, over a hundred guns with their caissons, and innumerable vehicles lined the riverbank over an area of several square miles. They tried to ford the river through the blocks of ice swept along by the current. The first cannon that made the attempt reached the opposite bank safely; but the water was rising higher minute by minute, and the wheels and the horses' struggles were digging a constantly deepening path at the point from which they crossed. One heavy ammunition wagon became hopelessly stuck in the mud, others piled up on it, and everything came to a stop.

But day was drawing to a close, and they were wearing themselves out in fruitless efforts. Pressed by the hunger, cold, and the Cossacks, the Viceroy had no choice but to order the abandonment of his artillery and all his supplies. It was a sorrowful sight. The owners of this wealth had scarcely time to part company with their possessions. While they were selecting the most indispensable objects and loading them onto their horses, a mob of soldiers fell upon the magnificent carriages and broke everything to pieces, avenging themselves for their poverty and suffering on this wealth, and keeping it from the Cossacks who were watching from a distance.

Most of the soldiers, interested chiefly in food, rejected embroidered garments, pictures, gilded bronzes, valuable ornaments in favor of a few handfuls of flour. That evening the riverbank presented a strange sight, with the riches of Paris and Moscow, the luxuries of two of the world's great cities, lying scattered and despised on the snowy waste.

Meanwhile the artillerymen, knowing there was no hope, were spiking their guns and scattering their powder. Others laid a trail with it across the snow to the ammunition wagons that had been left at a considerable distance behind our baggage. They waited till the greediest of the Cossacks had swarmed over and around the prize, then set fire to the trail of powder with brands from their campfires. The fire reached its destination in an instant; the wagons blew up, the shells exploded, and the Cossacks who were not killed on the spot dispersed in terror.

A few hundred men, still bearing the name of the 14th Division, were left to oppose these barbarians, and they were able to keep them at a respectful distance till the next morning. All the others, soldiers, administrators, women and children, sick and wounded, pursued by the enemy's fire, crowded to the edge of the torrent. But at the sight of the swollen waters and the enormous, jagged sheets of ice, they drew back, dreading to increase the already unbearable cold by plunging into the icy stream.

It was an Italian, Colonel Delfanti, who made the first move. Then the soldiers pressed forward, and the crowd followed. Only the weakest, the most cowardly, or the greediest remained on the bank. Such as could not bring themselves to part with their plunder, to abandon their fortunes, were punished for their hesitation. The next day, the savage Cossacks were seen in the midst of all this wealth, still covetous of the dirty, tattered garments of the unfortunate creatures who had become their prisoners. After taking all their clothes they collected them in bands and drove them naked through the snow, beating them cruelly with the shafts of their spears.

The army of Italy, divested of everything, dripping with the waters of the Wop, without food or shelter, spent the night in the snow near a village in which the generals tried in vain to find lodgings for themselves. The soldiers attacked the frame houses, falling in desperate swarms on every dwelling, taking advantage of the darkness that prevented them from recognizing their own officers or being recognized by them. They tore off the doors and windows, even the woodwork of the roof, caring little whether they forced others, regardless of their rank, to bivouac like themselves.

Their generals tried in vain to drive them off. The soldiers, even those of the royal and imperial Guards, bore their blows without complaining, without offering any opposition, but without desisting. Throughout the army similar scenes were repeated every evening.

The wretches applied themselves silently but stubbornly to their work, tearing off all four wooden sides of the houses, so that the officers were forced to leave them before they collapsed over their heads.

They spent that night drying themselves around the fires they had lit, listening to the cries, curses, and moans of those who were still crossing the torrent, or who rolled from the top of the steep bank to their death in the ice-filled waters.

It is a fact that reflects disgrace on the enemy, that in the midst of this chaos, within sight of so rich a prize, a few hundred men left a mile or so from the Viceroy, on the other side of the river, held both the courage and the cupidity of Platov's Cossacks in check for twenty-four hours. It is possible that the *Hetman* believed he had made sure of the destruction of the Viceroy on the following day. Indeed, all

his plans were so well laid that at the instant when the army
of Italy, at the end of a troubled and disorganized day's
march, caught sight of Dukhovshchina, one of the few towns
as yet uninjured, and were joyfully hurrying forward to
seek shelter in it, they saw swarming out of it several thousand
Cossacks with cannons who stopped them on the spot. At the
same time, Platov with the rest of his hordes galloped up
and attacked their rear and both flanks.

According to several eyewitnesses, the most terrible confusion ensued. The disbanded men, women, and attendants
rushed wildly on one another, stampeding through the
ranks. For a moment this unfortunate army was little more
than a formless mob, an ignoble rabble milling blindly round
and round. All seemed lost; but the coolness of the Prince
and the efforts of his officers saved the day. The crack troops
disengaged themselves from the confusion, ranks were re-
established. The army advanced under the protection of a
volley of shots, and the enemy who had everything on their
side, except courage — the only good thing we had left —
broke ranks and scattered, content with a useless demonstration.

We immediately took their place in the town, while they
pitched their camps outside and laid their plans for further
surprise attacks which were to last up to the very gates of
Smolensk; for the disaster at the Wop had made Eugène
give up the idea of remaining separated from the Emperor.
The Cossacks, emboldened by success, surrounded the 14th
Division. When the Prince tried to rescue them, the soldiers
and officers, benumbed and stiffened by sub-zero cold and a
cutting north wind, refused to budge from the warm ashes
of their fires. In vain he pointed out to them their surrounded companions, the approaching enemy and the shells
and bullets already falling around them. They still refused to

rise, protesting that they would rather perish there than bear such cruel suffering any longer. Even the sentinels had abandoned their posts. Nevertheless, Prince Eugène succeeded in saving his rear guard.

It was when he was moving back toward Smolensk with them that his stragglers encountered Ney's troops, to whom they communicated their panic. They all rushed toward the Dnieper and piled up at the entrance of the bridge, without thinking of defending themselves, when a charge made by the 4th Regiment stopped the enemy.

Its colonel, young Fezensac, had been able to arouse his half-frozen soldiers. One reproach from him had worked this change. There, as in all action, the superiority of the spiritual emotions over bodily sensations was very evident; for all the physical senses tended to encourage despondency and flight, and Nature urged it with a hundred insistent voices; yet a brief appeal to their honor sufficed to produce the most heroic dedication. The soldiers of the 4th Regiment advanced furiously upon the Russians, against mountains of ice and snow and in the teeth of the northern gale — indeed, they had everything against them, but Ney himself was obliged to moderate their zeal.

*

## Sufferings at Smolensk

At length the army came within sight of Smolensk again. The soldiers pointed it out to each other. Here was the end of their suffering, here was the land of promise where famine would be changed to abundance, and weariness would find rest. In well-heated houses they would forget the bivouacs in sub-zero cold. Here they would enjoy refreshing sleep, and mend their clothes, here shoes and uniforms adapted to the Russian climate would be distributed among them.

At the sight of the city only the *corps d'élite*, reduced to a few soldiers and the required officers, kept their ranks. All the others dashed madly ahead. Thousands of men, mostly unarmed, covered both the steep banks of the Dnieper, crowding together in a black mass against the high walls and gates of the city. But the unruly mob, their haggard faces blackened with dirt and smoke, their tattered uniforms or the grotesque costumes that were doing the duty of uniforms — in short, their frenzied impatience and hideous appearance frightened those inside. They believed that if they did not check this multitude of hunger-maddened men, the entire city would be given over to lawless plunder. Therefore, the gates were closed against them.

It was hoped also that by such rigorous treatment these men would be forced to rally. Then, in this poor remnant of our unfortunate army, a horrible conflict between order and disorder took place. In vain did the men pray, weep, implore, threaten, try to batter down the gates, or drop dying at the feet of their comrades who had been ordered to drive them back; they found them inexorable. They were forced to await the arrival of the first troops still officered and in order. These were the Young and Old Guard; the disbanded men were allowed to follow them in. They believed that their entrance had been delayed in order to provide better quarters and more provisions for these picked troops. Their suffering made them unfair, and they cursed the Guard, asking themselves, "Are we to be forever sacrificed for this privileged class, for this useless ornament never seen in the front rank except at reviews and festivities, or at the distribution of awards? Is the army never to get anything but their leavings? Must we wait forever to be fed until these favorites are satiated?" The only answer that could have been given them was that it was necessary to keep at least one corps intact, and that preference must be given to those who would be able to make the most powerful effort when the occasion required it.

Finally, all the unfortunate creatures were in Smolensk — Smolensk, city of their dreams! They left the riverbanks strewn with the half-dead bodies of the weak who had succumbed to impatience and the long hours of waiting. They left still others on the icy slope they had to climb to reach the upper part of the town. The survivors rushed to the regimental storehouses, where many more died outside the doors, for here they were repulsed again. "Who were they? . . . To what corps did they belong? . . . How could they prove it? . . ." The quartermasters were responsible for the rations. They were not to deliver supplies except to authorized officers bringing receipts for which they exchanged a stipulated number of rations. But these disbanded men around the doors had no officers, nor could they tell where their regiments were. Fully two thirds of the army were in this predicament.

So these men scattered through the streets, their only hope now being in pillage. But the carcasses of horses cleaned of meat down to the bone lying everywhere indicated the presence of famine. The doors and windows had been torn out of all the houses as fuel for the campfires, so the men found no shelter there. No winter quarters had been prepared, no wood provided. The sick and wounded were left out in the streets on the carts that had brought them in. Once again the deadly highroad was passing through an empty name! Here was one more bivouac among deceptive ruins, colder even than the forests the men had just left.

Finally these disorganized troops sought out their regiments and rejoined them momentarily in order to obtain their rations. But all the bread the bakers had been able to bake had already been distributed, as had the biscuits and meat. Rye flour, dry vegetables, and brandy were measured out to them. The best efforts of the guards were needed to prevent the detachments of the different corps from killing each other around the doors of the storehouses. When after interminable formalities the wretched fare was delivered to them, the soldiers refused to carry it back to their regiments. They broke open the sacks, snatched a few pounds of flour out of them, and went into hiding until they had devoured it. It was the same with the brandy. The next day the houses were found full of the corpses of these unfortunate warriors.

So it was that deadly Smolensk proved to be the beginning of our suffering, though we had hoped it would put an end to it. An immensity of woe stretched out before us. We were going to have to march forty days more under the weight of this iron yoke! Some of the men, already over-burdened with present miseries, were completely over-whelmed by the dreaded prospect. Others rebelled against their fate; no longer counting on anyone but themselves, they resolved to live at all costs.

From that time on, the strong plundered the weak, stealing from their dying companions, by force or by stealth, their food, their clothing, or the gold with which they had filled their knapsacks instead of provisions. Then these miserable wretches whom despair had driven to banditry, threw away their own weapons in order to save this infamous loot, tak-ing advantage of the common fate, the complete anonymity, the unrecognizable state of their uniforms, the darkness of night, and anything that might encourage cowardice and crime. I should not have mentioned these obnoxious details if reports exaggerating their horror had not already been published; for such atrocities were rare, and the guiltiest were executed.

The Emperor reached Smolensk on the ninth of November, when the disorder was at its height. He shut himself up in one of the houses on the new square, and never left it until the fourteenth, when he continued his retreat. He had counted on finding fifteen days' provisions and forage for an army of a hundred thousand men; there was not more than half that quantity of rice, flour, and spirits, and no meat at all. We heard him shouting in great fury at one of the men who had been entrusted with the responsibility of providing those supplies. This commissary, it is said, saved his life only by crawling on his knees at Napoleon's feet. The reasons he gave probably did more for him than his supplications.

"When I reached Smolensk," he explained, "the bands of deserters the army had left behind in its advance on Moscow had already invested the city with horror and destruction. Men were dying there as they had died on the road. When we had succeeded in establishing some sort of order, the Jews were the first to furnish some provisions. Some Lithuanian noblemen followed their example, inspired perhaps by a nobler motive. Then the long convoys of supplies collected in Germany began to appear. The light wagons, called *comtoises,* were the only ones that could get through the Lithuanian sands, and they had brought only ten tons of flour and rice. Several hundred head of German and Italian cattle were driven in at the same time.

"A horrible, death-dealing stench from the piles of corpses in the houses, yards, and gardens was poisoning the air. The dead were killing the living. The civil employees and many of the soldiers were stricken, some of them to all appearances becoming idiots, weeping or fixing their hollow eyes steadily on the ground. There were some whose hair stiffened, stood on end, all twisted into strings; then, in the midst of a torrent of blasphemy, or even more ghastly laughter, they dropped dead.

"We had to slaughter the greater part of the German and Italian cattle immediately. These beasts would neither eat nor walk. Their sunken eyes were glazed and set. They did not even flinch from the slaughterer's knife . . . Other misfortunes followed; several convoys were intercepted, some supply depots taken, and a drove of eight hundred oxen were recently seized at Krasnoye.

"You must also take into consideration the great number of detachments that have passed through Smolensk, and the long stay of General Victor with twenty thousand soldiers and fifteen thousand sick; the multitude of marauders that flocked into the city at the news of an insurrection and the approach of the enemy. All these have lived on our provisions. We have had to distribute nearly sixty thousand rations a day. Moreover, we sent supplies and cattle to meet the army at Mozhaysk on the road to Moscow, and at Elnia on the Kaluga road."

Some of these allegations were true. Various storehouses had been established at given distances along the way from Smolensk to Minsk and Vilna. These two cities held more supplies than Smolensk; and the garrison towns on the Vistula formed their first line. The total quantity of supplies distributed over this expanse of country was incalculable, and the efforts required to transport them were colossal; but they added up to almost nothing in this immense wasteland.

So great expeditions are crushed by their own weight. Human limits had been exceeded. Napoleon's genius, seeking to transcend time, climate, and distance, had as it were got lost in space. Great as his capacities were, he had gone beyond them.

He had no illusions concerning this destitution. Alexander alone had deceived him. Accustomed to overcoming everything by the terror of his name, and the admiration inspired by his daring, his army, himself, and his fortune, he had staked everything on Alexander's first move. He was still the same man as in Egypt, at Marengo, Ulm, or Esslingen. He was Hernando Cortez; he was the Macedonian burning his ships and in spite of his soldiers striking out into an unknown Asia; he was Caesar entrusting his whole fortune to a fragile bark!

# CHAPTER VII

************

## *Napoleon at Smolensk*

NAPOLEON LINGERED in Smolensk for five days. It was known that Ney had received the order to get there as late as possible, and Eugène, to halt at Dukhovshchina for two days. The marshals wondered at the Emperor's inaction, with famine, disease, winter, and three Russian armies stalking us. It was certainly not the necessity to wait for the Italian army that was causing the delay. One marshal complained, "What is there for us to do in this burned and deserted city but to take all the supplies and pass on quickly?" Another wondered, "Does the Emperor think that by dating his dispatches for five days from this city, he can give to his unruly flight the appearance of a slow and glorious retreat? He has ordered the destruction of the city walls to prevent us, he says, from being delayed by them again. As if there were any question of our returning to this place, when we don't know whether we shall ever get out of it!" And another, "Will anyone believe that he wishes to give the artillerymen the time to get their horses rough-shod? As if it were possible to get any work out of the smiths, exhausted by hunger and long marches, with broken forges, and no materials at all for so great an undertaking!"

And still another grumbled, "Perhaps the Emperor wants to give himself the time to get the multitude of disarmed

and useless soldiers on the road ahead of him, out of reach
of danger; then to rally the best of the troops and re-form
the army. As if it were possible to convey any sort of order
to men so widely scattered, or to rally them without lodgings or rations! or to dream of a reorganization for corps of
dying soldiers who have nothing to hold them together, and
who would be dissolved by the slightest touch!"

Such were the conversations of the generals around Napoleon, or rather their secret reflections; for their devotion
to him was to remain unshaken for two years longer in the
midst of even greater calamities and a general uprising of
the nations.

The Emperor, however, attempted something which was
not wholly fruitless: namely, to rally under one commander
the remaining fragments of the cavalry. Of the thirty-seven
thousand troopers present at the crossing of the Niemen,
there were now only eighteen hundred mounted men left.
Napoleon gave the command of this body to Latour-Maubourg, to which no one objected, either because of weariness
or the esteem in which this general was held.

As for Latour-Maubourg, he accepted this honor, or rather
this burden, with neither pleasure nor regret. He was a man
unlike other men: always ready, though never impatient;
calm, active, and remarkable for his high moral principles;
natural and unostentatious — a man simple and true in his
relations with others, associating glory with action, and not
with words. He preserved an unchanging order and measure even in the midst of excessive disorder. Nevertheless —
and this did honor to our age — he went as far, as high, and
as fast as anyone else.

This feeble attempt at reorganization, the distribution of
a part of the supplies and the loss of the rest by plunder, the
repose that the Emperor and his Guards were able to take,

the destruction of part of the artillery and baggage, and the dispatching of a number of orders — these were about all the benefits derived from that fatal halt. On the other hand, all the trouble we had anticipated came to pass. The few hundred men that had been rallied held together but for a short time: the explosion of the mines blew up only a few pieces of wall and served no other purpose than to drive out of the city on the last day the stragglers whom we had not been able to set in motion.

It was on the fourteenth of November that the Grand Army (or rather, thirty-six thousand combatants) began to leave the city. Many disheartened men, some women, and several thousand of our sick and wounded were left behind. The Old Guard and the Young Guard together could muster no more than nine or ten thousand infantrymen and two thousand troopers; Davout and the 1st Corps had five or six thousand; Prince Eugène and the army of Italy, five thousand; Poniatowski, eight hundred; Junot and his Westphalians, seven hundred; and Latour-Maubourg with the remains of the cavalry, fifteen hundred. There might also be added to these about one thousand light-horse and five hundred dismounted cavalry that we had succeeded in getting together.

This army had numbered one hundred thousand combatants on leaving Moscow. In twenty-five days it had been reduced to thirty-six thousand! The artillery had already lost three hundred and fifty of their guns; yet these wretched remains were still divided into eight armies, which were encumbered with sixty thousand unarmed stragglers and a long train of cannon and gear.

It is not known whether it was this clogging mass of men and vehicles, or — which is more likely — a mistaken sense of security that led the Emperor to leave an interval of one day between the departure of each marshal. In any case, it was arranged that Napoleon, Prince Eugène, Davout, and Ney should withdraw from Smolensk one after another. Ney was not to leave till the sixteenth or seventeenth of November, after having put out of commission and buried the guns we were leaving behind and destroyed their ammunition, driven all the stragglers out, and blown up the great walls of the city.

Meanwhile Kutuzov was lying in wait for us several miles away, prepared to cut down, one after another, the fragments of our greatly reduced, widely separated army corps.

On the fourteenth of November, at five o'clock in the morning, the imperial column finally left Smolensk. Their bearing was resolute, but gloomy and silent as the night and the still, colorless countryside through which they were passing. The silence was broken only by the crack of the whips applied to the horses, and the sharp, violent oaths that rang out when we dropped into hollows and had to climb back up the icy slopes, with men, horses, and cannon rolling over each other in the darkness. The first day we made only twelve miles, and it took the artillery of the Guard twenty-two hours to cover the same distance!

Nevertheless, this first column reached Korythnia without any great loss of men. It was there that Junot with his seven hundred Westphalians passed us. Advance troops had been sent on to Krasnoye, and the wounded and disbanded men were approaching Liady. Korythnia is some twelve miles from Smolensk; Krasnoye, twelve miles from Korythnia; and Liady ten miles beyond Krasnoye. The Dnieper flows five miles away on the right of the main road from Korythnia to Krasnoye. Abreast of Korythnia another road, the one from Elnia to Krasnoye, comes close to the main road.

That very day Kutuzov arrived by that secondary road,

his ninety thousand men covering its entire length. He marched parallel to Napoleon and soon outstripped him, while he sent his advances along the crossroads to intercept our retreat.

*

## Action before Krasnoye

Kutuzov himself, with the bulk of his army, had moved up and taken a position in the rear of these front line troops, within reach of them all, and was congratulating himself on the success of his maneuvers. His slowness, however, would have spoiled them if it had not been for our own want of foresight; for this was a battle of mistakes in which ours were so much more serious that we thought we must all perish. As matters stood, the Russian general had every reason to believe we were his for the taking, and this confidence saved us. Kutuzov failed himself when it was time to act, his age preventing him from carrying to success the plans he had so wisely formed.

While all these masses were taking their positions around Napoleon, he was resting quietly in a poor tumbledown house, the only building left standing in Korythnia, apparently ignorant of or indifferent to the movement of men, weapons, and horses that were hemming him in. At least, he did not send any order to the three corps remaining at Smolensk to hasten their departure, and he himself waited till it was daylight to set off.

His column was advancing without precaution, preceded by a crowd of marauders, all eager to reach Krasnoye, when at about five miles from that town a row of Cossacks, extending from the heights on the left and across the highroad,

suddenly appeared before them. Our soldiers halted, astounded. They had not expected anything of the kind; and
it seemed to them that the hand of adverse fate had traced
upon the snow between them and Europe that long, black,
motionless line, as an irrevocable end to all their hopes.

Some of the men, stupefied by suffering, devoid of feeling,
their eyes fixed on the home land, kept moving obstinately
and mechanically ahead, heedless of all warning. They were
about to give themselves up, but others drew together in a
compact mass, and for a moment they stood and looked
each other over. Some officers soon galloped forward and established a degree of order among the disbanded soldiers,
and seven or eight riflemen sent out in advance were sufficient to break through the threatening screen.

The French were smiling at the audacity of this idle
demonstration when suddenly a Russian battery posted on a
ridge at their left opened fire, sending its shot across the
road. At the same time thirty squadrons appeared on that
side, threatening the advance of the Westphalian corps,
whose general, losing his head, gave no orders whatever.

A wounded officer, Exelmans by name, a stranger to the
German troops, but who found himself among them quite
by chance, rallied the soldiers with indignant shouts and
seized the command. The enemy, seeing this head of a
column march forward in good order, were afraid to attack
them other than with their cannon, whose shots the brave
men disregarded, soon getting beyond their range.

When the turn of the grenadiers of the Guard came to pass
through the Russian fire, they closed their ranks around the
Emperor, like a moving fortress, proud of the honor of protecting their sovereign. The regimental band gave expression to this pride, by playing at the height of danger the song
whose words were then so well known: *"Ou peut-on être*

*mieux qu'au sein de la famille?"* \* But the Emperor, whom nothing escaped, interrupted the music with the exclamation, "It would be better to sing, '*Veillons au salut de l'Empire!*' " † — words much better suited, indeed, to his preoccupation and the situation of the army.

As the enemy's fire had become too deadly, a detachment was sent out to silence it; and two hours later the Emperor reached Krasnoye. The mere sight of Sebastiani and the first grenadiers who had gone ahead of him was sufficient to drive out the Russian infantry. Napoleon entered the town in a state of anxiety, not knowing what part of the enemy army he had been dealing with, as his cavalry was too weak to leave the highroad in order to reconnoiter and get him any information. He left Mortier and the Young Guard two miles in the rear, thus extending a helping hand — but too weak and too far away — to his army. He himself decided to wait for it to overtake him.

The passing of this column had not been too bloody, but we had not been able to conquer the terrain as easily as the men. The road was very hilly, and on every slope we lost guns we did not have the time to spike, and supply wagons which were plundered by our men before being abandoned. The Russians looking down from their hills saw into the very heart of our army, saw its weaknesses, its deformities, its most shameful aspects — all that an army usually hides with the greatest care.

Miloradovich, however, from his high position seemed to be satisfied with insulting the Emperor and the Old Guard that had for so long been the terror of all Europe. He did not dare to clean up their remains until they had marched past; but then he made bold to assemble his forces and come

---

\* Where could one be happier than in the bosom of the family? — J.D.T.
† Let us watch over the safety of the Empire. — J.D.T.

down from his hills, and took up a strong position with twenty thousand men across the main road. By this movement he separated the Emperor from Prince Eugène, Davout, and Ney, and closed the road to Europe against those three generals.

*

## March of Eugène from Smolensk to Krasnoye

While Miloradovich was making these preparations, Eugène was doing his best to assemble his scattered forces in Smolensk. With the greatest difficulty he succeeded in tearing them away from the plundering of the stores, and finally rallied eight thousand men; but by then the day of the fifteenth was drawing to a close. He had to promise rations and hold out the alluring bait of Lithuania to decide them to resume their march. Night overtook the Prince before he had covered more than seven miles. By that time half his soldiers had left the ranks. The next morning he took to the road again with all who had not frozen to death around the campfires during the night.

The rumble of cannon that they had heard the evening before had ceased. The royal column advanced with difficulty, adding their own corpses and abandoned gear to what was already on the road. At their head rode the Viceroy and his chief of staff, General Guilleminot. Completely absorbed in their gloomy reflections, they gave rein to their horses and by slow degrees left their troops behind them, without being aware of it; for the road was full of stragglers and men marching at will whom they had given up all hope of keeping in order. They rode on in this way until they were about five miles from Krasnoye, when they were suddenly brought up short by something that was happening in front of them. A number of the disbanded men had come to a stop; the ones behind had caught up with them and gathered around them, and others farther ahead had turned back and joined the group, soon forming a considerable mass. The Viceroy, alarmed, looked about him, and perceived that he was an hour's march ahead of his army, that around him he had only fifteen hundred men of all ranks and nations, without organization, without officers or weapons fit for combat, and that he was being summoned to surrender.

This summons, coming from a bearer of a flag of truce, was answered with a general cry of indignation. But the Russian, who was all alone, insisted, "Napoleon and his Guard have been beaten. You are surrounded by twenty thousand Russians. Your only safety is in accepting honorable conditions, and these General Miloradovich offers you."

At these words Guyon, one of those generals whose soldiers were either all dead or dispersed, sprang forward and shouted, "Go back where you came from! and tell whoever sent you that if he has twenty thousand men, we have eighty thousand!" The Russian, confused and speechless, turned away.

All this had happened in an instant, yet flashes of fire and clouds of smoke were already rising from the hills on their left. A rain of shells and grapeshot swept the high road, and the heads of threatening columns appeared with leveled bayonets. The Viceroy hesitated a moment. He was loath to abandon this miserable troop; but finally, leaving his chief of staff with them, he rode back toward his own division, determined to bring them forward to the combat and break through this barrier before it became insurmountable, or to die in the attempt. In the arrogance born of a crown and repeated victories, he could not think of surrendering.

Guilleminot called around him the officers who were mingled with the soldiers in the crowd. Several generals and colonels and a great number of other officers stepped forward and surrounded him. With one accord they recognized him as their leader, and began to separate into platoons the mass of troops which it was impossible to move in its present disorder.

This organization was effected under heavy fire. Superior officers took their places proudly in the ranks and became simple soldiers again. Inspired by another sort of pride, a group of the marines of the Guard would accept only one of their own number as commanding officer, while all the other platoons were commanded by generals. Up to then the Emperor himself had been their only colonel, and though so close to death now, they exercised a prerogative which nothing could make them forget, and which was respected.

This band of brave men, hastily organized, resumed their march toward Krasnoye. They had passed out of range of Miloradovich's cannon when the Russian general hurled his columns against their flanks, closing them in and forcing them to wheel about and take a defensive position. It must be said to the eternal glory of these warriors, fifteen hundred French and Italians, one against ten, that they were able to hold their enemies in check for over an hour, with only their courage and a few good firearms in their favor.

But there was still no sign of the Viceroy and the rest of his division, and it was becoming impossible to resist any longer. Again and again they were summoned to lay down their arms. During those brief truces they could hear the distant thunder of cannon in front of them and behind them. It seemed that the whole army was being attacked at the same time, that from Smolensk to Krasnoye there was just one massive battle. If they wanted assistance, they could not wait for it here, but must go and look for it. But where? Krasnoye was out of the question, it still being too far away; besides, there was every reason to believe our troops were fighting there, too. It would be better, then, to march straight back into Russia, since our faces were turned in the direction of Smolensk, and Prince Eugène was there somewhere; with closed ranks and concerted movements break through the Russians and rejoin the Viceroy, then all together turn back, defeat Miloradovich, and so reach Krasnoye.

The men gave their unanimous assent to their leader's proposal. The column immediately formed into a compact body and struck out through the enemy's ten thousand guns and muskets. The first reaction of the astonished Russians was to open a way for this handful of partially disarmed warriors into the very center of their ranks. But when they realized their intention the Russian soldiers on both sides of the road, either through admiration or pity, called out to them to stop and begged them to give themselves up. But our men replied only by a resolute march, a ferocious silence, and the points of their bayonets. Then all the Russians fired at once, point-blank, and half the heroic column fell lifeless or wounded.

The survivors kept on without a single soldier deserting the ranks or a single Muscovite daring to lay hands on them. Very few of those unfortunate men survived to see the Viceroy and his division advancing on the road. Only then did they break formation and rush headlong into the enfeebled ranks that opened to receive and protect them.

But they found little security there; for the Viceroy's skeleton army after a bloody encounter had been defeated and was now in the Russians' power. Yet victory was so novel to the enemy that, though they held it in their hands, they did not take immediate advantage of it, but waited till the next day to finish us off.

Prince Eugène noticed that the majority of the Russians, attracted by his demonstrations, were grouped at the left of the road. He waited till night, faithful ally of the weak, had chained their movements in sleep. Then, leaving his fires burning on that side to deceive the enemy, he swerved to the right, made a wide detour through the fields, and passed quietly around Miloradovich's left flank, while this general, too sure of success, was dreaming of the glory that would be his the next morning when he received the sword of Napoleon's son.

In the midst of this perilous maneuver there was one awful moment. At the most critical instant, while those men who had survived so many combats were stealing along the flank of the Russian army, holding their breath and walking on tiptoe; when their safety hung on a single look or cry of alarm, the moon suddenly came out from behind a thick cloud and lit up all their movements. At that moment a Russian voice called out, challenging them and asking them who they were. They gave themselves up for lost; but one Klisky, a Pole, ran up to the Russian and, addressing him in his own language, said in a whisper, "Be still, you fool! Don't you see that we belong to Ouvarov's corps, and that we're on a secret mission?" The Russian, satisfied, said no more.

Finally, after two hours of cruel floundering, the troops rejoined the highroad; and the Viceroy was actually in Krasnoye on the seventeenth of November, when Miloradovich, descending from his hilltop to seize him, found the field occupied by only a few stragglers whom no effort had been able to induce to leave their fires the night before.

*

## The Battle of Krasnoye

The Emperor had waited in Krasnoye all the preceding day for the arrival of the Viceroy. The sound of Eugène's battle had worried him terribly. An effort to break through the enemy in order to join him had not succeeded, and when night fell without bringing the young prince, his stepfather's distress increased. He asked himself, "Have Eugène and the army of Italy and this long day of hopeless waiting all come to an end together?" One hope remained — that Eugène, driven back to Smolensk, might have joined Ney and Davout there, and that the next day the three with united forces would make a decisive move.

In his anxiety the Emperor assembled the marshals whom he still had with him — Berthier, Bessières, Mortier, and Lefebvre. They had survived; they had overcome the final obstacle. Now they had only to continue their retreat through Lithuania, which lay open before them. But they would not abandon their companions to the mercy of the Russian army; so they decided to turn back into Russia, either to deliver them or perish with them.

Once this decision had been made, Napoleon set coolly about preparing for its execution. The large-scale maneuvers of which there were signs on every hand did not shake his determination. Everything indicated that Kutuzov was advancing with the intention of seizing him in Krasnoye. Already, during the night of the fifteenth, Ojarowski with an advance guard of the infantry had gone beyond the city and taken a position at Malievo, a village behind his left flank. Excited rather than depressed by this bad news, he called

Rapp, his aide-de-camp, and ordered him to set out immediately. Then instantly recalling him, he said, "No, you are not to go. Let Roguet and his division march alone. You will stay, for I don't want you to be killed here. I shall need you for Danzig."

As Rapp carried that message to Roguet he wondered that the Emperor, surrounded by eighty thousand enemy troops whom he planned to attack the next day with only nine thousand of his own, should have so little doubt of his success that he could think of what he was going to do in Danzig — a city separated from him by winter, two other Russian armies, starvation, and five hundred miles!

The nocturnal attack on Chirkova and Malievo was successful. Roguet knew from the position of the Russians' fires that they were occupying those villages, which were connected by a plateau and defended by a ravine. He disposed his troops in three columns of attack. Those on the left and right advanced stealthily as far as possible toward the enemy. Then, at a signal given by himself from the center, they were to charge with leveled bayonets, holding their fire.

The two wings of the Young Guard attacked simultaneously. While the Russians, surprised and not knowing where to defend themselves, wavered between the left and the right, Roguet and his column bore down on the center and penetrated to the very middle of their camp. In utter confusion the soldiers had just the time to throw the greater part of their weapons, heavy and light, into a neighboring lake and set fire to their shelters; but the flames, instead of saving them, only served to light up the scene of their destruction.

This action halted all movement of the Russian troops for twenty-four hours, and allowed the Emperor to remain in Krasnoye, where Eugène rejoined him in the course of the following night. Napoleon received the Prince with manifest joy; but he was soon overcome by fresh anxiety concerning the welfare of Ney and Davout.

The Russian camp around us presented the same spectacle as at Vinkovo, Malo-Yaroslavetz, and Viazma. Every evening the holy relics of Muscovite saints, surrounded by countless wax tapers, were brought out and set up near the tent of the general-in-chief for the adoration of the soldiers. While these recruits, as was their custom, were displaying their devotion by endless signs of the cross and genuflections, the priests inflamed them with exhortations which seemed ridiculous and barbarous to our more civilized ears.

We were informed that a spy had reported to Kutuzov that Krasnoye was filled with an enormous mass of Imperial Guards, and that the aged marshal feared to compromise his reputation by attacking us. But the sight of our distress emboldened Bennigsen, who was able to induce Strogonov, Galitzin, and Miloradovich with a force of over fifty thousand men and a hundred pieces of cannon to make an early morning attack — in spite of Kutuzov — on our fourteen thousand famished, enfeebled, and half-frozen French and Italians.

Napoleon fully understood the imminence of this danger. He could have escaped it, as day had not yet dawned. He was free to evade this deadly combat. With Eugène and his Guard he might have gained Orsha and Borisov where he would have found thirty thousand French troops under Victor and Oudinot, and the corps of Dombrowski, Regnier, and Schwartzenberg, as well as full storehouses, and where the following year he could have made his reappearance as formidable as ever.

Before daybreak on the seventeenth he gave his orders. Fully armed, he took to the road afoot, at the head of the Old Guard; but it was not toward Poland, his ally, that he marched, nor toward France where he would still be the founder of a dynasty and the emperor of the West. As he took up his sword he said, "I have played the Emperor long enough! It is time to play the General!" And he plunged deliberately into the center of the eighty thousand enemy troops in order to draw all their efforts upon himself and divert them from Ney and Davout, and so snatch the two marshals from the jaws that were closing on them.

Day dawned, disclosing the Russian battalions and batteries barring the horizon on three sides — in front, on our right, and behind us — and Napoleon and his six thousand Guards advancing with a firm step into the center of this deadly enclosure. At the same time Mortier, a few paces ahead of his Emperor, deployed the five thousand men that were left of his corps in the face of the whole Russian army.

Their objective was to defend the right side of the highroad from Krasnoye to the deep ravine, in the direction of Stachova. A battalion of troopers of the Old Guard, drawn up in a fortresslike square near the road, supported the left wing of our young recruits. To the right on the snow-covered plains surrounding the city the remains of the cavalry of the Guard, a few guns, and Latour-Maubourg's twelve hundred horsemen (since leaving Smolensk the cold had dispersed or killed five hundred of them) were doing their best to substitute for the battalions and batteries that the French army now lacked.

Then the battle began. But what a battle! Here the Emperor had no more of those sudden illuminations, no flashes of inspiration, none of those bold unexpected moves that had forced the hand of luck and brought him so many victories, and with which he had so often abashed, stunned, and crushed his enemies. Here the enemy's movements were free; ours, fettered; and this genius in the realm of attack was reduced to defending himself.

But here it was borne in on us that Fame is not a mere shadow, but a real force, doubly powerful by the inflexible pride it lends its favorites and the timid precautions it suggests to such as would venture to attack them. The Russians that day had only to march forward without maneuvering, even without firing, and their mass would have crushed Napoleon and his wretched troops; but, overawed by the sight of the conqueror of Egypt and Europe, they did not dare to come to close quarters with him. The Pyramids, Marengo, Austerlitz, and Friedland seemed to rise up and stand between him and their great army. It was quite conceivable that in the eyes of those submissive, superstitious men there was something supernatural in such extraordinary renown; that they thought him beyond their reach and not to be attacked except from a distance; that men would be powerless against the Old Guard, the living fortress, the *granite column* (as Napoleon had called them), which cannon alone could demolish.

The young soldiers, half of whom were seeing action for the first time, stood up to the deadly fire for three solid hours without taking a step backward or making a movement to get out of its way, and without being able to return it, as their cannon had been destroyed, and the Russians kept out of range of their muskets.

The voice of Claparède and the noise of cannon fire in the rear warned Napoleon that Bennigsen was getting control of the road to Liady on the farther side of Krasnoye, and cutting off his retreat. The enemy's fire flashed to the east, the west, the south. Only one side was open, the north, the side toward the Dnieper; this was barred by a ridge at whose foot ran the road now occupied by the Emperor. The enemy

seemed to be covering this hill with their cannon; thus they
were right over his head and might have crushed him at close
range. This danger being pointed out to him, he threw one
glance at it and said, "Well, let a battalion of my chasseurs
go and seize it!" Then, troubling himself no longer with
this matter, he gave his undivided attention to Mortier's
dangerous situation.

At that juncture Davout was seen approaching through a
swarm of Cossacks, whom he scattered by accelerating his
march. His troops disbanded as soon as they caught sight of
Krasnoye, and running across the fields, got beyond the right
of the Russian line behind which they had come up. Davout
and his generals could not rally them before reaching the
city.

So the 1st Corps was saved; but at the same time we
learned that our rear guard was at the end of its resistance
in Krasnoye, that Ney had probably not left Smolensk yet,
and that we ought to give up all idea of waiting for him.
Still Napoleon hesitated, unable to bring himself to make
this great sacrifice. But finally, as everything seemed lost,
he decided what to do. He called Mortier to him, took his
hand kindly, and told him, "There is not a minute to lose!
The enemy is breaking through on every side. Kutuzov may
reach Liady, even Orsha and the last bend of the Dnieper
before me. I must move rapidly with the Old Guard to occupy that passage. Davout will relieve you. Together you
must try to hold out at Krasnoye until nightfall. Then you
will rejoin me." His heart heavy with despair at having to
abandon the unfortunate marshal, he withdrew slowly from
the field of battle, entered Krasnoye where he made a brief
halt, then cut his way through as far as Liady.

Mortier was willing to obey, but the Dutch division of
the Old Guard had lost the important post they were defending, and with it a third of their men; and the Russians

had immediately covered it with their artillery. Roguet who was being cut to pieces by their fire thought he could silence it. The first regiment he ordered to charge the guns was repulsed. The second, the 1st Light Infantry, drove into the very center of the Russians. Two cavalry charges did not halt them. They pushed steadily on, till they were overwhelmed by a third charge and a hail of grapeshot. Roguet was able to save only fifty soldiers and eleven officers!

Mortier had lost half his men. It was two o'clock, but he still astounded the Russians by his resolute bearing. Finally the latter, emboldened by the absence of the Emperor, attacked with such violence that the Young Guard found themselves completely surrounded; they would soon be unable either to hold out or to fall back.

Fortunately, a few platoons rallied by Davout, and the sudden appearance of another large group of stragglers, attracted the attention of the enemy. Mortier took advantage of this respite to order the three thousand men still remaining to him to withdraw at a walk before the fifty thousand Russians. "Do you hear, men?" cried General Laborde. "The marshal says *at a marching step!* At a marching step, soldiers!" And the poor fellows, dragging many of their wounded with them, under a shower of bullets and grapeshot, withdrew as slowly from the field of carnage as if it had been a drill-ground!

When Mortier had put Krasnoye between himself and Bennigsen he felt safe. The enemy broke through the stretch of road separating that city from Liady only with the fire of their batteries which lined the left side of the highway. Colbert and Latour-Maubourg held them in check on the hills. In the course of this march a strange incident occurred. A shell plowed into the body of a horse, exploded, and blew the animal to pieces without wounding the rider, who landed on his feet and kept on walking.

*

## Halt at Orsha, Where Napoleon Waits for Ney

Our march the next day was by fits and starts. The impatient stragglers got ahead of Napoleon. As they passed him they saw that he was afoot, walking laboriously with the aid of a stick, and stopping every quarter of an hour, as if unwilling to tear himself away from Old Russia whose frontier he had crossed, and where he was leaving his unfortunate companion in arms.

In the evening we reached Dombrowna, a town built of wood and, like Liady, still inhabited. This was a novel sight for the troops who had seen nothing but ruins for the past three months. At last we were out of Old Russia, out of the boundless desert of snow and ashes, and were entering a friendly, populated region whose language we understood. At the same time the temperature moderated, a thaw set in, and we received some supplies.

So it was that winter, the enemy, loneliness and — for some — the bivouacs and starvation, all left us at the same time; but it was too late. The Emperor knew that his army was destroyed. The name of Ney frequently fell from his lips, accompanied by exclamations of grief. The night we settled in Dombrowna he was heard groaning and muttering, "The misery of my poor soldiers breaks my heart! Yet I cannot help them, unless I establish a permanent base . . . But where can we rest, without ammunition, food, or artillery? I am not strong enough to stay here: we must reach Minsk as soon as possible."

While he was speaking a Polish officer rushed in with the news that Minsk — Minsk, his storehouse, his retreat, his only hope — had just fallen into the hands of the Russians! General Tchitchakov had entered it on the sixteenth. Napoleon was speechless for a while, as if mortally stricken by this final blow. Then, rising to the situation, he said coolly, "In that case, there is no choice left us but to cut our way through with our bayonets!"

It was still far from dawn when Napoleon was awakened by an unusual noise. Some say they heard scattered musket shots, but that these had been fired by our own men to drive people out of their houses, so they could take their places. Others claim that, in keeping with an unruly habit in our camps where the men shouted freely to each other, the name of one Hausanne, a grenadier, had been spoken loudly in the midst of complete silence, and the soldiers had mistaken this for the warning cry of *aux armes* (to arms). Be that as it may, everybody saw, or thought they saw, Cossacks, and Napoleon found himself surrounded by clamors of war and terror. Without showing alarm, he told Rapp, "Go see what it is. Doubtless those miserable Cossacks again who are determined we shan't sleep!" But the noise had soon swollen to a tumult, with men running either toward battle or away from it and mistaking each other for enemies as they collided in the dark.

For a moment Napoleon thought we were really being attacked. He asked if the little remaining artillery had been set up on the other side of a stream with high banks which ran through the city. On being informed that this precaution had been neglected, he rushed down to the bridge and personally superintended the moving of his guns across that ravine.

He then returned to the Old Guard and addressed each battalion separately. "Grenadiers," he said. "We're retreating without being defeated by the enemy; let's not be defeated by ourselves! Set an example to the army. Several of you have already deserted your standards and thrown down your arms. I am not invoking military law to put a stop to this disorder, but am appealing to you personally. Dispense judgment amongst yourselves. I commit this discipline to your honor."

He had the other troops harangued in the same terms. Those few words sufficed for the Old Guard, who probably had no need of them. The rest of the men received them with cheers; but an hour later when the march was resumed they had quite forgotten them. Napoleon blamed the rear guard in particular for that false alarm, and angry words passed between him and Davout.

At Orsha we found well-filled storehouses, a bridge train of sixty boats with the necessary equipment, *which were all burned,*\* and thirty-six pieces of harnessed cannon that were distributed among Davout, Eugène, and Latour-Maubourg. Here for the first time we found officers and gendarmes posted on the two bridges over the Dnieper for the purpose of stopping the crowd of stragglers and making them rejoin their regiments. But these men avoided their standards which had once meant everything to them, as if they were evil omens.

Disorder had by now acquired an organization of its own, and enlisted in its ranks men who had become skillful at it. When a thick mass of stragglers had accumulated some of those rascals shouted, "The Cossacks are coming!" in order to quicken the march of those in front and to increase the tumult. Then they took advantage of the disorder to seize the provisions and cloaks of the poor wretches they had thrown off their guard.

The gendarmes who were seeing the army for the first time

---

\* The italics are the translator's. — J.D.T.

since the disaster, amazed at the sight of such misery and frightened by the confusion, soon gave up in despair; and the mob poured over the bridges to the friendly side of the river, which would have been given over to pillage, without the intervention of the Guard and the few hundred men left to Prince Eugène.

Napoleon entered Orsha with six thousand Guards — all that were left of the original thirty-five thousand. By now Eugène's forty-two thousand had been reduced to eighteen hundred; Davout's seventy thousand to four thousand. Davout himself had lost everything. He did not even have any linen, and was in a state of extreme exhaustion from hunger. He seized the loaf held out to him by one of his companions and devoured it. Someone gave him a handkerchief with which to wipe the frost from his face. "Only men of iron could bear such hardships!" he groaned. "It is physically impossible to hold out any longer! Human strength has its limits, and we have gone beyond them!"

It was he who at the outset had directed the retreat as far as Viazma; and he could still be seen, faithful to his habit, stopping at every pass and waiting till the last man had gone through, sending stragglers back to their ranks, struggling unceasingly against insubordination. He encouraged his soldiers to insult their comrades who laid down their arms, or to take their spoils from them, as the only way of restraining the former and punishing the latter. Some of us, however, considered his severe, methodical manner of proceeding incongruous in the universal confusion, and thought he allowed himself to be too deeply affected by it.

The Emperor tried in vain to check the discouragement. When he was alone he could be heard lamenting over the suffering of his soldiers; but in front of them he managed to appear inflexible, even on that point. He issued a proclamation ordering every man to rejoin his ranks. The officers who did not would be stripped of their commissions; the soldiers, put to death.

This threat had no effect at all on men who had become callous and desperate, and were fleeing not from danger, but from suffering, and who feared the sort of life that was offered them even more than the death with which they were threatened.

But Napoleon's confidence grew with the danger. To him, the poor handful of men lost in a desert of mud and ice was still the Grand Army, and himself the conqueror of Europe. Yet, underneath this show of firmness, he had no illusions, which was shown by the fact that while he was still at Orsha he burned with his own hands every article of clothing belonging to him which might serve as a trophy to the enemy, in the event of his fall.

There also were burned, unfortunately, all the documents which he had accumulated in view of writing a history of his life; for such had been his intention when he embarked on this fatal expedition. He had decided to stop as a conqueror at the Dwina and the Dnieper, to which he was now returning as a disarmed fugitive. The boredom of six long months of winter on the banks of those rivers had appeared to him then as the worst of enemies. To overcome it he, another Caesar, would dictate his commentaries.

But how everything had changed! Two of the enemy's armies were cutting off his retreat. The question which occupied him now was, through which of the two should he try to cut his way? As the Lithuanian forests into which he was about to plunge were unfamiliar to him, he called a council of the officers who had just crossed them on their way to join him.

The Emperor began by telling them that too great famili-

arity with success often opened the way to great reverses —
but that this was no time for recriminations. Then he spoke
of the fall of Minsk and, acknowledging the cleverness of
Kutuzov's persistent movement on his right flank, declared
he wished to abandon his line of operation in that direction,
rejoin the Dukes of Belluno and Reggio, make head against
Wittgenstein, and reach Vilna by marching north around the
sources of the Berezina.

Jomini, a German-Swiss general, opposed this plan, pointing out that Wittgenstein occupied such a solid position in
the long defiles that his resistance would probably be stubborn enough to consummate our ruin: He added that at this
season, in our present disorganized state, it would be fatal
for our army to change its route. We should certainly get
lost on the crossroads through the barren marshy forests. In
his opinion, only by keeping to the highroads could the army
preserve some semblance of order. As the bridge over the
Berezina at Borisov was still open, we should march at once
in that direction.

He then assured the Emperor that he knew of a road
branching off to the right of that city which crossed the
Lithuanian swamps over a series of wooden bridges. According to him, this road running through Zembin and Molodeczno was the only one that would take the army safely
to Vilna. By following it we would leave on our left Minsk
and the Minsk road, longer by a day's march, with fifty
broken bridges making it impassable, and Tchitchakov's
army occupying it. In that way we could pass through the
two Russian armies without coming into contact with either.

The Emperor's resolution was shaken; but, as the thought
of deliberately avoiding combat hurt his pride, and he did
not want to leave Russia without one decisive victory, he
summoned General Dode of the engineer corps. As soon as

that officer was within sound of his voice, he called out to him, "We have to choose between retreating by the Zembin road, or defeating Wittgenstein at Smoliany!" Knowing that Dode had just come from there, he asked him if that position was unassailable.

Dode informed him that Wittgenstein occupied a ridge overlooking the entire swampy region. To reach the Russian camp it would be necessary to beat back and forth out of the enemy's sight and range along the winding path, so that the right and left flanks of our attacking column would be alternately exposed to their fire. Their position was, therefore, unassailable from the front; to pass around it we should have to march back toward Vitebsk and make a very long circuit.

Disappointed in this last hope of glory, Napoleon decided on Borisov. He ordered General Eblé to go ahead with eight companies of engineer sappers and pontoniers to prepare a crossing for him over the Berezina. General Jomini was to act as his guide.

But Napoleon was slow in making up his mind to leave the banks of the Dnieper. It seemed to him that in so doing he would be abandoning the unfortunate Ney a second time, and bidding a definite farewell to this valiant companion-in-arms. As he had done at Liady and Dombrowna, he kept sending messengers at all hours of the day and night to inquire whether anyone had got news of the marshal; but no information whatever concerning his whereabouts had been able to pass the Russian lines. This silence of death had lasted four days, yet the Emperor persisted in hoping. Finally, on the twentieth of November, he was forced to quit Orsha, though he left Eugène, Mortier, and Davout behind. But after covering five miles he halted, inquired for Ney, and waited a little longer.

# CHAPTER VIII

********

## Ney Is Mourned as Lost

THE WRECK of the army remaining in Orsha shared
Napoleon's grief. When their most urgent duties allowed them a moment of leisure, all their thoughts and
eyes turned toward the Russian bank of the Dnieper. They
listened for any sign of battle which might announce Ney's
arrival, or rather, his last breath. But they saw only Russians,
who were already threatening the bridges over the river.
One of the three marshals wanted to destroy these bridges,
but the others were strongly opposed to it. That would have
meant placing a still wider distance between themselves and
their unfortunate comrade, and would have been tanta-
mount to admitting that he could never be saved. Dismayed by the prospect of such a terrible misfortune, they
could not bring themselves to accept it.

But hope died with the passing of the fourth day. Night
brought them more fatigue than rest. The marshals began
blaming themselves for Ney's undoing; as if it would have
been possible for them to wait for the 3rd Corps any longer
on the plains of Krasnoye, where they should have had to
fight twenty-eight hours longer with ammunition and forces
enough for only an hour!

Already, as in all times of cruel loss, the mourners were
reviving memories. Davout was the last to have seen the

unfortunate marshal, and Mortier and the Viceroy asked what his final words were. At the sound of the first cannon fired at Napoleon on the fifteenth of November, Ney had wanted them to evacuate Smolensk immediately, behind the Viceroy. Davout had refused to do so, recalling the Emperor's orders, and their obligation to blow up the walls of the city. The two generals quarreled violently. As Davout had insisted upon remaining until the next morning, Ney, who was to bring up the rear, had been forced to wait for him.

It is true that on the sixteenth Davout had sent to warn him of his danger, but then, either because he had changed his mind, or because he was angry at Davout, Ney had replied, "All the Cossacks in the universe will not prevent me from carrying out my instructions."

When they had exhausted all their memories and conjectures, the three marshals relapsed into gloomy silence. Suddenly the gallop of horses was heard, then a joyous shout, "Marshal Ney is saved! He is in sight! Here are some Polish troopers with the news!" The next instant one of Ney's officers appeared and informed us that the marshal was advancing along the right bank of the Dnieper, and was asking for help. But night was falling. Davout, Eugène, and the Duke of Trévise had counted on that short period to revive and warm their soldiers. For the first time since leaving Moscow, these poor men had received sufficient rations. They were going to cook them, then lie down and spend a warm night under cover. How was it going to be possible to induce them to take up their arms again and tear themselves from their shelters, to make them give up this night of rest whose wonderful relief they had only just begun to enjoy? Who would persuade them to retrace their steps and go back into the Russian darkness and cold?

Eugène and Davout contended for the honor of perform-

ing this act of devotion, and the former won out only by the
right of his superior rank. Shelter and the distribution of
rations had accomplished what threats could never have
done — rallied the stragglers — so that the Viceroy found
four thousand of his men who were willing to march for
Ney's sake. But this was to be their last effort!

They advanced in total darkness, over unfamiliar ground,
for about five miles, stopping frequently to listen. Their
anxiety began to grow. Had they got lost? Were they too
late? Had their unhappy comrades all perished? Was it the
victorious Russian army they were going to meet? In his
uncertainty Prince Eugène directed some cannon to be fired.
Back over the sea of snow came a signal of distress. It was the
3rd Corps who, without artillery, were answering the cannon
of the 4th with fire by platoons. The two corps at once began
to walk toward each other. Ney and Eugène, ahead of their
troops, were the first to meet. They rushed into each other's
arms — Eugène, with more alacrity than Ney. The former
wept, the latter gave vent to his feelings in words of anger.
One was happy, touched to the heart, exalted by Ney's
martial heroism and by his own chivalry in coming to the
rescue; the other was still heated from the combat, incensed
at the risk the army had taken for his sake, and laying all the
blame on Davout, whom he wrongly accused of having
deserted him.

Several hours later when Davout tried to exonerate himself, all he could get out of Ney was a disagreeable look and
the words, "Monsieur le Maréchal, I do not reproach you
with anything. God is our witness and our judge!"

As soon as the two corps came within sight of each other
they broke ranks. Soldiers, officers, generals — all rushed
forward. Eugène's men shook hands with Ney's, touched
them with joy mingled with astonishment and curiosity, and

pressed them compassionately to their breasts. They gave them the rations and brandy they had just received, and plied them with questions. Then they marched back to Orsha together, Eugène's army impatient to hear, Ney's impatient to tell what had happened.

\*

## Details of Ney's Retreat from Smolensk

Ney's men told how they had left Smolensk on the seventeenth of November with twelve cannons, six thousand armed men, and three hundred horses, abandoning their five thousand disabled men to the mercy of the enemy. If it had not been for the roar of Platov's cannon and the explosion of the mines, they would never have been able to tear some seven thousand disarmed stragglers away from the ruins of the city in which they had taken refuge. The soldiers dwelt on their commanding officer's care for the wounded and the women and children, showing once again how the bravest was also the most humane.

At the gates of the city an infamous act had filled them with horror from which they had not yet recovered. A mother had abandoned her five-year-old son, pushing him out of her overloaded sleigh, in spite of his cries and tears. "He has never seen France!" she had cried in frenzy. "He will not miss it. But I know France — I want to see it again!" Twice Ney had had the poor child picked up and placed in his mother's arms, and twice she had thrown him out on the frozen snow. But this crime (the only one noted among a thousand acts of sublime devotion) did not go unpunished. The unnatural mother herself was abandoned on the snow from which the little victim had been picked up.

This orphan had been entrusted to another mother, and was later seen with the troops at the Berezina, Vilna, and even at Kovno. He actually survived all the horrors of the retreat.

Eugène's officers continued questioning Ney's staff who went on with their story. They depicted their corps advancing with their marshal toward Krasnoye through the masses of debris we had left behind us — followed by one lamentable mob and preceded by another whom hunger had driven at a quicker pace. They told how they had found every hollow and gully filled with helmets, shakos, opened chests, articles of clothing, wagons and cannon, some overturned, others still harnessed, some of the poor horses still alive, though half devoured by wolves. Near Korythnia at the end of their first day a violent cannonading and the whistling of bullets over their heads had led them to believe they were being attacked. This outburst seemed to proceed from a spot on the road just ahead of them, yet there was no sign of the enemy. Ricard and his division went ahead to reconnoiter. They only found two French batteries which had been abandoned with their ammunition in a bend of the road. In a neighboring field a band of miserable Cossacks were running away frightened by their own daring and the noise they had created in setting fire to the powder.

At this point Ney's officers paused and took their turn at asking questions. What had happened? What was the cause of our general discouragement? Why had the cannon been abandoned to the enemy in perfect condition? Had we not had the time to spike the guns, or at least to spoil the ammunition?

They went on to say how until then — up to the end of the first day — they had found nothing but the traces of disastrous flight. But on the second day all had changed, and they confessed their gloomy presentiments at finding the snow reddened with blood, strewn with shattered weapons and badly mutilated corpses. The dead bodies marked the different ranks and places of battle; the men pointed them out to each other. Here had stood the 14th Division; the torn caps left on the snow bore the number of that regiment. Over there, the Italian Guard; all the dead were wearing that uniform. But where were the survivors? . . . In vain they questioned this bloody field, the lifeless bodies, the dreadful frozen silence of the realm of the dead; they could gather nothing concerning the fate of their companions or what was in store for themselves.

Ney hurried them over these ruins, and they proceeded without encountering any real obstacle until they reached a spot where the road dipped down into a deep gully, then rose again to cross a wide plateau. This was the battlefield of Katova where, in their triumphant march eastward three months earlier, they had beaten Neverovski and fired a salvo for Napoleon with the guns taken from the enemy the day before. The men said they had recognized the field despite the snow that lay so thick over it.

Their disbanded men were running wildly back toward them, pointing out a black mass of enemy troops occupying those snow-covered plains, when a solitary Russian officer left the main body and walked down the hill toward them. Shown into the presence of the marshal, he summoned him to surrender. Either in affected politeness or out of respect for our leader, he couched his summons in flattering terms. "I have come from Kutuzov," he said. "Our field marshal would not have had the presumption to make such a cruel proposal to so great a general, so famous a warrior, if there had been the slightest chance of your saving yourself. But eighty thousand Russians are in front of you and around

you. If you doubt it, Kutuzov will allow you to send someone to inspect his ranks and count his forces."

The Russians had not ceased speaking when forty volleys
of grapeshot were suddenly fired from the right of his army,
cutting our ranks to pieces and putting an end to his speech.
A French officer sprang forward to kill the man whom he
considered a traitor. Ney, checking this impulse but yielding
to his own, shouted at him, "A marshal never surrenders.
And we do not parley under fire. You are my prisoner." The
unfortunate officer, disarmed, was left exposed to the fire of
his own men. He was not set free until we reached Kovno,
twenty-six days later, during which time he shared all our
miseries, at liberty to escape but restrained by his word of
honor.

Then the enemy opened fire from all sides and, as the narrators said, the hills which had been cold and still a moment
before became volcanoes in full eruption; but this only inflamed Ney. The soldiers, growing enthusiastic every time
the marshal's name came up in their story, declared that
in the midst of all that fire, the man of fire had seemed in his
natural element.

Kutuzov had not deceived them. Against them were eighty
thousand men, in deep, unbroken, well-armed ranks, numerous squadrons, a powerful artillery in a formidable position.
And facing this mass, five thousand soldiers in a disorderly
column, separated into several parts, weary, discouraged,
with dirty, defective weapons mostly unloaded and shaking
in weakened hands.

Yet the French general had no thought of yielding, nor of
dying; but only of cutting his way through that barrier —
and without the least idea that he was making a sublime
effort.

All that day his wretched forces held out somehow against the stubborn fire and repeated charges of the enemy. Night began to blur everything; winter, favorable to our retreat in this one respect, brought it on quickly. Ney had awaited it anxiously; but when he took advantage of this respite to order his men to march back toward Smolensk, all his officers were paralyzed with amazement. His own aide-de-camp could not believe his ears. Speechless, as if not understanding the marshal's words, he stood and stared at him. But Ney repeated the order, and from his curt, imperious tone they realized that it was the fruit of calm resolution and freshly tapped resources, the sort of self-confidence which inspired confidence in others, and a spirit which prevailed in even the most critical situation. Therefore they obeyed immediately, turned their backs on Napoleon and France, and re-entered deadly Russia. They had marched backward for about an hour when for the second time they came upon the field of battle marked by the remains of the army of Italy. There they halted a short time, and their marshal, who had remained alone at the rear, rejoined them.

The officers followed his every movement with their eyes. What was he going to do? How was he to carry out his plans, whatever they were, in an unfamiliar region, without a guide? But Ney, with a warrior's instinct, stopped on the edge of a stream flowing at the bottom of a narrow ravine. He had the snow cleared away and the ice broken; then, after observing the direction of the current, he cried, "This is a tributary of the Dnieper! Here is the guide we must follow! It will lead us to the river, which we must cross. We shall be safe on the other side," and they set out at once in that direction.

At a short distance from the highroad they halted again at a village whose name they did not know. The narrators thought it was Fomina, or it might have been Danikova. There they rallied their troops and built fires, as if they intended making it their quarters for the night. The Cossacks who were following them believed that to be their intention, and evidently sent someone to inform Kutuzov of the spot where a French marshal would surrender his arms to him the next morning; for shortly afterward the boom of his cannon was heard.

Ney listened. "Can that be Davout at last?" he asked. "Has he finally remembered me?" He listened again. The regular intervals of the firing told him it was a salvo. Then he realized that the Russian camp was rejoicing in advance over his capture, and he swore to spoil their joy. He ordered his army to resume their march. At that moment his Poles who had been ransacking the village produced a lame peasant, the sole inhabitant to be found. Here was a stroke of unexpected good luck. The peasant told them that the Dnieper was only a couple of miles distant, but that it was too deep to ford and was probably not frozen over. "It will be!" cried the marshal. But when his staff reminded him that a thaw had set in, he added, "That doesn't make any difference. We shall cross anyway, since there's no alternative."

At about eight o'clock they passed through another village, the gully came to an end, and the lame man who was leading them stopped, and pointed to the Dnieper. (The men thought it was between Syrokorenye and Gusinoye.) Ney and his escort hurried to the bank; the river was sufficiently frozen to bear a man's weight. The blocks of ice carried along by the current had jammed in a sharp bend of the river and the cold had frozen them together; but at only one point, for both above and below it the surface of the water was in motion. Dared they trust the treacherous appearance of the enemy's river? One of the officers risked his

life to find out. With no little difficulty he reached the opposite bank, and came back to report that the men, and perhaps
some horses, could cross, but that everything else would have
to be abandoned. They must work quickly, as the ice was
beginning to give way.

Then as Ney looked around he realized that only a small
portion of his troops were with him. In the course of that
silent, nocturnal flight across the fields, his column composed
of greatly weakened men, many wounded, and women with
their children had not been able to keep together, but had
scattered widely and the different groups had lost sight of
each other in the darkness. Nevertheless, he might still have
made sure of his own safety by crossing the river and waiting
on the other side for the stragglers to come up. Such an idea
never entered his head. Someone suggested it to him, but he
brushed it aside. He allowed three hours for the rallying of
the stragglers. Apparently indifferent to the dangers of
waiting, he wrapped his coat around him, lay down on the
riverbank, and spent those three perilous hours in unbroken
sleep. His was the temperament of great men — a strong
mind in a strong body, and that vigorous health without
which there would be few heroes.

Finally at midnight the crossing began. But the first men
who ventured out from the bank called back that the ice was
giving way under them, that it was sinking, that they were
in water up to their knees. Shortly afterward, this frail
support split with a frightening crack which echoed in the
distance, as in the breaking up of a frost. Everybody stopped
in consternation.

Ney gave the order that they were to cross one at a time.
They advanced cautiously, not knowing in the dark whether
they were placing their feet on blocks of ice or in the cracks between them. There were places where they had to cross

wide gaps by leaping from one floating sheet to another, at the risk of falling between two of them and disappearing forever. The ones in front faltered, but the crowds in the rear pushed ahead and shouted to them to hurry.

When at length, after such cruel experiences, they did reach the other side, they found themselves faced by a vertical slope covered with a coat of sleet that prevented them from climbing to safety. Many fell back on the ice, which gave way under them or on which they were crushed. According to Ney's men, the Russian river and its banks seemed to have lent themselves reluctantly, as if by compulsion, to their preservation.

As they told their story they dwelt with particular horror on the anguish of the women and the sick at being forced to leave behind with the baggage the remains of their fortunes and provisions, all their resources for the present and future. They had watched them rummaging wildly through their possessions, selecting certain articles, throwing them aside, picking them up again, finally falling with exhaustion and grief on the frozen riverbank. The speakers shivered at the recollection of the awful sight of all those human beings scattered along the abyss; of the sound of one body after another crashing down on the ice, of their screams as they sank; and especially of the hopeless weeping of the wounded who held out their arms from their carts, which had not dared to venture out on that frail support, and implored their companions not to abandon them.

The marshal then tried to get several of the carriages loaded with these poor creatures across, but in the middle of the river the ice gave way and split open. The men on the opposite bank listened to the long drawn-out, agonized shrieks that dwindled to intermittent moans, then fell to silence. All had disappeared!

Marshal Ney, staring in consternation down into this gulf, thought he saw something still moving among the shadows. It was one of the victims of the catastrophe, an officer named Briqueville, who was prevented from rising to his feet by a deep wound in his groin. A sheet of ice had lifted him to the surface. Soon he could be clearly seen crawling on his hands and knees from one floating ice cake to another, slowly approaching. Ney himself drew him to safety.

In the last twenty-four hours three thousand armed men and four thousand stragglers had either died or strayed from the ranks. The guns and all the baggage were lost, and Ney found that he now had hardly more than three thousand soldiers and an equal number of disbanded men. Finally, when all these sacrifices had been consummated and everybody that had been able to make the crossing had been brought together, they set out again, and the vanquished river became their ally and guide.

They were following a random, uncertain course when one of the men, having fallen forward on his hands, reported that they were on a traveled road. This was all too true: the soldiers at the head of the column stooped down, and using their eyes as well as their hands, found ruts made by a great number of guns and horses. So, then, they had only escaped from one army to run into another, and were going to have to fight again when they were scarcely able to walk! So war was all around them! Ney, however, without showing alarm, urged them forward on the dangerous trail.

It led them to the village of Gusinoye, which they took by surprise. There they found all the things they had lacked since leaving Moscow — people, food, beds, warm houses. They seized everything, including a hundred sleeping Cossacks who woke up to find themselves prisoners. Ney made a brief halt there to hear reports and re-form his ranks. By ten

o'clock they had occupied two more villages, and were resting in them when the surrounding forests suddenly came to
life. While our men were calling each other and concen-
trating on the hamlet nearest the Dnieper, thousands of
Cossacks slipped out from behind the trees and surrounded
the wretched little army with their spears and cannon.

It was Platov with all his hordes that had been following
this bank of the river. They might have burned the village,
exposed the weakness of Ney's forces, and utterly destroyed
them; but they stood for three hours without moving or
firing — we never knew why. They said they had not been
given any specific order, their commanding officer being
disabled; and in Russia nobody dares to take anything on
himself.

Ney's resolute bearing held them in check; he and a few
soldiers sufficed. He went so far as to order his other troops
to go on resting until nightfall. Then he had the order to
decamp in absolute silence circulated; the men were to pass
this on in whispers and to gather into a compact body. They
moved forward all together; but their very first step was like
a signal given the enemy, whose muskets went off with a
great roar as all their squadrons charged.

Our unarmed stragglers, still numbering about three
thousand, were terrified by the noise. This herd of men
surged madly back and forth and rushed into the ranks of
the soldiers, who beat them off. Ney succeeded in keeping
them between himself and the enemy, whose fire the useless
mass absorbed. Thus the timid served as a protection for
the brave. Making a rampart of those poor wretches for his
right flank, the marshal moved backward toward the Dnieper,
which became a cover for his left. He advanced cautiously
between the two, moving from one clump of trees to another,
from gully to gully, taking advantage of every twist and

turn, every rise and fall in the earth's surface. He was often forced to leave the riverbank; then Platov's hordes would surround him on all sides.

So for two whole days (in which time they covered fifty miles) six thousand Cossacks hovered constantly about this column, reduced to fifteen hundred armed men. Night brought them some little relief, and they plunged into the dark with a sort of joy. But if anyone dared to halt an instant to bid a last farewell to those who had fallen from exhaustion or wounds, he lost all trace of his comrades. There were indeed many cruel moments, many scenes of despair; but finally the Cossacks slackened their pursuit.

From midnight until ten in the morning on the nineteenth they marched without encountering any adversary other than a very hilly stretch of country. Then suddenly Platov's columns came in sight again, and Ney halted and faced them under cover of the skirts of the forest. All day long the soldiers were reduced to lying and watching the Russian cannon balls knock down the trees that were protecting them or roll through their bivouacs. Their light firearms — all they had left — were inadequate to keep the enemy at a safe distance. As soon as night fell the marshal gave the signal, and the troops set out again toward Orsha. In the course of the previous day fifty horsemen under Pchebendowski had been sent ahead to demand assistance. They should have reached Orsha by now, unless the enemy had already occupied that town . . .

Here Ney's officers ended their story, with the final statement that nothing worthy of note had happened after that, though they had encountered other cruel obstacles . . . Orsha was separated from Smolensk by a mere five days' march. Yet how much glory had been crowded into that brief journey! Indeed, a short distance and very little time are required to earn eternal fame!

When Napoleon, who had halted five miles beyond Orsha, heard the good news of Ney's reappearance he leaped for joy and cried, "So I have saved my eagles! I would have given three hundred millions from my treasury to ransom such a man!"

So for the third and last time the Grand Army had crossed the Dnieper, a river half Russian, half Lithuanian, but of Muscovite origin. It flows from east to west as far as Orsha, where it seems to want to enter Poland. But the Lithuanian highlands block its course, forcing it to turn sharply southward and form the frontier of the two countries.

Kutuzov's eighty thousand Russians halted before this insignificant obstacle. Up to that point they had been the spectators rather than the authors of our calamities. We never saw them again, and our army was delivered from the torturing spectacle of their joy. In this war Kutuzov's character had been of more service to him than his military genius. So long as it was a question of deceiving and temporizing, his crafty nature, laziness, and advanced age worked of themselves and he rose to the occasion. But when it was a question of moving rapidly, pursuing, forestalling, or attacking, he fell short of the mark.

Platov, however, after passing Smolensk had crossed over to the right side of our road, as if he intended to join Wittgenstein. All the war lay on that side now.

The twenty-second of November found us toiling along the road from Orsha to Borisov, between a double line of giant birches, through melted snow and deep liquid mud in which the weak got drowned, and which trapped and held as prisoners for the Cossacks those of the wounded who, believing that the frost had definitely set in, had exchanged their carts for sledges or sleighs at Smolensk.

In the midst of this general decay and discouragement an action of antique grandeur stood out. Two marines of the Guard had got separated from their column by a band of Cossacks who seemed bent on their destruction. One of the marines lost heart and was about to give himself up, but the other shouted to him that if he committed this act of cowardice, he would kill him. And he did: when he saw his companion throw his musket away and put up his hands, he shot him down in the very arms of the Cossacks. Then, taking advantage of their surprise, he quickly reloaded his musket which he kept leveled on the bravest of the band as he walked backward, stealing from tree to tree, and so succeeded in rejoining his company.

It was during the first days of the march toward Borisov that the news of the loss of Minsk spread through the army. Then the marshals themselves looked around them in consternation, their imagination, made sensitive by such a long succession of frightful spectacles, foreseeing an even more sinister future. In their private conversations several of them expressed their fear that "like Charles XII in Ukrania, Napoleon has led his army to destruction in Moscow!"

# CHAPTER IX

********

## *The Berezina River*

WHILE HE WAS at Toloczina, Napoleon had the position of Borisov described to him. He was told that at that point the Berezina ceased to be a river and became a lake covered with ice floes; that the Borisov bridge was about a third of a mile long, and that it had been destroyed beyond hope of repairs, making the crossing there impossible. A general of the engineers' corps, coming from the Duke of Belluno, arrived at that juncture. Napoleon called him in and questioned him. It was this general's opinion that our only hope of escape was through Wittgenstein's army. The Emperor said, "I must proceed in such a way that my back will be turned to all of them — Kutuzov, Wittgenstein, and Tchitchakov." And he pointed out on his staff map the portion of the Berezina just above Borisov, declaring that it was there he wished to cross. When the general reminded him that Tchitchakov occupied all the right bank, the Emperor indicated another spot below the first, and still a third, nearer the Dnieper. Realizing that he was approaching the country of the Cossacks, he desisted. "Ah yes!" he cried. "Poltava! . . . Like Charles XII!"

Indeed, every calamity that Napoleon might possibly have foreseen had occurred; and this similarity of his situation and the Swedish conqueror's threw him into such despair that he fell ill, afflicted even more cruelly than at Malo-Yaroslavetz. In his distress he was heard to mutter, "This is what happens when one heaps one mistake upon another!"

This, however, was the only sign he gave of his inner disturbance, and the valet who ministered to him at that time was the only person to sense his trouble. Daru, Duroc, and Berthier all said they knew nothing about it, as he appeared calm and unshaken to them; which was true, he being still sufficiently master of himself to repress his anxiety. The strength of a man, the greater part of the time, consists in concealing his weakness.

A conversation which took place that night will give an idea of the gravity of his situation and the manner in which he bore it. The hour was late. Napoleon had gone to bed. Duroc and Daru who had remained in his room, thinking him asleep, were exchanging in whispers the most gloomy conjectures. But he was listening, and at the words *prisoner of state* he sat up. "What!" he cried. "You believe they would dare?"

Daru, taken by surprise, hesitated a moment before answering, "If we are forced to surrender, we may expect anything. I have no faith in the generosity of an enemy. We all know that high state politics have their own ethics and recognize no law."

"But France," asked the Emperor. "What would France say?"

"Oh, as for France," Daru replied. "We could make a thousand guesses, all more or less disagreeable; but none of us can know what would take place there." Then he added, "The best thing for the Emperor's marshals, as well as the Emperor himself, would be for him to get back to France by flying or some other means, since all ways by land are closed to him. He would be of more use to his marshals in France than if he remained with them."

"So I'm in your way?" Napoleon said with a smile.

"Yes, sire."

"And you don't want to be made a prisoner of state?"

"I'd be satisfied to be a prisoner of war," Daru replied in the same tone.

The Emperor was silent for a time, then he asked with a more serious air, "Have all the reports of my ministers been burned?"

"Sire, until now you have not allowed us to do so."

"All right . . . go destroy them. For you must admit we are in a sorry plight."

This was the sole avowal of his defeat that adversity wrung from him. On those words he fell asleep, possessing the ability to put off things till the morrow, when it was necessary.

In all his orders he evinced the same firmness. He approved Oudinot's intention to rout Lambert, and urged him to get control of some fording place either above or below Borisov. He wanted him to have decided on a place of crossing by the twenty-fourth, and to have begun making preparations for it. Then he was to be informed of the plans in order that he might move accordingly. Instead of thinking of escaping from the enemy's armies, he was now wholly bent on defeating Tchitchakov and retaking Minsk.

It is true that, eight hours later, in a letter to the Duke of Reggio he appeared to be resigned to crossing the Berezina at Veselovo and retreating directly toward Vilna through Vileika, so avoiding the Russian admiral. On the twenty-third, Napoleon began to make preparations for what was evidently a desperate move. First he had the standards of all the different corps brought to him and burned. Then he rallied in two battalions eighteen hundred dismounted troopers of the Guard of whom only eleven hundred and fifty-four were armed with muskets or carbines. The cavalry of the army of Moscow was so nearly nonexistent that Latour-Maubourg could muster a mere hundred and fifty men with horses! The Emperor gathered around him all the officers of this branch of the service. He called that troop composed of about five hundred commissioned men his *sacred squadron*. Grouchy and Sebastiani were given command of it, and several generals of divisions served in it as captains.

But on the twenty-fourth, Napoleon learned that the crossing could be attempted only near Studzianka, at a spot where the Berezina was about a hundred yards wide and six feet deep. The disadvantage was that the army would land on the other side in a swamp, fully exposed to the fire of the enemy who occupied an advantageous position. All hope of passing between the Russian armies had faded. With Kutuzov and Wittgenstein forcing us up to the Berezina, we were going to have to cross the river, despite Tchitchakov's troops drawn up along the other bank.

*

## Approaching the Berezina

Once more Napoleon ordered that all unnecessary vehicles be burned: no officer was to keep more than one carriage, and half the supply wagons were to be destroyed in order that the horses might be given to the artillery of the Guard. The officers commanding those troops were to seize all the draft horses they could lay their hands on, including the Emperor's, rather than abandon a single cannon or ammunition wagon.

Then we plunged into the dark interminable Minsk forest, broken only at rare intervals by a clearing with a hamlet or a miserable settlement. Wittgenstein's cannon filled the woods with their echoing roar, and the threatening sound quickened our step. The Russian general was marching from the north and rapidly approaching the right flank of our dying column. He seemed to be bringing with him the severe winter which had left us when Kutuzov abandoned the pursuit. Forty or fifty thousand men, women, and children drifted through those woods with as much speed as their weakness and the sleet-covered ground would allow.

Our forced marches, begun before dawn and continued as long as there was any light, completed the work of dispersal of our troops; they simply disappeared in the gloom of the vast forest and the long nights. We did halt at nightfall, but we set out again while it was still dark, proceeding at random, without any given signal. The remains of our different corps melted away, and the utmost confusion reigned.

As we were approaching Borisov in this supreme degree of exhaustion and disorder, we heard loud shouts coming from the road in front of us. It was Victor's army that Wittgenstein had pursued halfheartedly up to the right side of our road, who were waiting for the passing of Napoleon. These troops, still fresh and intact, greeted their sovereign with the old cheers which had not been heard among us for a long time.

Our disasters had been carefully concealed even from their officers. When, therefore, instead of the expected column of splendid warriors, conquerors of Moscow, they saw in Napoleon's wake a mob of tattered ghosts draped in women's cloaks, odd pieces of carpet, or greatcoats burned full of holes, their feet wrapped in all sorts of rags, they were struck with consternation. They stared in horror as those skeletons of soldiers went by, their gaunt, gray faces covered with disfiguring beards, without weapons, shameless, marching out of step, with lowered heads, eyes on the ground, in absolute silence, like a gang of convicts.

What amazed them most was the sight of so many straggling isolated colonels and generals who were paying no attention to anyone but themselves, intent on saving either their poor possessions or their persons, marching among the soldiers who took no notice of them, to whom they gave no orders and from whom they could no longer expect anything, all ties between them being broken and all difference of rank effaced by a common misery.

The soldiers of Victor and Oudinot could not at first believe their eyes. The officers, with tears of pity running down their cheeks, seized hold of any of their companions whom they recognized in the crowd, offering them their own food and clothing. Then they asked where the corps of their army were; and when these were pointed out to them, and they saw only a wretched platoon of officers and non-commissioned officers around a general, instead of thousands of armed men, they went on looking for them.

The sight of such disaster began to unsettle the 2nd and 9th Corps from the first day. Disorder, most contagious of all diseases, spread among them, for it would seem that order is an exertion against nature. Yet these unarmed, even dying men, knowing that they were going to have to fight their way across a wide river, past a powerful enemy, still had no doubt but that they would win.

Theirs was only the ghost of an army; but it was the ghost of the Grand Army! They felt that they had been defeated only by Nature, and the sight of their Emperor restored their courage. For a very long time they had been accustomed to looking to him not only for their existence, but for victory. This was their first disastrous campaign; and they had enjoyed so many successful ones. They had only to follow him, who had lifted his soldiers so high and brought them so low, and he would save them! He still lived in the midst of his army, like hope in the human breast.

And so he rode fearlessly in the midst of all those men who could have reviled him as the cause of their misery. From time to time he spoke simply to one of them, sure of being respected as long as there existed any respect for glory and realizing that he belonged to us as much as we belonged to him, as his fame was a sort of national property. We would have preferred turning our weapons against ourselves — as, indeed, some of the men did — which would have been less of a suicide.

Several fell dead at his very feet; and, though they were raving in delirium, their suffering entreated but never reproached him. Was he not sharing our common danger? Who among us was risking more than he, or losing more by the disaster?

The critical moment was approaching. Victor was now in the rear with fifteen thousand men; Oudinot had gone on ahead with his five thousand, and was already close to the Berezina; the Emperor was between the two with seven thousand soldiers, forty thousand stragglers, and an enormous mass of baggage wagons and artillery, the greater part of which belonged to the 2nd and 9th Corps. As he neared the Berezina his march became hesitant. He halted every few minutes on the high road waiting for darkness to conceal his arrival from the enemy, and to give Oudinot the time to evacuate Borisov.

When this marshal entered the city on the twenty-third, he found the bridge, which was about a third of a mile long, broken in three places; and the proximity of the enemy made it impossible for him to attempt to repair it. He learned that

on the left, two miles farther downstream, he would find a
ford near Oukoholda, but that it was dangerous; one mile
above Borisov, at Stadhof, there was another, equally impracticable. Finally there was the third ford, which he had
known of for two days, at Studzianka, five miles below
Stadhof.

Oudinot made his choice without delay. During the
night of the twenty-third the general commanding the
artillery, a company of pontoon engineers, an infantry regiment, and Corbineau's brigade occupied Studzianka. Meanwhile the other two spots had been reconnoitered and found
to be under close observation by the enemy. The important
thing, then, was to deceive the Russians, and draw them away
from Studzianka. As we could not prevail by force, we
resorted to cunning. Three hundred soldiers and seven
hundred stragglers were sent toward Oukoholda on the
twenty-fourth with instructions to collect all the material
necessary to build a bridge, making as much noise as possible
about it. At the same time a whole division of cuirassiers
marched with great pomp up and down the riverbank in
full view of the enemy.

We did more: the chief of staff, General Lorencé, had
several Jews brought to him. With an exaggerated show of
interest, he questioned them concerning the ford at Oukoholda and the roads leading from there to Minsk. Pretend-
ing to be highly satisfied with their replies, apparently
convinced that there was no better spot for the crossing, he
retained some of the traitors as guides and had the others
conducted beyond our outposts. Sure that the latter would
not keep their word, he had them swear that they would
meet us somewhere on the lower Berezina to inform us of
the enemy's movements.

*

## Preparations for the Crossing

While we were trying in that way to attract Tchitchakov's attention to the left, we were secretly preparing for a crossing at Studzianka. At five o'clock in the evening on the twenty-fifth, General Eblé arrived followed by only two wagons of charcoal, six covered wagons of tools and nails, and several companies of pontoniers. While at Smolensk he had had each of his workmen take a tool and some cramp irons.

The trestles they had been building since the day before, out of beams from Polish cottages, proved to be too weak, and the work had to be begun all over again. It was simply impossible to complete the bridge in that one night: it must be set up the next morning by daylight and under the enemy's fire, but we had no choice.

At dusk on that decisive day Oudinot, leaving Napoleon to occupy Borisov, took his position with the rest of his corps at Studzianka. His men had marched in inky darkness without making any noise, speaking to each other only in whispers. At eight o'clock he and Dombrowski took their stand on the hills overlooking the place of crossing, while Eblé moved down the slope and occupied the riverbank with his pontoniers and a wagonload of cramps which he had had forged from the steel rims of abandoned cartwheels. He had sacrificed everything else to keep this poor resource — which in the end saved the army.

At dawn on the twenty-sixth the first trestle was planted in the muddy river bed. But, to complete our misfortune, the swollen waters had blotted out all traces of the ford. This necessitated herculean efforts on the part of our poor engineers, who worked in water up to their mouths, struggling against the ice carried down by the current. Some of them died of the cold or were forced under by the great cakes of ice. They had everything against them — except the enemy. The temperature was at the right degree to make the crossing of the river most difficult, without freezing it over completely or hardening the mud through which we should have to wade to approach the bridge. As on other occasions, winter proved itself a more formidable enemy than the Russians, but they failed to make use of their season which was always on their side.

The men toiled all night by the light of the enemy camp-fires burning brightly on the opposite bank, within range of the muskets and guns of Tchaplitz who, no longer doubting our intention, sent a messenger to inform his commander-in-chief of it. The presence of a Russian division destroyed all hope of our having deceived the Admiral (Tchitchakov). At any moment we expected his artillery to open fire on our workmen. They were not interrupted; but the work was not sufficiently advanced when day dawned, and the low, swampy opposite shore was too well exposed to Tchaplitz's positions for us to attempt a surprise crossing.

When Napoleon left Borisov at ten o'clock he firmly believed that he was heading for a desperate encounter. With his remaining ten thousand four hundred Guards he pitched his camp at Staroi-Borisov in an estate belonging to Prince Radziwill, situated to the right of the road, halfway between Borisov and Studzianka. He spent the rest of the night on his feet, going out every few minutes to listen or pay a visit to the crossing where his fate was to be decided. His hours were so filled with anxiety that as each one struck he thought it was morning, and his attendants were obliged to advise him of his mistake.

He rejoined Oudinot at the break of day. As was always the case with him, he was calmed by the presence of danger. But his most resolute generals, Rapp, Mortier, and Ney, were filled with apprehension at the sight of the Russian fires and their favorable position. "If the Emperor gets out of this predicament," they said, "we shall certainly believe in his star!" Murat himself was convinced that the time had come to think of saving Napoleon's life, as certain Poles had suggested to him.

The Emperor was waiting for morning in one of the houses along the river, built against the steep slope of the hill occupied by Oudinot's artillery, when Murat burst in upon him. "I consider it impossible to cross here," he told his brother-in-law. "You must save yourself while there is still time! Several miles above Studzianka there is a spot where you can cross the Berezina without danger. In five days you could be in Vilna. Certain brave Poles who know the road have offered to escort you, and will answer for your safety."

Napoleon rejected this proposal as a shameful course, a cowardly flight, and became indignant at the idea that anyone could have believed he would abandon his army so long as it was in danger. He did not, however, hold this against Murat: perhaps he was gratified that the Prince had given him an opportunity to display his courage, or perhaps he interpreted the offer as a simple sign of devotion, and the finest quality in the eyes of a sovereign is attachment to his person.

By now the light of dawn was putting out the Muscovite fires. Our troops got under arms, the artillerymen took their positions before their guns, the generals studied the situation. All turned their eyes toward the opposite shore in that perfect stillness which accompanies the tense moment of waiting before some grave event. The noise of our hammering which had begun the day before must have echoed all night among the wooded hills and attracted the attention of the enemy. We were certain that the first light of day would reveal their battalions and artillery drawn up in front of the frail scaffolding of the bridge, to the construction of which Eblé had to devote eight more hours. Without doubt they had only held their fire during the night because their aim would be surer by daylight . . . Morning came. And we saw abandoned campfires, a deserted riverbank, and, up on the hills, thirty pieces of cannon in retreat! A single one of their shells would have been enough to shatter our sole road to safety, but their artillery was retiring as fast as our own formed a battery.

Farther off we could see the end of a long column that was marching toward Borisov without looking back. However, one infantry regiment and twelve guns still faced us, though without taking a position, and a flock of Cossacks were wandering along the skirt of the wood. These formed the rear guard of Tchaplitz's division, six thousand strong, that was voluntarily withdrawing, as if to let us pass.

The French troops did not dare to trust their eyes at first. Then, overcome with joy, they cheered and clapped their hands. Rapp and Oudinot rushed into the Emperor's presence with the news: "Sire, the enemy have broken camp and given up their position!"

"It isn't possible!" cried the Emperor.

But Ney and Murat came in to confirm the report. Napoleon darted out of his quarters in time to see the tail end of Tchaplitz's division disappear into the woods. Beside himself with joy, he exclaimed, "I have outwitted the Admiral!"

At that moment two Russian cannon were pushed out on

the opposite shore and trained on us. A single volley sufficed
to drive them off. This act of imprudence on our part was
not repeated, lest the noise of firing should recall Tchaplitz,
for the bridge was hardly more than begun. It was eight
o'clock, and the pontoniers were only sinking their first
trestles.

The Emperor, impatient to take possession of the opposite
bank, pointed it out to a group of his bravest men. Jacqueminot, an aide-de-camp of the Duke of Reggio, and Count
Predzieczki, a Lithuanian nobleman, plunged into the river
first, and despite the sharp cakes of ice which tore the flanks
and chests of their horses, succeeded in landing on the other
side. Major Sourd and fifty chasseurs of the 7th, each one
carrying a light-infantryman behind, followed close after
them. Two frail rafts, making twenty trips, managed to ferry
another four hundred across.

The Emperor wanted a prisoner whom he could question.
Jacqueminot, who had heard him express that wish, had no
sooner got across the river than he fell on one of Tchaplitz's
soldiers, disarmed him, bound him, threw him across his
saddle, and brought him back through the ice floes to
Napoleon.

By one o'clock the last Cossack had been driven from the
riverbank, and the bridge for the infantry was finished.
Legrand's division hurried across it with their cannon, accompanied by cheers of *Vive l'Empereur!* Their sovereign
assisted in getting the artillery across by encouraging the
brave soldiers with his words and example. Seeing them at
last in possession of the opposite bank, he cried, "My star
again!" for like all conquerors, he believed in fate.

As soon as the first bridge, which was intended for the
infantry alone, was finished, a second was begun, a few
hundred feet farther upstream, for the artillery and baggage

trains. This was not completed until four o'clock in the afternoon.

Napoleon with six thousand Guards and Ney's corps, reduced to six hundred armed men, crossed the Berezina at two o'clock. He posted himself in reserve to Oudinot and secured the outlets from the bridges against any future attack by Tchitchakov. A mass of baggage wagons and stragglers had preceded him, and others continued to stream over after him as long as daylight lasted. Meanwhile General Victor's troops had taken the place of the Guards on the hills above Studzianka.

*

## The Annihilation of Partouneaux's Division

Up to that point everything had gone well. But when Victor passed through Borisov he left General Partouneaux and his division there with the order to stop the enemy behind the town, drive out the stragglers who had taken refuge in its houses, and then rejoin him before the end of the day. Partouneaux * was seeing for the first time the terrible disorder of the Grand Army; and, as Davout had done at the beginning of the retreat, he tried to conceal it from Kutuzov's Cossacks who were at his heels. This futile effort, the repeated attacks by Platov along the road from Orsha and by Tchitchakov at the burned bridge, kept him in Borisov until nightfall.

He was finally preparing to leave when he got the order

---

* Louis Partouneaux (1771–1835), courageous French general. Previously wounded and taken prisoner by Suvarov, during the Italian campaign. — J.D.T.

to spend the night there. This came from the Emperor, who doubtless hoped to concentrate the attention of the three Russian generals upon that city until all our forces had succeeded in crossing the river.

Now Wittgenstein had allowed Platov to follow our army on the main road, while he had taken a secondary road on the right. That evening he made his appearance on the hills running along the river between Borisov and Studzianka, occupied the road connecting those two points, and seized everything within sight. A crowd of stragglers rushing back in terror toward Partouneaux let him know that he was cut off from the rest of the army.

Partouneaux did not falter. Though he had only three cannon and three thousand five hundred combatants with him, he made the immediate decision to cut his way through the Russian lines, disposed his forces, and marched forward. His advance was slowed up by the slippery condition of the road, confused masses of baggage wagons and stragglers, a strong, icy head wind, and inky darkness. Soon the fires of thousands of enemies on the hills at his right gave proof of a fresh obstacle. Yet he kept on, as long as he was attacked only from that side; but in a short time the road in front was blocked by a mass of troops, advantageously posted, whose shots tore through his column from one end to the other.

The ill-fated division was trapped in a hollow, with a long line of five or six hundred wagons impeding its progress, and some seven thousand terrified stragglers, howling with despair, throwing themselves wildly against its thin lines. They broke through, dispersed the platoons, and drew more and more discouraged combatants into their confusion. The order to fall back was given, in order to rally and take a better position; but as they marched backward they ran into Platov's cavalry. By now half the combatants had perished, and the fifteen hundred soldiers who were left found themselves hemmed in by three armies and a river.

At this juncture a bearer of a flag of truce appeared and summoned the French to surrender in the name of Wittgenstein and fifty thousand armed men. Partouneaux spurned the summons, and called on the few stragglers still bearing arms to take their stand with him. He was determined to make one last attempt to cut a bloody path through to the Studzianka bridge. But those soldiers, once so bold, were now so demoralized by suffering that they were unable to make use of their weapons. At that moment the general commanding the advance guard informed Partouneaux that our bridges had been set on fire: an aide-de-camp named Rochez swore that he had seen them burning! Partouneaux believed that false report, for where calamity is concerned, misfortune is credulous.

Convinced that he had been abandoned and betrayed, he gave the order to three of his brigades to try to save themselves by slipping along the enemy's flank under cover of the darkness. With the fourth brigade, reduced to four hundred men, he scaled the steep wooded hills on his right, hoping to steal through Wittgenstein's troops and either rejoin Victor at Studzianka or pass around the Berezina at its sources.

But turn where he would, he ran into the enemy's fire. For several hours he wandered blindly over the snow-covered plain through the raging blizzard, seeing his men, half dead from hunger, cold, and fatigue, drop one after another into the hands of the Russian cavalry. Still the unfortunate general continued to struggle against the elements, men, and his own despair. Suddenly he felt the earth give way under his feet. Deceived by the smooth snow, he had walked out on a frozen lake, and the ice, not yet thick enough to bear his weight, began to crumble beneath him. Only then did he surrender.

Meanwhile, the other three brigades had got so closely hemmed in on the main road that they were unable to make a movement in any direction. Still, they held out until morning — fighting for a while, then parleying; but in the end they, too, laid down their arms, and they and their general were united in a common misfortune. A single battalion out of the entire division escaped, one that had been left behind in Borisov . . . Its commanding officer, carried along by a crowd of stragglers fleeing toward Studzianka, taking the wrong road and leaving on his right the one the army was following, stole along the windings and turnings of the river and, protected by the darkness and the resistance of his less fortunate companions, managed to escape from the enemy and bring the news of Partouneaux's surrender to Victor.

Napoleon was cruelly affected by this bad news. "When everything appeared to be saved as by a miracle," he groaned, "why did this *defection* have to spoil it all?" The expression was unfair; but it was torn from him by suffering, either because he anticipated that the enfeebled Victor would be unable to hold out long enough the next day, or because he esteemed it a point of honor to leave none but unarmed stragglers in the hands of the enemy during the whole retreat. In fact, this was the first and only division to lay down its arms.

This victory encouraged Wittgenstein. Also, two days of feeling about, the report of a prisoner, and the taking of Borisov by Platov had given Tchitchakov the information he needed. Now the three Russian armies — of the north, the east and the south — felt themselves to be one united force, with close communication between their generals. Wittgenstein and Tchitchakov were bitterly jealous of each other, but they detested us even more. It was hatred rather than friendship which held them together. Those generals were now ready to make a simultaneous attack on the Studzianka bridges from both sides of the river.

*

## Crossing the Berezina

It was the twenty-eighth of November. The Grand Army had had two whole days and nights in which to effect the crossing, and it should have been too late for the Russians to do any harm. But chaos reigned in our midst; besides, there had not been enough material for the two bridges. Twice during the night of the twenty-sixth the bridge for heavy vehicles had broken apart, and the crossing had been interrupted for seven hours. It had collapsed again on the twenty-seventh, at four in the afternoon. Moreover, the stragglers and disbanded men scattered through the surrounding woods and villages had not taken advantage of the first night, but at daybreak on the twenty-seventh they had all moved toward the bridges and tried to cross at the same time.

It was then that the Old Guard by whom they regulated their movements began to cross. Their departure was like a signal. The wretched crew poured in from all sides and accumulated on the riverbank. In a few minutes an immense confused mass of men, horses, and vehicles besieged the narrow entrances to the bridges and began to flow over them. Those in front, pushed by the weight of those behind or halted by the river, were crushed, trampled on, or forced into the ice-filled water of the Berezina. From the horrible, formless mob there arose a sort of dull murmur which swelled at times to a wild clamor mingled with groans and awful imprecations.

The best efforts of Napoleon and his lieutenants to save those poor distracted men by restoring order in their ranks were fruitless. The confusion was so great that when Napoleon himself wished to cross at two o'clock, it was necessary to use force to clear a passage for him. Latour-Maubourg and one corps of grenadiers of the Guard, moved to pity, gave up trying to break a way for themselves through the miserable crowd.

The hamlet of Zaniwki, situated in the depth of the forest a couple of miles from Studzianka, became the imperial headquarters. Eblé had made a survey of the baggage covering the riverbank, and he warned the Emperor that six days would be insufficient to get so many vehicles across. Ney who was present cried out, "Then they must be burned at once." But Berthier, inspired by the evil genius which dwells in courts, objected to this, insisting that we were far from being reduced to such an extremity. The Emperor, swayed by the opinion most agreeable to him, and thinking of all the men whose supplies and worldly goods were in those wagons, and for whose misfortune he blamed himself, was willing to listen to Berthier.

On the night of the twenty-seventh the disorder was brought to a close by a reverse movement, the crowd leaving the bridges and flowing back again toward Studzianka. In a wink the village had disappeared — had been torn to pieces and turned into fuel for a countless number of fires. Paralyzed by cold and hunger, the poor creatures refused to stir from them, so that one more night was lost for the crossing.

Meanwhile Victor with his six thousand soldiers was de-

fending them against Wittgenstein. When, by the first light
of day, they saw this general making preparations for a battle,
when they heard Wittgenstein's cannon thunder over their
heads and Tchitchakov's guns answer from the other side,
they rose as one man and poured wildly down the slope toward the bridges again.

Their terror was well founded. The last day for many of
these unfortunate beings had come. Wittgenstein and Platov
with forty thousand men of the armies of the north and east
were attacking the hills along the left bank which Victor
with only six thousand combatants was trying to defend. At
the same time, on the other bank, Tchitchakov with twenty-
seven thousand Russians of the army of the south, issued
from the Stachova road and took their stand against Oudinot,
Ney, and Dombrowski, the three of whom had been able to
muster a mere eight thousand armed men. These were supported by the *sacred squadron* and the Young and Old
Guards — in all, three thousand infantrymen and nine hundred troopers.

The two Russian armies meant to seize the two ends of
the bridges simultaneously and lay hold of all the troops that
had not succeeded in getting beyond the Zembin marshes.
Over sixty thousand well-dressed, well-fed, and completely
armed soldiers were facing eighteen thousand half-naked,
starving men, divided into two bodies by the river, surrounded by swamps, and hampered by our fifty thousand
stragglers, wounded and sick, and an enormous number of
baggage wagons.

During the last few days the cold had been so severe that
the Old Guard had lost one third, and the Young Guard one
half of their combatants. This loss and the destruction of
Partouneaux's division explain the terrible reduction of
Victor's forces. Yet the marshal held out against Wittgen-

stein all that day; and on the other shore Tchitchakov was beaten by Ney, whose eight thousand French, Swiss, and Poles were a match for twenty-seven thousand Russians!

The Admiral's * attack was slow and halfhearted. His guns swept the road, but he did not dare follow after the shells and rush into the breaches they made in our ranks. Yet the Vistula Legion in front of his right wing gave way before the charge of one of his strong columns. Oudinot, Dombrowski, and Albert were wounded. Claparède and Kosikowski soon suffered the same fate. We began to fear that all was lost. But suddenly Ney appeared on the scene, and hurled Doumerc and his cavalry through the woods and upon the flank of that Russian column. They took two thousand prisoners and cut down the rest and, by this vigorous action, decided a battle which had been uncertain. Tchitchakov was pushed back to Stachova.

Most of the generals of the 2nd Corps were wounded, for the fewer soldiers they had the more they felt called upon to expose their persons. That day many officers took up the muskets of their wounded soldiers and stepped into their places in the ranks. Among the losses, that of young Count de Noailles, Berthier's aide-de-camp, who was killed on the spot by a bullet, was particularly noted. He was one of those officers of unusual worth but perhaps a trifle too energetic, who spend themselves without stint and are sufficiently rewarded by just being given something to do.

During this action Napoleon at the head of the Guard stayed in reserve at Brilowa, protecting the outlets of the bridges — between the two battles, but nearer to Victor's. This marshal, though attacked in a perilous position by a force four times greater than his own, lost little ground . . . Night fell before Wittgenstein's forty thousand men had suc-

* Tchitchakov. — J.D.T.

ceeded in routing the Duke of Belluno's six thousand. The latter were still in possession of the Studzianka hills, and still preserved the bridges from the attacks of the Russian infantry, though they could not conceal them from the artillery of the left wing.

During all that day the situation of the 9th Corps was all the more critical as a weak and narrow bridge was its only means of retreat, and the approaches to this were blocked with baggage wagons and demented stragglers. As the combat grew hotter and hotter the terror of those poor people increased the disorder. At first they were frightened by the noise of a serious battle; then by the sight of the wounded being brought back from it; finally, by the Russian battery on the left whose shells began to fall in the midst of their confusion.

They plunged madly down the hill, one on top of another; and this multitude piled up on the riverbank with horses and vehicles of all sorts in an inextricable jam. It was around noon that the first enemy shots fell among them and unleashed universal despair.

Then, as in all extreme situations, hearts were laid bare, and both infamous and sublime actions were witnessed. Some there were who, determined to pass at all costs, cut a horrible way for themselves with their swords. Others opened an even crueler road for their carriages, driving them pitilessly through the helpless crowd, crushing men and women, in their odious greed sacrificing their companions in misery to save their possessions. Still others, overcome by unmanly fright, wept, implored, and sank helplessly down, terror wiping out the little strength they had left. There were some especially among the sick and wounded who went apart and sat down resignedly, staring at the sifting snow which was soon to be their tomb.

Many of those in the front line of the desperate mob had missed the bridge and fallen into the water. When they tried to climb up the sides of the trestles, most of them were pushed back into the river. Women were seen among the floating ice sheets with children in their arms, holding them higher and higher as they sank. When their bodies were under water their stiffened arms still held the little ones up.

At the height of this ghastly scene the artillery bridge parted in the middle. The column that was crossing the narrow thoroughfare at the time tried in vain to turn back, but the stream of men in the rear, unaware of the disaster, heedless of the cries of those in front, kept pushing on and forced them over the edge; only to be themselves forced over a second later.

Then everybody rushed toward the other bridge. An enormous number of heavy caissons, supply wagons, and pieces of artillery were also flowing in toward it from all sides. In spite of their drivers' efforts to guide them, they dashed down the steep rough bank into the mob of human beings, crushing all who were unable to get out of their way, then colliding with each other and killing everybody around them as they overturned.

All the time successive waves of human beings kept rolling in and piling up, to the accompaniment of shrieks of rage and pain. In the unspeakable chaos, men who had been thrown down and were being smothered attacked with nails and teeth the legs of their comrades who were trampling on them, only to be pitilessly kicked aside, as if they were enemies.

Among them wives and mothers called in heartrending tones for their husbands and children from whom they had got hopelessly separated. Holding out their arms toward them, they implored the crowd to let them get through; but they were swept back and forth by the surging tide of human beings, and were not even noticed when they went down. In the indescribable uproar made by the boom of cannon, the bursting of shells, the shriek of the wind, vociferations, groans, and awful curses this soulless mob could not hear the moans of their victims!

The more fortunate succeeded in reaching the bridge by walking over heaps of prostrate half-smothered wounded men and women and children. When they set foot on that frail passage they imagined they were saved; but they were still impeded at every step by fallen horses and broken or missing planks. Also, on the other side the bridge ended in a miry swamp in which countless horses and vehicles had got stuck, creating a fresh obstacle and checking their flight.

Then in the column of desperate men crowded together on this one narrow way of escape, a monstrous struggle took place, in which the weak and the ones nearest the edge were forced into the river by the strong; and the latter, without so much as turning their heads, carried away by the instinct of self-preservation, pressed savagely on, deaf to the cries of rage and despair of their companions or officers whom they were sacrificing to their own ends.

But on the other hand, how many acts of self-sacrifice did we note! Why must we lack time and space to describe them? There were soldiers, even officers, who hitched themselves to sleds and pulled their sick or wounded comrades away from the deadly riverbank. A little apart from the crowd a group of motionless soldiers watched over a dying officer who had been entrusted to their care. In vain he begged them to leave him and think of saving themselves; but they refused to do so, and rather than abandon their leader, waited for death or captivity. . . A frail little boat made of birch bark containing a mother and her two children sank among the ice floes. An artilleryman, fighting his own way across the bridge, saw it and, heedless of his own safety, plunged into the water and succeeded in saving one of the victims — the younger of the children. The poor little fellow began screaming for his mother, and the brave gunner was heard to say as he carried him along in his arms, "Don't cry: I didn't save you from drowning just to leave you on the riverbank. I'll see that you're taken care of. I'll be a father and family to you."

The night of the twenty-eighth of November added to our calamities. Darkness did not hide the victims from the Russian guns. On the contrary, the black mass of men, horses, and vehicles standing out clearly against the snow covering the riverbanks, and the noise rising from it only helped the enemy artillery to take better aim. Desolation reached its peak around nine o'clock when Victor began his retreat and his divisions opened a tragic path through the miserable hordes whom until then they had been defending. However, a rear guard having been left at Studzianka, the multitude, either because they were benumbed by the cold or would not leave their supplies, refused to take advantage of this last night to get across to the opposite side. The supply wagons and carriages were burnt in order to force their unfortunate owners to leave them, but to no avail. Dawn alone sent them all flowing back together toward the entrance to the bridge which they once more besieged. It was half past eight in the morning when Eblé, seeing the Russians approaching, finally set fire to it.

The disaster had reached its utmost limit. An immense quantity of wagons, three heavy guns, several thousand men, and some women and a few children were abandoned on the enemy's side of the river. We could see them wandering in desperate groups up and down the bank. Some plunged into the water and tried to swim; others trusted themselves to the drifting cakes of ice. Still others rushed straight into the flames on the bridge which crumbled under their feet. Burned and frozen at the same time, they died from two opposite forms of torture, and their bodies soon piled up with the ice and beat against the trestles of the bridge. The rest of the crowd just stood and waited for the Russians. About an hour after Eblé's crossing, Wittgenstein showed himself on the hills, and, without having won the battle, he garnered the spoils.

*

## Napoleon Decides to Return to Paris

While this catastrophe was being enacted the disorganized remains of the Grand Army on the opposite side of the river began to drift confusedly down the high road leading to Zembin. That region is one vast wooded plain on which the water, draining down from several different slopes, forms an interminable marsh. The army crossed this in wonder mingled with fright and the beginnings of joy at their escape, over three consecutive bridges, more than a third of a mile long.

These splendid bridges, built of pitch pine, which began several miles from the place of crossing, had been occupied by Tchaplitz for several days. A number of felled trees and piles of dry combustible brushwood placed before the entrances to the bridges told what he had intended to do. A spark from a Cossack's pipe was all that was needed to set fire to them. Had that happened, all our struggles and the crossing of the Berezina would have been to no avail. Trapped in a narrow space between the river and the swamp, without shelter, in a raging storm, the Grand Army and our Emperor would have been forced to surrender without a battle.

In this desperate situation, when all France seemed fated to be taken prisoner in Russia, with everything against us and in favor of the enemy, the latter did nothing but by halves. Kutuzov did not reach Kopis, on the Dnieper, until the day when Napoleon arrived at the Berezina; Wittgenstein let himself be kept in check as long as was required for the crossing; Tchitchakov was defeated; and Napoleon succeeded in saving sixty thousand of his eighty thousand men.

Until the last minute he had remained on the riverbank near the ruins of Brilowa, wholly without shelter, at the head of his Guard that had lost a third of its number in the catastrophe. During the day they took up their arms and stood in battle array; at night they camped around their sovereign with the old grenadiers keeping the fires burning. They sat on their knapsacks, their elbows on their knees and their heads in their hands, sleeping all doubled up in order that their limbs might keep each other warm, and that they might feel the emptiness of their stomachs less keenly.

During those three days and nights Napoleon's attention wandered unceasingly from one to another of the three battle fronts. He encouraged the 2nd Corps with his orders and his presence, protected the 9th and the crossing with his artillery, and seconded Eblé in his attempt to save as much debris as possible from the shipwreck. Then he personally led what was left of the army toward Zembin, where Prince Eugène had preceded him.

We marveled to see the Emperor ordering the marshals whose troops were nonexistent to take such or such a position on the road, as if they were still in command of armies. One of them pointed this out to him with some bitterness

and began to enumerate his losses. But Napoleon, determined to refuse to listen to all reports, lest they should de-
generate into complaints, interrupted him angrily with the
words, "Why do you want to destroy my peace of mind?" As
the marshal persisted, he silenced him by repeating the question, this time in a reproachful tone, "I asked you, sir, why
you wanted to destroy my peace of mind?" These words
spoken in the depth of his misery gave an idea of the attitude
he imposed on himself and expected of others. During those
mortal days the spot of every one of his bivouacs was marked
by heaps of corpses.

Gathered around him were men of all conditions, ranks,
and ages — ministers, generals, administrators. Particularly
conspicuous among them was an elderly nobleman, a remnant
of those bygone days when grace and charm and brilliance
had reigned supreme. As soon as it was daylight this sixty-
year-old general * could be seen sitting on a snow-covered
log performing his morning toilet with imperturbable gaiety.
In the midst of the tempest he would adjust his well-curled
and powdered wig, scoffing at disaster and the unleashed
elements that were buffeting him.

Near this gentleman, officers of the technical corps engaged in endless dissertations. Ours being a century in
which, because of a few discoveries, we are emboldened to
think we can explain everything, these men sought a reason
for the constant direction of the north wind as it inflicted
the sharpest pain on them. Others would be attentively
studying the regular hexagonal crystals of the snowflakes
covering their clothing. The phenomenon of the *parhelia,* or
appearance of several simultaneous images of the sun, due to
the presence of ice crystals in the air, was also the subject of

* Probably Count Louis de Narbonne-Lara (1755–1813), Minister of War
in 1791. — J.D.T.

frequent conversations, all of which served to distract the officers from their suffering.

It was on the twenty-ninth of November that Napoleon left the banks of the Berezina, pushing on before him a mob of disbanded men, and marching with the 9th Corps, itself completely disorganized. The 2nd and 9th and Dombrowski's division had still numbered fourteen thousand soldiers the day before. With the exception of possibly six thousand other armed men, the rest of the Grand Army had nothing in the shape of divisions, brigades, or regiments; we were still sixty thousand strong but wholly without organization. We marched in confusion, cavalry, infantry, artillery, French, Germans — all mixed up, without either flank or center. The artillery and baggage trains rolled along with the formless mass, never having received any other instruction than to advance as far as possible.

The road wound uphill and down dale, sometimes so narrow in the defiles that the men were crushed against each other, then crossing plains on which the crowd dispersed in the hope of finding shelter and a little food. In this way Napoleon came to Kamen, where he slept along with the prisoners taken the day before, who were parked in the open. Those poor wretches, reduced to devouring their own dead, almost all perished of hunger and cold.

On the morning of the third of December Napoleon reached Molodeczno, the last spot where Tchitchakov could have cut him off. We found some food there, and abundant forage: the day was fair, the sun shone brightly, and the cold was bearable. Also, several couriers, the first we had seen in a long time, arrived together. The Poles were immediately ordered to Warsaw by the way of Olita, and the dismounted cavalry by the way of Mercez, on the Niemen.

The rest of the troops were to follow the high road which we had rejoined at Molodeczno.

Until then, as far as anyone knew, Napoleon had not conceived the idea of leaving his army. But in the middle of the day he announced point-blank to Daru and Duroc that he intended to set out at once for France. Daru saw no necessity for it. "Our lines of communication are re-opened," he said, "and the most serious dangers behind us. All along the way now we shall be meeting the reinforcements that are being sent from Paris and Germany."

To this the Emperor replied, "I no longer feel strong enough to leave all Prussia between myself and France. And why should I remain at the head of a retreat? Murat and Eugène are well able to lead it, and Ney to protect it. It is absolutely necessary that I return to France, to reassure and arm the people, and to insure the allegiance of all the Germans. Then, I shall come back with fresh adequate troops to save what is left of the Grand Army . . . But to reach Paris I shall have to cross a thousand miles of allied territory alone. In order that this may be accomplished without danger, my intention must be kept secret: no one must know the road I am to take, and the disastrous news of our retreat must not be made public. I must ride ahead of that news, because of the effect it would have and the general defection which would result, were it known. Therefore, there is not a minute to lose; the time for my departure has come."

His only hesitation was over the choice of a commander for the army: he wavered between Murat and Eugène. While he admired the wisdom and devotion of the latter, he knew Murat to be more brilliant, more dynamic; and in our present situation the leader must be able to overawe. Eugène would remain with the King: his age and inferior rank would be security for his submission, and his character, for his zeal. He would set a good example for the other marshals.

Moreover, Berthier, through whom all imperial orders and rewards were habitually channeled, would also stay with them. Thus nothing in the form or organization of the army would be changed. This arrangement, while promising his speedy return, would hold his most impatient generals faithful to their duty and keep his most determined enemies in a state of wholesome fear. Such were Napoleon's designs. Caulaincourt at once received the order to prepare secretly for his departure. The place chosen for it was Smorgony; the time, the night of the fifth of December.

Although Daru was not to accompany the Emperor, and was to be burdened with the full responsibility of administrating the army, he listened in silence, finding no reasonable objection to such impelling motives; but it was not the same with Berthier. This elderly general, now greatly enfeebled, who had not left Napoleon's side for sixteen years, was shocked at the idea of this separation, and there resulted a violent scene between the two. The Emperor was indignant at his resistance. In his anger he cast in Berthier's teeth the favors he had heaped upon him. The army, according to him, stood in need of the reputation which he had made for him — which, of course, was only a reflection of his own.

"I will give you twenty-four hours in which to make up your mind, sir," he cried, "after which, if you still persist in your folly, you may retire to your estate — and stay there, for I shall forbid you ever to return to Paris or enter my presence!" . . . The next day, the fourth of December, Berthier, excusing himself for his opposition on the grounds of his age and impaired health, sorrowfully submitted to his sovereign's wishes.

The very day that Napoleon decided on his departure, the terrible cold returned, as if the Russian weather, seeing him about to make his escape, had increased in severity to strike him down and destroy all the rest of us. The thermometer stood at ten below zero when we reached Bienitza, on the fourth of December.

Napoleon left Count Lobau and several hundred of the Old Guard behind at Molodeczno. It was here that the road from Zembin crossed the main road from Minsk to Vilna, and it was important that we should hold that junction until the arrival of Victor, who would then take command until Ney finally came up; for it was to this marshal and the 2nd Corps under General de Maison that the rear guard had again been entrusted.

When Napoleon reached Smorgony he found himself in the midst of crowds of dying men. Though filled with sorrow at the sight of their distress, he gave no sign of his feeling; nor did they let him hear a word of complaint. Such a thing as a mutiny was out of the question at that time. That would have required an additional effort, and everybody's strength was used up in combating hunger, cold, and fatigue. The men found it easier to plod along in complete silence, employing all their resources against an inimical nature, than to wear themselves out in provocations or complaints. Their simple physical needs absorbed all their moral strength. They lived like automatons on impressions received in better days — many of them on a certain conception of honor and glory, the result of twenty years of victories, the warmth of which still survived and struggled within them.

Besides, the authority of their generals was still absolute, still respected, because it had always been paternal, because all dangers, triumphs, and suffering had been shared. We were just one unhappy family, whose leader, perhaps, was most to be pitied. The Emperor and the Grand Army, therefore, preserved toward each other a melancholy, dignified silence, both parties being too proud to complain and too experienced not to feel the uselessness of complaint.

Napoleon made haste to set up his last headquarters, where he completed his final instructions and his twenty-ninth bulletin in which he reported the condition of his spent and frozen army. The greatest precautions were taken to prevent any of his plans from getting beyond the four walls of his apartments until the next day. Nevertheless, a presentiment of some supreme misfortune possessed the officers, all of whom would have liked to accompany him. They were hungry for a sight of France and yearned to be with their families again, and to escape from that atrocious climate. But, being governed by duty and honor, they did not dare to express that wish.

While they were all making a brave pretense at resting, night fell, and the time had come for Napoleon to make his plan known to the commanding officers of the army. He summoned all the marshals, and as they entered spoke to each one privately, winning them over to his project by opening his heart to them. As soon as Davout appeared, for instance, he advanced to welcome him, asking why he had seen him so rarely of late, and if he had deserted him. When Davout answered that he feared he had displeased him in some way, the Emperor quietly explained the reasons for his behavior, received his replies graciously, and went so far as to tell him the route he had planned to take, and to listen to his advice.

He was affectionate with them all. Having seated them around his table, he praised them warmly for their splendid conduct during the campaign. He acknowledged his own temerity in a single sentence: "If I had been born on the throne, if I were a Bourbon, it would have been easy for me not to make any mistakes!"

After the meal he had Eugène read Bulletin 29. Then he

told them all together what he had already imparted to each one privately: "This very night I am leaving for Paris, accompanied by Duroc, Caulaincourt, and Lobau. My presence in that city is absolutely indispensable for the good of France and the remnant of my poor army. There, and there only, can I hope to maintain the Austrians and Prussians in a state of submission. These nations will certainly think twice before they make war on me, when they see me at the head of the French nation and an army of twelve hundred thousand men." He went on: "I am sending Ney ahead to reorganize everything in Vilna. Rapp will help him, then will move on to Danzig. Lauriston will proceed to Warsaw; Narbonne to Berlin; my personal staff will remain with the army. You may expect action at Vilna where you will have to check the enemy. You will find Loison and De Wrede there with reinforcements, supplies, and all sorts of ammunition. You will make your winter quarters behind the Niemen. I sincerely hope the Russians will not cross the Vistula before I return . . . I leave the King of Naples in command of the army. I trust you will obey him, as you have obeyed me, and that perfect harmony will reign among you."

By now it was ten o'clock. The Emperor rose, pressed their hands affectionately, embraced them, and withdrew. . . . Outside he found a crowd of officers drawn up on either side of his path. His farewell to them was expressed by a sad forced smile, while their wishes for his success were confined to respectful gestures. He and Caulaincourt entered a closed carriage, with his mameluke * and Captain Wonsowitch of the Guard on the box. Duroc and Lobau followed in a sleigh.

---

*Mameluke: faithful manservant that Napoleon brought back from Egypt with him. — J.D.T.

# CHAPTER X

********

## *The Army without Napoleon: From Smorgony to Vilna*

COMRADES, I confess that at this point my mind, disheartened, refused to go on with the recollection of so many horrors. Having got as far as Napoleon's departure, I was convinced that my task was finished. I had set myself up for the historian of that great epoch in which, from the zenith of glory, we were hurled down into the pit of deepest misfortune; but now that there is nothing left for me to relate but frightful sufferings, why should we not both be spared — you the pangs of reading them, and myself the painful strain on my memory which has nothing but ashes to stir up, nothing but disaster to recount, and nothing but gravestones to write on?

Yet, as it was our fate to carry misery as well as happiness to the very limit of likelihood, I will try to keep the promise I made you. Since the history of great men gives an account of their last moments, what right have I to suppress the dying gasp of the Grand Army? Everything about it belongs to posterity, these last terrible groans as well as the shouts of victory. Everything about it was great, and it is our lot to astound the centuries with its splendor and its grief. Poor consolation, but all that is left us; for, never doubt it, comrades, the noise of such a fall will echo down the ages in which great misfortunes bring immortality as surely as great glories.

The Poles escorted Napoleon for the first few miles. Then it was the turn of the Neapolitans of the Royal Guard. There were six hundred men in this corps when they came out from Vilna to meet the Emperor; they perished to the last man at the hands of winter in the short distance between Smorgony and the Lithuanian capital. During the first night of the journey the Russians seized Youpranoui (some say it was Osmiana), a town through which the Emperor's escort had to pass, though they abandoned it immediately. If Napoleon had reached there one hour earlier, he would have fallen into the midst of that skirmish.

He met the Duke of Bassano * at Miedniki. The Emperor's first words to him were, "I have no army any more! For many days I have been marching in the midst of a mob of disbanded, disorganized men, who wander all over the countryside in search of food. We could still rally them by giving them bread, shoes, uniforms, and arms; but my administrative personnel has not provided against anything of the sort, and my own orders have never been executed."

Maret replied by giving him a report on the quantity of supplies in the great Vilna depots. "You restore life in me!" the Emperor exclaimed. "I shall count on you to convey to Murat and Berthier the order to stay in that capital a full week, long enough to rally the army, and give it sufficient courage and strength to continue the retreat in a little less deplorable condition."

The rest of Napoleon's journey was effected without difficulty. He passed around Vilna through the suburbs, halted

* Hugues-Bernard Maret, Duke of Bassano, Minister of Foreign Affairs under Napoleon. — J.D.T.

at Wilkowiski to exchange his carriage for a sleigh, stopped at Warsaw on the tenth to demand of the Poles a levy of ten thousand Cossacks, in return for which he granted them certain subsidies and promised that he would soon be back at the head of three hundred thousand men. He crossed Silesia at top speed, visited the Saxon king at Dresden, then halted at Hanau and Mainz. On the nineteenth he made his sudden appearance in Paris, two days after the publication of his twenty-ninth bulletin.

From Malo-Yaroslavetz to Smorgony, the master of all Europe had been just the general of a dying, disorganized army: from Smorgony to the Rhine, he was an unrecognized fugitive in a hostile land: beyond the Rhine he became once more the conquerer of Europe, and one last breath of prosperity puffed out his drooping sails.

The generals left behind at Smorgony approved of his departure, and, far from letting it discourage them, they pinned their hopes on it. In their thinking, the army had only to continue the retreat, the way was open, the Russian frontier not too far distant. They would soon get reinforcements in the form of eighteen thousand fresh troops, and were nearing a large city containing immense stores. Murat and Berthier, left to their own devices, believed themselves capable of directing the retreat . . . But in that condition of supreme disorder only a Colossus could have served as a rallying point, and *he* had disappeared! In the empty space left by his going, Murat was hardly visible.

We realized then — and only too well — that a great man cannot be replaced; either because his subordinates' pride forbids them to obey another, or because, having habitually thought of everything, foreseen and ordered everything himself, he has formed only able lieutenants, but no leaders.

On the very first night one general refused to obey. The

marshal commanding the rear guard reached the royal headquarters practically alone. Three thousand men of the
Young and Old Guards were still in fighting condition; but
that was the entire Grand Army. Of the once gigantic body,
only the head remained. When the news of Napoleon's departure spread among them, even those veteran warriors
were unsettled, and soon fell into disorder. Accustomed to
being directly commanded by the conqueror of Europe, they
scorned to serve another.

The majority of the colonels whose conduct until then had
been praiseworthy, still marching with four or five officers
and soldiers round their standards, in their proper places, refused to obey anyone but themselves. Each one believed
himself responsible for his own safety, and looked to himself alone for preservation. There were men among them
who marched five hundred miles without turning their
heads. From now on it was *every man for himself.*

It must be said, though, that the disappearance of the Emperor and Murat's inadequacy were not the only causes of
this dispersion: the violence of winter which at that moment became extreme, was largely responsible for it. The
great cold made everything worse; it seemed to have vowed
that the army should not reach Vilna.

Up to Molodeczno where we halted on the fourth of
December and where the hand of winter fell heavily on us
again, we had been leaving fewer corpses strewn along our
path, though the going was still rough. This respite was
owing to a rise in temperature, to a few supplies provided by
this less devastated region, to the vigor of Ney and De
Maison in holding the enemy in check, and, possibly, to the
fact that only the strongest men had survived the Berezina.

The puny organization which had been established within
our disorder had been maintained. The mass of fugitives

toiled ahead in a multitude of small groups of eight or ten men apiece. Some of these bands still had horses, either to carry their food, or to be used as food themselves. A few rags, some utensils, a pack, and a stick formed the gear of those poor wretches — all their arms and armor. Of the soldier there was nothing left, neither weapon nor uniform, nor the will to resist any other foe than hunger and winter. But there still remained in them some degree of resolution, a familiarity with danger and suffering, and an alert, resourceful nature which enabled them to make the most of the situation. Also, among the soldiers still carrying arms, the dread of a certain nickname with which they themselves ridiculed their disorderly comrades had some restraining influence.

But after Molodeczno and the departure of Napoleon, winter shut down with utmost severity. As it attacked us, all the associations against misery broke down, and there remained only a multitude of isolated individual struggles. The best of the men lost all self-respect: they stopped at nothing. Conventions no longer restrained them. Their misery was without hope of relief, even without regret. Discouragement had neither judge nor witness; all were victims.

From now on there existed no fraternity of arms, no society, no human ties. An excess of hardship had made brutes of our men, and hunger, ravenous, devouring hunger, had killed everything in those unfortunate beings but the instinct of self-preservation, sole driving force of the fiercest animals, to which everything else is sacrificed. A harsh, violent, merciless nature seemed to have communicated her fury to them. Like true savages, the strong despoiled the weak: they crowded around the dying, often not waiting to rob them until they had breathed their last. When a horse fell, you would have thought you were witnessing the fatal moment of a hunt, as the men swarmed upon the animal and tore it into scraps, over which they fought like famished hounds!

However, the majority did still have enough moral strength left to enable them to seek their own safety without harming anyone else; but that was the extreme effort of their humanity. If an officer or comrade fell by their side or under the wheels of the cannon, he called in vain for help; in vain he invoked the name of a common religion, country, or cause. No one so much as looked at him. All the icy inflexibility of the climate seemed to have entered their hearts; its rigidity had frozen their feelings as well as their faces. All, with the exception of a few high officers, were completely absorbed in their own suffering, and terror left no room for pity.

Selfishness which is generally attributed to an excess of prosperity was produced here by an excess of misery — much more excusable in the latter case. The former is voluntary; the latter, almost forced: the former is a crime of the heart; the latter, an impulsion of the instinct, purely physical. Certainly it was a matter of life or death to stop for a single minute. In this universal desolation the stretching out of a hand to a dying comrade or leader was an admirable act of generosity. The slightest humane gesture became a sublime action.

Fortunately there were those among us who stood firm against heaven and earth, and continued to protect and comfort the weak; but such were very rare.

On the sixth of December, the day following the departure of the Emperor, the sky became still more terrible. The air was filled with infinitesimal ice crystals; birds fell to the earth frozen stiff. The atmosphere was absolutely still. It seemed as if everything in nature having movement or life, down to the very wind, had been bound and congealed in a universal death. Now not a word, not a murmur broke the dismal silence, silence of despair and unshed tears.

We drifted along in this empire of death like accursed phantoms. Only the monotonous beat of our steps, the crunch of the snow, and the feeble groans of the dying broke the vast mournful stillness. Among us was heard neither raging nor cursing, nothing that would imply a trace of warmth: we had hardly enough strength left to pray. Most of the men fell without a word of complaint, silent either from weakness or resignation; or perhaps because men only complain when they have hopes of moving someone to pity.

The soldiers who had been most resolute until then lost heart completely. At times the snow opened up under their feet. Even where it was solid, its ice-coated surface gave them no support, and they slipped and fell, and got up to fall again. It was as if this hostile earth refused to carry them any longer, laid snares for them in order to hamper them and retard their flight, and so deliver them up to the Russians, who were still on their trail, or to their terrible climate.

When exhaustion compelled them to halt a moment, the icy hand of winter fell heavily on its prey. In vain the miserable victims, feeling themselves grow numb, staggered to their feet, already without voice or feeling, and took a few steps, like automatons. Their blood was freezing in their veins, like water in a brook, and slowing up their hearts. Then it rushed to their heads, and the dying men reeled along as if they were drunk. Actual tears of blood oozed from their eyes, horribly inflamed and festered by loss of sleep and the smoke of campfires. Their chests were racked by deep sighs. They stared at the sky, at us, at the earth with a wild, frightened look in their eyes; this was their farewell to a merciless nature that was torturing them, perhaps also a reproach. Before long they fell to their knees, then forward on their hands. Their heads wagged stupidly from side to side for a little while, and a gasping rattle issued from their lips. Then they collapsed in the snow, on which appeared the slow-spreading stain of blackish blood — and their suffering was at an end.

Their comrades passed them without taking a single step out of their way, lest they should lengthen their journey by a few feet — without so much as turning their heads, for their beards and hair were bristling with icicles, and the least movement was painful. They did not even feel pity for those who fell; for what had they lost by dying? What were they leaving? We were suffering so much! We were so far from France, so out of our element in this bleak land, that tender memories were snapped and hope all but wiped out. The majority had grown indifferent to death, by necessity, from having looked on it so often, everywhere — even treating it contemptuously at times. Generally we just thought, when we saw those poor fellows lying stiff in the snow, that they had no more needs, that they were resting and not suffering any longer. The quiet, normal, customary sort of death is usually looked upon as an extraordinary event, a frightening contrast, and a terrible revolution; but in this confusion, in the violent and continuous movement of a life filled with action, danger, and pain, it seemed a mere transition, a slight alteration, one more change of place, and it no longer shocked us.

Such were the last days of the Grand Army: its last nights were still more frightful. The groups of soldiers, overtaken by darkness far from any human habitation, halted at the edge of the forest. There, they lit their fires around which all night long they sat, stiff and motionless as ghosts. They could not get enough of this heat. They drew so close to it that their clothing took fire, as well as their frozen extremities, which the flames scorched. Soon the dreadful pain forced them to lie down — a fatal move — and the next morning they tried in vain to get up again.

Meanwhile those whom winter had left nearly intact, who still preserved a remnant of courage, were preparing their sorry evening meal. This was composed, as it had been since Smolensk, of some slices of broiled horsemeat, and rye meal made into gruel with snow water or rolled into pancakes which the men, having no salt, seasoned with powder from their cartridges.

All night long the light of these fires attracted other specters whom the first comers did not allow to approach. These miserable creatures wandered from one fire to another until, overcome by cold and despair, they gave up altogether and lay down in the snow behind the circle of their more fortunate companions, and breathed their last. Some of the men, without tools or strength to cut down the tall firs of the forest, tried in vain to set fire to their trunks. Death caught them in all sorts of attitudes around those trees.

Even greater horrors were seen in the spacious barns and sheds dotted here and there along the way. Soldiers and officers alike poured into them until they were filled to bursting. There, like so many cattle, they crowded together around two or three fires. The living, unable to drag the dead away from the circle, lay down on them and died in their turn, and served as deathbeds for still other victims.

Bands of stragglers kept arriving; and when they could not enter those sanctuaries of suffering, they besieged them. Generally they were satisfied to crouch out of the wind in the shelter of the buildings, but sometimes they tore off the dry wooden siding to keep their fires burning. Soon the flames

spread to the structures themselves, and the soldiers confined within them, half dead with the cold, were finished off
by the fire. The next day those of us who had been saved
by these shelters found our frozen comrades piled in heaps
around their cold hearths. To get out of those charnel
houses one literally had to climb over heaps of human
bodies, some of them still breathing.

At Youpranoui — that same town where the partisan
leader Seslawin had missed the Emperor by an hour — our
soldiers burned whole houses as they stood to get a few
minutes' warmth. The light of these conflagrations attracted
some poor wretches whom the intensity of the cold and
suffering had made delirious. They dashed forward in a
fury, and with gnashing teeth and demoniacal laughter,
threw themselves into those raging furnaces, where they
perished in dreadful convulsions. Their starving companions watched them die without apparent horror. There were
even some who laid hold of bodies disfigured and roasted by
the flames, and — incredible as it may seem — ventured to
carry this loathsome food to their mouths!

And this was the army that had issued from the most
civilized nation in Europe, that army once so brilliant, victorious over men up to the last moment, and whose name
still inspired respect in so many conquered capitals! Its most
glorious warriors, those who had borne themselves so hero-
ically on the world's great battlefields, had now lost all their
noble bearing. Covered with rags, their feet naked and torn,
they staggered along, supporting themselves on branches cut
from fir trees; and all the strength and perseverance they had
once put to the service of victory, they now employed in running away.

The army was in this utmost state of physical and moral
distress when the first fugitives reached Vilna. Vilna! their

storehouse, their base of supplies, the first rich inhabited city they had found since entering Russia. Its mere name and its nearness had kept a spark of hope glowing in their hearts.

On the ninth of December the majority of the stricken army at length caught sight of the capital. Thereupon, some crawling, some running, they poured headlong into the suburbs, crowding in and piling up with such obstinacy that within a short time they formed a hopeless jam of men, horses, and vehicles.

The disgorging of this multitude by one narrow passage became impossible. Those in the rear, guided by stupid instinct, increased the obstruction, without ever thinking of entering the city by its other approaches of which there were several. Everything was so disorganized that all that cruel day not one staff-officer appeared to regulate the ceaseless flow.

For ten long hours, with the thermometer at sixteen or seventeen below zero,* thousands of soldiers who fancied they had finally reached safety fell dead, either frozen or smothered in the crowd, as had happened at the gates of Smolensk and before the bridge over the Berezina. Sixty thousand men had crossed that river, and twenty thousand recruits had since joined them. Of those eighty thousand men, fully a half had perished — and the majority in the last four days, between Malodeczno and Vilna!

The capital of Lithuania was still totally ignorant of our disasters, when suddenly these forty thousand starving men filled its streets with groans and lamentations. At this unexpected sight the inhabitants became alarmed and closed their doors. It was a terrible thing to see those miserable hordes wandering about the town, some furious, others

* —27° or —28° Centigrade. — J.D.T.

apathetic, threatening or begging, trying to break down the doors of houses or the magazines, or dragging themselves toward the hospitals; but everywhere they were repulsed.

At the commissary depots they were checked by ridiculous formalities; for, the regiments being dissolved and the soldiers hopelessly scattered, no regular distribution of any sort was possible. These storehouses contained enough flour and bread for forty days, and meat for thirty-six days, for a hundred thousand men. But no leader dared to give the order to distribute these supplies to those who came to claim them. The administrators who had charge of them were afraid to take the responsibility; others feared the excesses to which starving troops give themselves up when everything is theirs for the taking. These administrators, it must be said, were not aware of the desperate situation of the army; and for several hours they let our unfortunate companions die of hunger in sight of those great heaps of provisions, which the enemy was to seize on the morrow.

At the barracks and hospitals also they were turned away, though not by the living, for death reigned supreme there. A few of the doomed inmates were still breathing: they complained that for a long, long time they had been without beds, even without straw, and almost totally without attention. The yards, the corridors, and all the wards, filled with piles of corpses, were nothing more than charnel houses.

At last, however, a few doors were opened to the fugitives, thanks to the efforts of some of the high officers, Eugène and Davout among others, the pity of the Lithuanians, and the avarice of the Jews. Then it was a touching thing to witness the wonder of those poor fellows on finding themselves once again in an occupied house. A loaf of leavened bread seemed to them the most delicious of foods; and what unutterable pleasure did they take in eating it seated at a table! Then,

they were filled with admiration at the sight of a small battalion of soldiers carrying arms, marching in order, and wearing uniforms. They seemed to have returned from the ends
of the earth, so thoroughly had the violence and endless
succession of hardships alienated them from their old ways
of living, so terribly deep was the abyss from which they were
emerging.

But they had no more than begun to enjoy the sweetness of
this truce when Russian cannon were thundering anew over
them and the city. Then the threatening explosions, the
shouts of the officers, the drums calling the soldiers to arms,
the clamor of the crowds of fugitives who kept pouring in,
filled Vilna with fresh confusion. The advance guard of
Kutuzov and Tchaplitz commanded by Orurk, Landskoy,
and Seslawin, was attacking Loison's division that had been
given the double duty of defending the city and holding in
check a column of unhorsed cavalry.

*

## From Vilna to Kovno

At first some attempt at resistance was made. De Wrede and
his Bavarians had just rejoined the army. But close behind
them came Wittgenstein who had been marching on our
right flank at about the same speed as Kutuzov and Tchitchakov, directly behind us. De Wrede had only two thousand
men left; and Loison's division, together with the garrison
from Vilna that had come out as far as Smorgony to meet us,
three days before, had been reduced by the cold from fifteen thousand to three thousand men.

De Wrede defended Vilna on the side toward Rukoni, but
was forced to yield after a noble effort. Loison's division,

nearer the city, held the enemy in check for a while. We had succeeded in arming a reluctant division of Neapolitans, and had even got them out of the city. But the muskets slipped from the numb hands of those men transplanted from a sunny land to this region of snow and ice. In less than an hour they returned without weapons, the majority of them disabled.

In the meantime drums were vainly beating a general call to arms through the streets. The Old Guard itself, now reduced to a few platoons, was hopelessly dispersed. These men now thought more of defending their lives against starvation and cold than against human enemies. Then the cry, *The Cossacks are coming!* was heard. For a long time this had been the only signal which most of the men would obey. It spread quickly through the city — and the dread flight was on again.

This was the fault of De Wrede who had rushed into the presence of Murat with the news: "The Russians are at our heels! The Bavarians have been forced back into the city, and are no longer able to defend it!" At the same moment the uproar in the street reached the King's ears, and he lost his head. Believing himself no longer master of the army, he ceased to be master of himself. He was seen leaving the palace afoot and forcing his way through the crowd. He probably feared there would be bloody skirmishes in the streets, packed to suffocation, as he had seen them the day before. He stopped, however, at the last house in the suburbs where he issued his orders and waited for dawn and the army, leaving all other cares to Ney.

If we had been able to hold out twenty-four hours longer in Vilna, many lives would have been saved. That deadly city cost us nearly twenty thousand men, including three hundred officers and seven generals. The majority were stricken by winter rather than by the Russians, though the latter reaped the benefits. Others, physically sound in appearance, were at the end of their moral resistance. After having had the courage to overcome so many hardships, they lost heart in sight of port, only four days' march away. They had reached a civilized city at last, and rather than set forth into the wilderness again, they chose to stay and trust to Fortune. In their case she was cruel!

On the tenth of December, Ney, who had voluntarily taken command of the rear guard, left the city, and immediately Platov's Cossacks overran it, massacring the unfortunate wretches whom the Jews, fearing reprisals, threw into the streets as they passed by. In the midst of this butchery a picket of Frenchmen appeared on the scene, coming from the bridge over the Viliya where they had been overlooked. At the sight of this fresh prey thousands of Russian cavalrymen galloped up, surrounded the little band with savage cries, and attacked them from all sides.

But the French officer had drawn up his men in a circle. Without a second's hesitation he gave the order to fire; then they charged with leveled bayonets. In a wink they had routed the aggressors and were masters of the city. Not stopping to wonder at the cowardice of the Cossacks, taking advantage of the momentary lull, they turned sharply around and succeeded in joining the rear guard without having lost a man.

This part of our army had come to grips with Kutuzov's advance guard and was attempting to stop them; for a fresh calamity which they were trying in vain to conceal, had kept them near the city.

At Vilna, as in Moscow, Napoleon had not had any official order given for retreat. He wanted our rout to be unan-

nounced, wanted it to make itself known, to take our allies
and their monarchs by surprise, so that we might avail ourselves of their confusion and get safely through their territory before the people were disposed to join with the Russians to overpower us.

That is why everybody in Vilna — Lithuanians, foreigners, the prime minister himself — had been deceived. They
did not believe in our defeat till they saw it, and the almost
superstitious faith of Europe in the infallibility of Napoleon's genius gave him an advantage over his enemies. But
this same confidence had lulled his friends with false security, for in Vilna, as in Moscow, none of them had made
preparations for any action whatever.

This city contained a great part of the equipment and the
treasury of the army, its supplies, a number of immense covered wagons with the Emperor's possessions, much artillery,
and a great many wounded men. Our sudden appearance
had fallen like a thunderbolt on those in charge of all this.
Some were galvanized into action by terror, others were
paralyzed by consternation. Out of it came orders and
counterorders of all sorts, and men, horses, and vehicles became tangled in an inextricable jam.

In the midst of this chaos several officers succeeded in
getting as much as could be set in motion, out of town and
on the road to Kovno. But when this bewildered, heavily
loaded column had gone about two miles they were stopped
by the hill and narrow pass of Ponari.

In our conquering march eastward this wooded knoll had
seemed to our hussars little more than a slight irregularity in
the earth's surface from the top of which the entire plain of
Vilna could be seen, and the strength of the enemy estimated.
In truth, its steep but short slope had hardly been noticed.
In a regular retreat it would have been an excellent position

for turning around and checking the enemy; but in a chaotic flight, where everything that could be of use became a hindrance, when in blind haste we turned everything against ourselves, this hill and defile were an unsurmountable obstacle, a wall of ice against which our best efforts were broken. It stripped us of everything — supplies, treasury, booty, and wounded men. This misfortune was serious enough to stand out above all our long succession of disasters; for it was here that the little money, honor, discipline, and strength remaining to us were irrevocably lost.

When, after fifteen hours of fruitless struggle, the drivers and soldiers forming the escort saw Murat and the column of fugitives go past them on the hillside; when they saw Ney himself withdrawing with the three thousand men remaining to De Wrede and Loison; when they turned around and saw the hill behind them littered with wagons and guns shattered and overturned, men and horses on the ground, dying on top of each other — then they no longer thought of saving anything, but only of forestalling the avidity of the foe by pillaging themselves.

The bursting of a wagon carrying loot from Moscow acted as a signal. Everybody fell upon the other wagons, broke them open, and seized the most valuable objects. The soldiers of the rear guard coming upon this confusion, threw down their arms and loaded themselves with the plunder. So furiously intent were they on this that they failed to heed the whistling bullets or the shrieks of the Cossacks who were pursuing them. It is said that the Cossacks mingled with them without being noticed. For a few minutes Europeans and Tartars, friends and foes, were united in a common lust for gain. Frenchmen and Russians were seen side by side, all war forgotten, plundering the same wagon. Ten million francs in gold and silver rapidly disappeared!

But along with these horrors, acts of noble devotion were noticed. There were men that day who forsook everything to carry off the wounded on their backs; others, unable to get their half-frozen companions out of the struggle, perished in defending them from the brutality of their fellow soldiers and the blows of the enemy.

On the most exposed spot of the hill a colonel of the Emperor's staff, Count de Turenne, held the Cossacks at bay, disregarding their wild shouts and their shots, while he distributed Napoleon's personal treasury among the guards who stood within sight and hearing. These brave men, fighting with one hand and holding the riches of their leader in the other, succeeded in saving all of it. Long afterward, when we were out of danger, each one returned the amount that had been entrusted to him: not a single gold coin was lost.

The catastrophe at Ponari was all the more shameful as it could have been easily foreseen, and even more easily avoided; for it was possible to pass around the hill on either side. Our debris served at least one purpose — to stop the Cossacks. While they were collecting this booty Ney at the head of several hundred Bavarians and French defended the retreat as far as Evé. Since this was the last effort he was to make, it would be well to outline Ney's method of retreat, the one he had observed since leaving Viazma on the third of November, that is, for thirty-seven days and nights.

Every day at five o'clock in the afternoon he halted and held the Russians at bay while his soldiers ate and rested, then set off again at ten. All night long he urged on the horde of laggards by dint of threats, supplications, or blows. At daybreak, about seven o'clock, he halted again, took up a position, and rested under arms and on guard till ten. Then generally the Russians would come in sight again, and we had to keep up a constant flight until nightfall, gaining as much ground as possible in a backward direction. At first this was in pursuance of definite marching orders, but later according to circumstances. The rear guard had been progressively reduced from two thousand men to one thousand, then to five hundred, and finally to sixty! Yet Berthier, either through design or habit, had not altered his procedure. It was still to a corps of thirty-five thousand soldiers that he addressed himself, imperturbably giving detailed instructions concerning all the different positions which nonexistent regiments or divisions were to take or hold till the next day; and every night when, on Ney's insistence, he had to wake up the King (Murat) to force him to get under way again, he always showed the same astonishment.

In this manner Ney directed the retreat from Viazma up to a spot several miles beyond Evé. There, as was his habit, the marshal had stopped the Russians and was giving his men their evening rest, when at about ten o'clock he and De Wrede suddenly realized that they were absolutely alone. Their soldiers had abandoned them, leaving their weapons in shining stacks around the forsaken fires. Fortunately, the extreme cold, while it put a finishing touch to the discouragement of our own army, had also benumbed the enemy. Ney had considerable trouble overtaking his column. Then all he found was a disorganized band of fugitives, running away from a handful of Cossacks who were making no effort to capture them or kill them — either through pity (for one grows weary of everything), or because our abysmal suffering had terrified even the Russians, and they thought their vengeance was too great (for many had shown themselves generous). Or were they finally satiated with loot and tired of carrying it? or had they, despite the dark, simply noticed that they were dealing with unarmed men?

Winter, terrible ally of the Muscovites, had sold her favors dear. Russian disorder pursued our disorder! We came in contact with prisoners who had escaped from their hands several times over. These had for a while marched in the midst of their shuffling columns without being noticed. Some of them, availing themselves of favorable opportunities, had ventured to attack isolated Russian soldiers and seize their provisions, their weapons, and even their uniforms, which they had put on. Under this disguise they had mingled with their captors; and so complete was the disorganization, the stupid carelessness, and the torpor into which the Russian army had fallen that these prisoners had marched along with them for a whole month without being recognized.

Kutuzov's hundred thousand men had by now dwindled to thirty-five thousand. Of the fifty thousand soldiers commanded by Wittgenstein there remained barely fifteen thousand. Wilson affirmed that out of the ten thousand armed men who had marched from the interior to reinforce the Russian army, only seventeen hundred ever reached Vilna — despite all the precautions they knew how to take against winter. But the head of a column was enough to defeat our unarmed soldiers. Ney attempted in vain to muster a small force; and he who had until then, single-handed, maintained some sort of order in the rout was now swept along with it.

*

## From Kovno to Paris

On the thirteenth of December they reached Kovno, frontier city of the Russian Empire. After a final crucifying march of forty-six hours, they found themselves again on friendly soil. Immediately, without pausing, without casting a glance behind them, the majority of the men dispersed and plunged into the forests of Polish Russia. But some did turn around when they reached the other side of the river, and look back on the land of suffering from which they were escaping. It is said that when they found themselves on the very spot from which, five months before, their innumerable eagles had victoriously set out, tears ran down their cheeks and groans broke from their chests.

Here were the same valleys down which had poured those three long columns of dragoons and heavy cavalry, three streams of steel and brass, flashing in the hot sunlight. But now, men, weapons, eagles, horses, sunlight, even the frontier river they had crossed in such ardor and hope — everything had disappeared. The Niemen was just a long mass of blocks of ice piled up and welded together by the breath of winter. In place of the three French bridges brought fifteen hundred miles and erected with such daring speed, there was only one Russian bridge. Instead of the four hundred thousand companions who had fought so many successful battles with them, who had rushed so valiantly into Russia, they saw issuing from the white, ice-bound desert only one thousand foot soldiers and troopers still armed, nine cannon, and twenty thousand beings clothed in rags, with bowed heads, dull eyes, ashy, cadaverous faces, and long ice-stiffened beards. Some of them were fighting in silence for the right to cross the bridge which, despite their reduced number, was still too narrow to accommodate their precipitous flight. Others had rushed down the bank and were struggling across the river, crawling from one jagged cake of ice to another. And this was the Grand Army!

Two kings, one prince, eight marshals, followed by several generals afoot and unattended, then a few hundred of the

Old Guard still bearing arms, were all that remained of the original host. It might be said, though, that it lived on incarnate in the person of Marshal Ney. Friends, allies, enemies — I call on you to witness! Let us render the homage that is due to the memory of this unfortunate hero * . . . In Kovno he found a company of artillery, three hundred Germans belonging to the garrison, and General Marchand with four hundred armed men, of whom he took command. His first act was to scour the city looking for possible reinforcements. All he found were the wounded who were making a pitiful attempt to keep up with our wild flight. For the eighth time since leaving Moscow he had to abandon them in a body in the hospitals, as he had abandoned them individually along the road, on the battlefields, and around all the campfires.

Several thousand French soldiers were crowded together in the great square and the streets adjacent to it; but these were stretched out cold and stiff in front of the brandy shops which they had broken open, and in which they had imbibed death, instead of the life they had hoped to find. Here was the only relief that Murat had left him! So Ney found himself alone in Russia at the head of seven hundred foreign recruits. At Kovno, as at Vilna, the honor of our arms and the dangers of the last retreat were committed to his care, and he accepted them.

At dawn on the fourteenth of December the Russians attacked. While one of their columns blocked the road from Vilna, another crossed the Niemen on the ice at a spot above the city and set foot on Prussian soil. Proud to be the first

---

* Ney was sent to oppose the advance of Napoleon after his escape from Elba, but he deserted the Bourbons and joined up with his old commander. He was condemned to death for high treason and shot the next day. This incident was undoubtedly fresh in Ségur's memory when he was writing his history. — J.D.T.

to pass that frontier, they marched on the Kovno bridge in order to close this way of escape and completely cut off Ney's retreat.

Ney called upon his infantry; but only one of its weak battalions, the garrison of three hundred Germans, was armed. These he disposed, shouting words of encouragement, and was about to give the order to fire when a Russian cannon ball came crashing over the stockade and shattered the thigh of their commanding officer. This brave soldier fell to the ground and, knowing himself lost, coolly seized his pistol and blew his brains out, in full sight of his troops. At this stroke of misfortune the soldiers lost their heads, and threw down their arms and fled in terror.

Still Ney, deserted by everybody, surrendered neither his person nor his post. After a vain attempt to check the flight of the Germans, he gathered up their loaded muskets and faced the horde of Russians alone. His boldness halted them and shamed some of his own artillerymen who followed the example of their marshal. This gave his aide-de-camp and Gérard the time to assemble thirty soldiers and set up two light cannon, while Generals Ledru and Marchand rallied the one remaining battalion.

At that moment — it was half past two — the Russians made a second attack on the bridge. Ney sent Ledru and Marchand with their four hundred men to protect this way of escape, while he himself, giving no further thought to what lay behind him, with his thirty men held the gate opening on the Vilna road till nightfall. Then still fighting, withdrawing but not fleeing, marching with his men, he crossed Kovno and the Niemen. So, to the very last he upheld the honor of the army, and for the hundredth time in forty days and nights, bravely exposed himself to danger of death or imprisonment in order to save a few more of his countrymen. He was the last of the Grand Army to leave that deadly land, demonstrating to the world the powerlessness of fate against great hearts, and showing how everything, even the most dreadful disaster, turns to glory for the hero.

It was eight o'clock at night when he reached the friendly bank of the river. There, realizing that the catastrophe was complete, seeing Marchand driven back to the entrance of the bridge, and the Vilkowiski road which Murat had taken, blocked by the enemy's troops, he turned to the right, plunged into the wood, and disappeared.

When Murat reached Gumbinnen he was surprised to find Ney there before him, and to learn that the army had come all the way from Kovno without a rear guard. Fortunately for us, the Russian pursuit slowed up once they had won back their territory. They seemed to hesitate on the Prussian frontier, undecided as to whether they should enter as friends or enemies. Murat took advantage of their indecision to stop a few days in Gumbinnen, while he dispersed the other corps of his army through the several towns on the banks of the Vistula.

On the eve of the final dispersal of the Grand Army Murat assembled the general staff. I do not know what evil genius inspired that council. We should like to believe that it was shame, before the generals, for his precipitous flight, and spite against the Emperor who had saddled him with so great a responsibility; or humiliation at having to appear defeated in the midst of people who had been most oppressed by our successes. But as his words on that occasion were of a most troublemaking nature and were never contradicted by his actions, and as they were the first signs of his defection, they cannot be suppressed.

He, the great warrior, elevated to the throne by the sole

virtue of his victories, returning broken and beaten! A thousand times during this campaign he had exposed himself to the gravest dangers; but though, as a king, he had not feared to die like a soldier in the front line, he could not bear the thought of living without a crown. Standing before the generals over whom his brother-in-law had given him command, he denounced the ambition of the latter (which he had shared) to exonerate himself.

"It is no longer possible to serve a madman!" he cried. "There is no hope of success in his cause. In all Europe there is not one prince who still has faith in his treaties. I am sorry that I rejected the proposals of the English. If I had not done that, I should still be a great monarch, like the Emperor of Austria or the King of Prussia!"

He was interrupted by Davout. "The King of Prussia and the Emperor of Austria," he shouted brutally, "are princes by the grace of God, the age, and the acceptance of the people. But you — you are king only by the grace of Napoleon and your French blood! The only way you can keep your title is through Napoleon and by remaining faithful to France. Black ingratitude has made you blind. I swear I will denounce you to your Emperor!"

The other generals were silent. Within themselves they excused this outburst of suffering on the part of the King, and attributed his words — which Davout's hatred and suspicious nature understood only too well — to his habitual impetuosity. Murat, feeling himself guilty, was visibly embarrassed. So this first spark of treason, which later was to be the undoing of France, was quietly snuffed out. History records it with regret, as the repentance and suffering involved were equal to the crime.

We were soon forced to drag our abasement through Koenigsberg. The Grand Army that for twenty years had been marching triumphantly through the capitals of Europe was reappearing for the first time in full flight, mutilated, disarmed, in one of the cities it had most humiliated by its glory. The inhabitants ran out as we went by to count our wounds, to evaluate their hopes of liberation by the extent of our misfortune; and we had to satiate their greedy eyes with the sight of our misery, bear the insult of their hopes, parading our failure before their odious merrymaking and marching under the crushing weight of disaster . . . But the poor vestige of the Grand Army did not sink beneath the burden. This mere shadow managed somehow to make an imposing show, to preserve its air of sovereignty. Though defeated by the elements, we paraded before man our victorious dominating formation.

The Germans, inspired either by fear or sluggishness, received us submissively. Their hatred was confined to a show of cold indifference, and as they rarely act of themselves, they were obliged to minister to our distress while awaiting some signal. Then winter, that had followed us as far as Koenigsberg, suddenly deserted us, and in one night the thermometer went up * forty degrees!

This sudden change was fatal to us. A great many soldiers and officers, whom the tension of the atmosphere had kept going by a sort of continual irritation, gave up and went to pieces all at once. La Riboisière, general commanding the artillery, succumbed, as did Eblé, the glory of the entire army. Every day, every hour we were dismayed to hear of some fresh loss.

It was not till the twenty-second of January that the Russians reached the banks of the Vistula. During their slow advance, from the third to the eleventh of January, Murat

* *Descendit* (fell) in the text. This must be a typesetter's mistake. — J.D.T.

remained at Elbing. In this most critical situation the King wavered back and forth, at the mercy of the events which were brewing around him. At times they carried his hopes to the sky, at times they plunged him into an abyss of doubt.

He had fled from Koenigsberg in a state of complete discouragement, but the temporary halt of the Russian forces and the joining of MacDonald's * troops with his, suddenly filled him with groundless hope. The day before he had believed that everything was lost, now he wanted to take the offensive again; and he immediately set about making his plans. His was one of those natures that make new decisions every minute. One day he resolved to push ahead; the next, to retreat to Posen.

This latter decision, which he acted on, was not made lightly. The rallying of the army on the Vistula had been illusory. The Old Guard numbered five hundred combatants at the most; the Young Guard was practically non-existent; of the first corps there remained eighteen hundred men; of the second, a thousand; of the third, sixteen hundred; and of the fourth, seventeen hundred. Moreover, the majority of these soldiers — all that were left of an army of six hundred thousand — were just about able to use their weapons.

While we were in this powerless state the right and left wings of our army broke away at the same time, Austria and Prussia having deserted us; and Poland became a trap which could be easily sprung on us. On the other hand, Napoleon, who had never willingly surrendered anything, expected us to defend Danzig; and we were obliged to rush all the forces that could still keep the field to that city.

When Murat at Elbing entertained the brief hope of re-

* Marshal Alexandre MacDonald (Duke of Tarente) who had remained behind in the region of Riga, in command of Prussian troops. — J.D.T.

forming the army, even dreamt of victory, he found that
the greater part of his officers were weary and disheartened.
Misery, which inclines a man to fear all things, and then to
believe all that he fears, had stricken their hearts. A number
of them were already expressing concern for their rank,
their standing, or the estates they had acquired in conquered
countries; and the only wish of most of them was to recross
the Rhine.

The recruits that kept coming in were an assemblage of
men from the several German states. To reach us they had
had to cross Prussia, where they breathed an atmosphere
poisoned by hatred. As they drew nearer they had encountered our discouragement and far-flung confusion.
After joining up with our troops they found to their surprise
that they were not surrounded and supported by trained
soldiers, but were alone, exposed to all sorts of discomforts,
and fighting to uphold a cause that had been abandoned by
those who should have been most interested in its success.
Therefore most of those Germans deserted at the first
bivouac.

Even MacDonald's seasoned troops were shocked at the
sorry sight of the army returning from Moscow. Nevertheless, this corps, along with the division commanded by
Heudelot, still maintained orderly formation. All these
remnants were hastily assembled in Danzig — thirty-five
thousand soldiers from seventeen different nations. The remainder, a small number, were to begin to rally only at
Posen and on the Oder.

Until now Murat had done everything humanly possible
to keep some semblance of order in our retreat; but as he
was crossing Marienwerder on the way to Posen, he was
handed a letter from Naples which upset all his plans. The
effect on him was terrible and instantaneous. As he read it,

bile mixed with his blood in such quantities that a few minutes later he was found to have been stricken with a severe attack of jaundice.

It appeared that the Queen had ventured to perform some act of government which touched Murat in one of his most vulnerable spots. Though he was not jealous of the Queen herself, despite her great beauty, he was furiously jealous of her authority. It was as the sister of the Emperor that he feared her.

It was strange to see this prince, who up to that day had appeared to sacrifice everything to the glory of battle, suddenly allow himself to be mastered by a less noble passion. In this instance his solicitude for his authority prevailed over his love of glory, carrying him off posthaste to Posen, where he definitely abandoned us.

This defection took place on the sixteenth of January, twenty-three days before Schwartzenberg also split off from the French army, of which Prince Eugène now took the high command.

Alexander stopped the march of his troops at Kalisch. Then the violent and continuous warfare which had followed us all the way from Moscow abated. Until spring the fighting was only by fits and starts, intermittent, halfhearted. The force of evil seemed spent, while in truth it was only the combatants who were exhausted. An even greater conflict was in preparation, and this truce was not a period devoted to peace, but rather to the premeditation of slaughter.

After fifteen hundred years of victories, the Revolution of the fourth century (that of the kings and nobles against the people) had been overthrown by the Revolution of the nineteenth century (that of the people against the kings and nobles). Napoleon was born of this conflagration, and he had allied himself so closely with it that it seemed as if the great convulsion had been nothing more than the labor pains of the birth of one man. He commanded the Revolution as if he were the genius of that terrible element. At his voice it came under subjection. Ashamed of its excesses, admiring itself in him, and attaching itself to his glory, it — the Revolution — united all Europe under his rule. And at a sign from him Europe rose to drive Russia back within its ancient boundaries. It seemed then that the North was about to be defeated in its icy vastness.

But this great man in those great circumstances was unable to subdue nature. In his powerful effort to make that steep ascent, his strength failed him, and just as he reached the frozen wastes of Europe, he was driven out headlong. And this North, victorious over the South in a defensive war, as it had been in the Middle Ages in its offensive wars, now boasts that it is invincible! Comrades, do not believe it! You could have triumphed over this land and its wide spaces, this harsh, gigantic climate as you did over her soldiers. But certain mistakes were made, which were punished by abysmal suffering. I have spoken at length of them. On this ocean of disaster I have erected a melancholy beacon with a lurid beam; and if my weak hand has not been equal to the painful task, I have at least attempted to give this warning, that those who came after us may see the peril and avoid it.

Comrades, my task is finished. I leave it to you to attest to the truth of the picture I have painted. Its colors will doubtless seem pale to your eyes and hearts, still filled with memories of such heroic exploits. But who among you does not know that an action is always more eloquent than any account of it, or that great historians are far rarer than great men, of whom they are born?

# INDEX

********

Adlerfeld, Gustave, 44
Agaponovtchina, 16
Albert, 257
Alexander, Czar, 8, 19, 23, 45, 49,
    91–92, 94, 107, 121–22, 124, 126,
    177, 194, 299; proclamation of,
    25–26
Anthouard, Count d', 12
Armistice, 129, 131, 135
Army of Italy, 55, 58, 183–88
Atrocities, 167

Bagawout, 66, 137
Bagration, Petr, 15, 27, 28, 49, 54,
    68, 71
Balloon, 92
Barclay de Tolly, Michel, 15, 26,
    27, 28, 33, 45, 48, 50–51, 71,
    74, 75
Beauharnais, Eugène de, Viceroy
    of Italy, 2, 12, 13, 16, 25, 57,
    65, 68, 69, 72, 73, 74, 75, 76, 78,
    79, 101, 113, 125, 143, 148, 149,
    169, 170, 171, 173, 183–84, 186–
    88, 195, 197, 198, 202–6, 208,
    216, 220, 222–24, 263, 266, 269,
    282, 299
Belliard, Augustin Daniel, 13, 29,
    30, 31, 46, 47, 72, 78, 79, 85

Bennigsen, Levin A. T., 127, 128,
    153, 209, 211
Béranger, 137
Berezina River, 237, 240, 247–50;
    crossing of, 254–62
Berthier, Louis-Alexandre, Prince
    of Neuchâtel, 16, 21, 22, 45, 47,
    74, 80, 88, 113, 116, 132, 136,
    142, 147, 149, 152, 158, 163,
    207, 238, 255, 267, 273, 289
Bessières, Jean-Baptiste, Duke of
    Istria, 2, 62, 72, 76, 88, 116,
    144–45, 149, 150, 152, 182, 207
Bialystock, 2
Bonnamy, Charles Auguste, 74, 75
Borelli, 34–35, 69
Borisov, 220, 237, 243, 250, 253
Borodino, 49, 164; Battle of, 52–
    81, 88
Borovsk, 142
Brilowa, 257, 263
Briqueville, 232
Broussier, Jean Baptiste, 75
Bruyères, Jean Pierre, 11, 67

Carigan, 10
Caulaincourt, Auguste J. G. de,
    21, 55, 77, 164
Caulaincourt, Marquis Louis de,

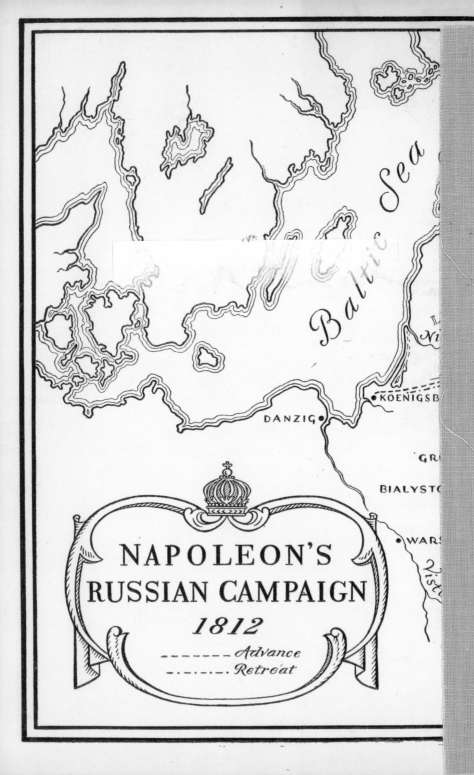

Baltic Sea

DANZIG

KOENIGSB

Ni

GR

BIALYSTO

WARS

Vistu

NAPOLEON'S
RUSSIAN CAMPAIGN
*1812*
------- *Advance*
-·-·-·-· *Retreat*